# STORIES OF NEWMARKET

# STORIES OF NEWMARKET

An Old Ontario Town

## ROBERT TERENCE CARTER

DUNDURN
NATURAL HERITAGE
TORONTO

Editor: Jane Gibson
Copy Editor: Cheryl Hawley
Design: Courtney Horner
Printer: Webcom

**Library and Archives Canada Cataloguing in Publication**

Carter, Robert Terence
    Stories of Newmarket : an old Ontario town / Robert Terence Carter.

Includes bibliographical references.
Issued also in electronic format.
ISBN 978-1-55488-880-1

    1. Newmarket (Ont.)--History. I. Title.

FC3099.N47C373 2011        971.3'547        C2011-900946-3

1  2  3  4  5     15  14  13  12  11

Conseil des Arts du Canada  Canada Council for the Arts    Canada    ONTARIO ARTS COUNCIL CONSEIL DES ARTS DE L'ONTARIO

We acknowledge the support of the **Canada Council for the Arts** and the **Ontario Arts Council** for our publishing program. We also acknowledge the financial support of the **Government of Canada** through the **Canada Book Fund** and **Livres Canada Book**, and the **Government of Ontario** through the **Ontario Book Publishers Tax Credit**, and the **Ontario Media Development Corporation**.

Care has been taken to trace the ownership of copyright material used in this book. The author and the publisher welcome any information enabling them to rectify any references or credits in subsequent editions.
*J. Kirk Howard, President*

Printed and bound in Canada.
www.dundurn.com

**Cover top left image:** The Old Town Hall and Market was built in 1883. Doors similar to this one were located on all four sides and opened into the main floor market space. Stalls were also located in the basement. *Photo by author.*
**Cover top centre:** All of the towers in Newmarket's downtown heritage district can be seen in this photo: the Old Town Hall bell tower, the twin towers of Trinity United Church, the towering steeple of the Christian Baptist Church, and the clock tower on the former post office. *Photo by Robert Buchan.*
**Cover top right:** The bell tower on the Old Town Hall is an exact duplicate of its original. The old tower, which was deemed unsafe and removed, was replaced in 1983 as part of the town's centennial celebrations. *Photo by author.*
**Cover bottom:** The electric cars of the Metropolitan Railway Company ran up Newmarket's narrow Main Street from 1899 to 1905. Merchants complained they restricted traffic and scared shopper's horses, so the tracks were moved to behind the west-side stores. *Author's collection.*

| Dundurn | Gazelle Book Services Limited | Dundurn |
| 3 Church Street, Suite 500 | White Cross Mills | 2250 Military Road |
| Toronto, Ontario, Canada | High Town, Lancaster, England | Tonawanda, NY |
| M5E 1M2 | LA1 4XS | U.S.A. 14150 |

To all those recorders of Newmarket's history who have gone before me, people such as Erastus Jackson, who recorded the recollections of the first pioneers; Ethel Trewhella, who spent years ferreting out the history of our town; Ned Roe, who proudly passed on the stories of his family; and many others.

# CONTENTS

*Acknowledgements ... 13*
*Introduction ... 15*
*Map of Nineteenth-Century Newmarket ... 17*

**Chapter 1: The Earliest Days** ... 19
Brûlé Walked Holland Trail Four Hundred Years Ago ... 19
The Mystery of Our First Settlers ... 21
The Trading Tree ... 24
Grinding the First Bushel ... 26
The 24th Regiment of Foot Often in Newmarket ... 28
Sword Led Way to Victory on Plains of Abraham ... 30

**Chapter 2: The Real Pioneers** ... 31
Beman Was a Hustler ... 31
Teenager Saved the Colony's Gold ... 34
Some Srigleys Dropped Their *H* ... 35
First Doctor a Mystery Man ... 37
Eli Gorham Brought His Machines with Him ... 38
First Settler's House Still on Eagle Street ... 40
Peter Robinson Was a War Hero: A Family Compact Man ... 42

**Chapter 3: Landmarks and Other Artifacts** ... 45
The Pond: The Jewel Downtown ... 45
Fairy Lake and Other Local Lakes ... 48
The Vanished Communities ... 50
Road to Uxbridge Lost ... 52
First School Had Eight Pupils ... 54
Earliest Pioneers Buried on Eagle Street ... 57
Gravestone Marks Resting Place of Renowned Fur Trader ... 59

**Chapter 4: Who Were These People?** ... 62
Area's First White Child: A Matter of Debate ... 62
Newmarket Storekeeper Fought Bravely in War of 1812 ... 63
Settler Had Noble Blood ... 67
Wellington Trained This Trooper Well ... 69
Washington Wanted to Hang This Pioneer Landowner ... 70
Richest of Old Stagecoach Landlords ... 71
Doctor Arrived with Shipload ... 73

**Chapter 5: Things Happen** ... 76
The War of 1812 Created Prosperity ... 76
Booze to Blame for Town's First Homicide ... 78
How Agnes Defeated the Ghost ... 80
Murder Rare in Quaker Community ... 82
Switch for Oxen Grew into Giant Willow ... 84
Gifts to First Nations Distributed at Holland Landing ... 85
Stories of 1837 Rebels ... 88
Wellington Veterans Saved Lount Home ... 90
Salt Well Boon to Pioneers ... 92
Fire Brought Renewal to Colonial Main Street ... 92

**Chapter 6: In Victoria's Reign** ... 96
Bogarttown: Rival for Newmarket ... 96
Mud-Brick Mansion Boasted Wine Cellar ... 98
Butcher's Fair Made Main Street a Cowtown ... 99
Water Street at the Foot of Main: An Early Industrial Area ... 101
Fur Trader Brought Seven Hundred to Party ... 103

Mansion House: A Meeting Place for Rebels ... 103
Riding Key to Fight for Responsible Government ... 106
Friends and Colleagues Until Chips Are Down ... 108
Gold on That Thar Creek ... 113
Newmarket's Fair: Biggest in the County ... 114
May 24th Just Isn't What it Used to Be ... 117
Everybody Skated on the Pond ... 118
Stranger at Station Set Off Fenian Scare ... 119
Citizens Opposed Riel ... 120

**Chapter 7: Fascinating Folks ... 123**
Buffalo Bill: Almost a Newmarket Boy ... 123
First Lawyer Had Famous Name ... 124
Holland River Named for Dutch Surveyor ... 125
Bishop's Throne Now in Museum ... 128
"Fleetfoot" Corbière: Fastest Mailman on the Frontier ... 130
Pioneer Colonel Was Canadian-Born ... 132
Heroes Risked All to Fight Plague ... 132
Samuel Morse and His New Telegraph ... 133
Reeve Gorham Had Faced Treason Charge ... 135
Her Church Bell First Rang Her Own Funeral ... 137
Farm Boy Became Renowned Artist ... 137

**Chapter 8: Growing Into a Town ... 140**
Newmarket Has Long Military History ... 140
Village Clerk Predicted Boom Times ... 142
The Era: Most Enduring of Newmarket's Newspapers ... 144
Three Generations of Canes Were Mayors ... 149
Photo May Be One of Cane's Former Slaves ... 151
Charcoal Maker Had Found Freedom in Upper Canada ... 152
Citizens Band Founded in 1872 ... 154
Pomp and Ceremony Greeted Governor General ... 156
Stickwood Brick Built Old Newmarket ... 157
Strange Societies Appeared on Great Occasions ... 160

**Chapter 9: More Life in the Nineteenth Century** ... 162

Artesian Well Went Wild ... 162

Early Railway Could Have Had Its Own Lottery ... 163

Oldest Companies Started in the Mid-Nineteenth Century ... 165

Telephones Came Early ... 166

Newmarket Regatta: An Annual Event ... 168

Politicians Didn't Keep Their Promise ... 169

Glenville Once a Thriving Village ... 171

Merchant Found Shot Through the Heart ... 173

Department Store King Started on Main Street ... 176

"Old" Town Hall Really Our Third ... 178

Boer War Victory Celebration Ended With a Bang ... 182

Minnie Murdered Susie ... 184

**Chapter 10: A New Century** ... 187

The 1899 Electric Train: To Toronto in an Hour ... 187

Amusement Park at Bond Lake ... 191

Area Families Colonized the West ... 192

Sir William Mulock: Father of Penny Post ... 193

Canal Almost Finished Then Abandoned ... 195

First Toronto Santa Claus Parade Started in Newmarket ... 198

Salvation Army Soldiers Took Newmarket by Storm ... 199

Gas and Oil Beneath Newmarket ... 203

Steam Whistles Sounded Daily ... 206

First Subdivision a Flop ... 208

First Hospital on Main Street ... 209

**Chapter 11: War and Depression** ... 211

The 127th Was Newmarket's Battalion ... 211

Little Town Lost Eighty-Three on Europe's Battlefields ... 212

Riding Refused to Re-Elect Prime Minister ... 215

Holland Marsh Became Canada's Salad Bowl ... 218

Redmen Won the 1933 National Title ... 219

Remember the 1940s ... 222

Six Weeks to Become an Army Town ... 224

Fifth Column Scare Triggered Wartime Paranoia ... 226
Young Flyer First Lost in Action ... 228

**Chapter 12: Later in the Century** ... 230
Davises Sparked Toronto's Theatre Life ... 230
Tall Tales About Past Pranks ... 231
National Film Board Documentary Focused on Citizens Band ... 233
Hagen Taught Generations of Canadian Artists ...234
Marsh Moonshine ... 236
Women's Christian Temperance Union Thought Water Best ... 237
Race to Build First Mall ...240

*Epilogue* ... 241
*Sources and Notes* ... 243
*Selected Bibliography* ... 263
*Index* ... 267
*About the Author* ... 277

# ACKNOWLEDGEMENTS

THIS BOOK IS the product of my fascination with the history of my town and could not have been undertaken and completed without the support, advice, and encouragement of many people.

First and foremost, I would like to thank my wife, Louise, who patiently put up with my many long hours "doing history" to see this project completed, and then volunteered to proofread the manuscript.

Creighton S. Henry, who did the wonderful drawings included in this work, is one of my oldest friends. When he was studying at the Ontario College of Art and I was a Ryerson journalism student, we had apartments in a Victorian mansion on Jarvis Street, but our friendship goes back beyond that to adventures on Lake Simcoe's south shore. I am very grateful to have his work in this book.

I am also grateful to Richard MacLeod, the nephew and executor of renowned Newmarket artist and historian the late George Luesby. George was generous in allowing me to use his drawings in my first book, *Newmarket: The Heart of York Region*, and Richard has been equally generous during the preparation of this one.

Robert Buchan and Mayor Tony Van Bynen have both provided support and encouragement and Robert has offered his excellent photographs, one of which appears on the cover. Lisa Lo, former chief librarian of the Newmarket Public Library system, got the ball rolling in the mid-1970s when she pushed for the founding of an historical society, and put a few interested folks into the same room one evening. The Society that resulted in now almost forty years old.

The late David Haskell, during the 1970s when he was publisher of *The Era* and I was the editor-in-chief, cut me a good deal of slack in regard to researching the town's heritage, although in the beginning readership surveys showed not many people read the articles I wrote. He stuck with me and eventually they built a strong following. I appreciate it. Today, many of the back issues of *The Era* are available on the Internet and there are hardly any citizens of old Newmarket such as Ned Roe left to interview, so the time was certainly right. I am also grateful to the Newmarket Public Library, where all the back issues of *The Era* and other local newspapers are available on microfilm.

A particular thanks to my editor, Jane Gibson, whose remarkable eye for detail has resulted in many a long search by me to fill in the gaps she found, allowing me to build a stronger manuscript. My appreciation also goes to my copy editor, Cheryl Hawley, for the many hours she spent on this manuscript.

While every effort has been made to ensure accuracy of information, any errors brought to the attention of the author or the publisher will be corrected in future editions.

# INTRODUCTION

I GREW UP in Newmarket, and although I lived and worked "away" for quite a number of years at various times, I always seemed to wind up back here. I think I can trace my interest in the stirring events of our history and the people involved to a particular elementary schoolteacher who claimed to be descended from a family of 1837 rebels and so taught those events with a fine flare. My interest was kindled. By the time I was in high school I had started collecting books on the history of this part of the world.

On moving back, in 1968, to become editor of *The Era* I discovered that local history wasn't a popular topic in town despite many reminders scattered around. The remains of the radial railway line were still apparent in many places, and the unfinished Newmarket Canal works were a "scar" on the river. The ornate town hall and market building, although run down, was still in use for civic purposes. Main Street itself followed an ancient Indian trail. However, I soon learned that the first editor of *The Era*, Erastus Jackson (1853–83) had shared my interest, and many of his reports peopled his time and many earlier events for me. What newspaperman could resist finding story leads like these and following them! They led me to people like Ned Roe, grandson of one of Newmarket's founders, and the realization of how close we really are to those pioneer days.

Over the years heritage has become popular, and Newmarket now has a historical society with a fine archives, a museum, and a group dedicated to preserving the record of our built heritage, and protecting the buildings themselves.

I have maintained my interest in the heritage of Newmarket throughout, written many columns about the community, and built an extensive resource collection on the people and the key happenings in the town's history. Finally, I decided to write another book on Newmarket to make the incredible stories marking the growth of the town available to the public. Some stories are funny, some are tragic, and some bear little-known historical detail, but all contribute to the legacy of Newmarket, the town that eventually emerged after Brûlé's early passage through the area.

Robert Terence Carter
Newmarket, Ontario

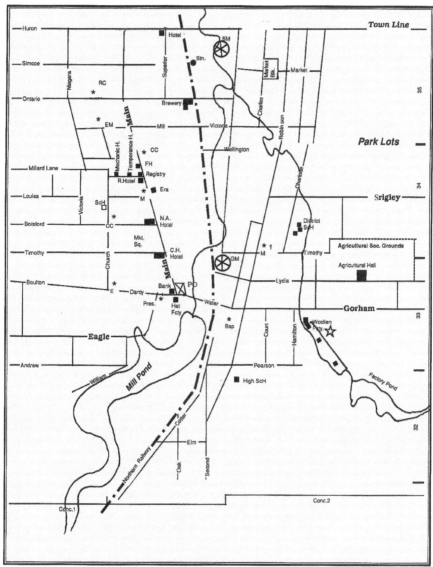

*Map of nineteenth-century Newmarket. Adapted from a map in the* County of York Illustrated Historical Atlas, *published by Miles & Co. of Toronto, 1878, page 29.*

*Chapter One*

# THE EARLIEST DAYS

## ❧ Brûlé Walked Holland Trail Four Hundred Years Ago ❧

IT'S BEEN OVER four hundred years since the first white man paddled up the Holland River. He was a French adventurer who, at Samuel de Champlain's behest, had come to live among the Huron in their villages around Georgian Bay in order to learn their language and their way of life. Étienne Brûlé was a farm boy of sixteen when he left his parents, peasant farmers living on the outskirts of Champigny, a small town south of Paris, to join the ship Champlain was outfitting at Honfleur for a voyage to the New World. It is not known how this teenage farm boy came to be chosen as one of the crew of adventurers who were preparing to sail off to the unknown wildernesses of the vast new continent beyond the sea. They left in April 1608.

Champlain settled at Quebec that winter and built his famous Habitation. During this period Brûlé had ample opportunity to become acquainted with the Montagnais people and found he could easily learn their tongue. It was probably there that young Brûlé began the loose relations with Native women and girls that would later bring him such ill repute. However, his facility for languages and smooth relations with the First Nations people were to lead him to his greatest adventures and, ultimately, to his death.

By the summer of 1610 Champlain and his small band of adventurers were thoroughly involved in the wars between the Huron, Algonquin, and Montagnais, the groups with whom they had built their fur-trading relationships, and their hereditary enemies, the Iroquois, who lived to the south. Champlain sent the eighteen-year-old Brûlé to winter with the Huron chief Iroquet. His mission, according to Champlain's journal, was "to learn what the country was like, see the great lake, observe the rivers, and what tribes lived on them, explore the mines and the rarest things among the tribes in those parts, so that on his return we might be informed of their truth."[1]

Brûlé spent the next twelve months living with the Huron. He adopted their dress, their food, and their customs, and thoroughly enjoyed himself. Although the records are unclear, the young Frenchman apparently returned to Quebec, had a falling out with Champlain, then came back to Huronia with his new friends and lived among them for the next four years.

From the beginning of his relationship with the Huron, Champlain promised to aid them against the Iroquois, an act that also benefited the French in their territorial ambitions, and, on a number of occasions, went into battle with them. On his return from France in the summer of 1615, the Huron again reminded him of his promise and pointed out that Iroquois warriors were constantly lying in wait for them along the trails between Huron country and Quebec. Intertribal warfare was one thing, but when it endangered his hard-won fur trade, it became quite another for Champlain. That July he set out from Quebec for Huronia. Once there, the French governor agreed to lead an expedition against the Iroquois town of Onondaga, south of Lake Ontario. He needed the assistance of the Huron allies, the Andastes who lived on the banks of the Susquehanna River in what is today eastern Pennsylvania. Étienne Brûlé, always eager for adventure and the chance to see new territory, volunteered to go with the mission. A date was set for the attack. Brûlé's role was to recruit the Andastes and have them at Onondaga at the appointed hour. The journey took him through the heart of Iroquois country.

He left with twelve Huron warriors on September 8, 1615. They travelled down Lakes Couchiching and Simcoe and up the west branch of the Holland River, making Brûlé the first white man on record travelling that river. From the Holland, the party shouldered canoes for the twenty-nine-mile portage to the mouth of the Humber River, following the long-established Carrying Place Trail south through present-day King Township.

This "bad boy" of early exploration had many other adventures, and it probably never occurred to him that one of his marks on history would be this short trip up this shallow river, which led him to that tortuous portage. Records of those days are sketchy but, according to J.H. Cranston, Brûlé may have lived among the Huron for twenty-three years until, reaping the rewards of his own treachery and debauchery, he ultimately lost their friendship. According to long-held speculation his end was a sticky one. The Huron were not kind to those they considered enemies. As the oft-told tale goes, Brûlé was tortured and killed, his remains put into a pot, boiled, then eaten. Perhaps there was nothing quite so lurid. It is likely he was murdered "for political reasons, possibly because of his dealings with the Seneca or another tribe feared by the Huron."[2]

## The Mystery of Our First Settlers

WHO GOT HERE first? Who were Newmarket's founding citizens? Many are well-known, but there is evidence to suggest that there were more than we know.

Timothy Rogers was one, of course. He brought the early Quaker settlers from Vermont and upper New York State to Yonge Street in 1801. But he didn't live in the village. Timothy and his family farmed on Yonge Street at Lot 95, King Township, today the southwest corner of Yonge Street and Davis Drive.

Joseph Hill, who dammed the Holland River and built the first gristmill for the area in 1801, seems almost certainly to have been the first citizen. He built a large frame house for himself and his family, and a store shortly after he constructed the mill. However, Hill returned to Pennsylvania rather than support the British side in the War of 1812, for reasons that will be shared later.

By Christmas 1801, James Kinsey, the miller at Hill's establishment, had ground the first bushel of wheat. It is safe to assume he lived near the mill. His family was still in the community in 1847 when his daughter,

Hannah, helped fight an epidemic, possibly typhoid, as noted in a story related in the *History of the Town of Newmarket* by Ethel Trewhella.

William Roe, born in the United States (his father was last British mayor of Detroit), recorded that when he arrived from York in 1814 to establish his fur-trading post, Newmarket, then known as Beman's Corners, consisted of two frame houses and several log buildings. One of the frame houses (formerly the Joseph Hill home) belonged to twenty-nine-year-old Peter Robinson and the Bemans (Elisha Beman was his stepfather). The other belonged to Timothy Millard, after whom Timothy Street is named, and who was Robinson's miller at the time. James Kinsey may have had one of the log cabins. It is not known who else was living nearby.

Joseph Hill had built the Robinson house, but sold it to the Beman-Robinsons in 1804. Elisha Beman, an American, married Christopher Robinson's widow. Christopher, a United Empire Loyalist from Virginia,[3] had been one of Simcoe's Queen's Rangers and later became surveyor general of Woods and Forests in Upper Canada. He died, almost broke, in 1798, leaving six children — three boys and three girls. The boys, Peter, William, and John Beverley, all became prominent members of the Family Compact and played a major role in the history of Upper Canada. Beman took on responsibility for them all when he married their mother and moved the family from York to Newmarket. The only son not to live in Newmarket was John Beverly, as he was attending school in eastern Ontario at the time.

The house was moved from its original site by the mill pond to a location farther west on Eagle Street in the 1850s. Interestingly, the house remains in its second site on Eagle Street and today is rental accommodation. Unfortunately, despite several attempts, the building is not designated as a heritage site.

It is not known where Hill lived after he sold the Robinson house, but it must have been nearby as he still had a tannery and other interests. In 1804, a man named Morris Lawrence (or Laurence) had settled here and became Hill's partner, which, as shall be seen in a later story, proved to be Hill's undoing.

Robert Srigley, born in Bucks County, Pennsylvania, originally had immigrated with his parents to Pelham Township, Niagara District, Upper Canada. In 1802, by then an adult, he brought his family to the area to establish a farm east of today's Main Street.

As noted, Elisha Beman established himself and his family here in 1804. His family included his wife, the former Esther Robinson, and her six children. The Beman stepsons Peter and William Robinson, then aged seventeen and five respectively, and their sisters, Mary (fifteen), Sarah (thirteen), and Esther (seven) lived in Newmarket,[4] while the middle son, John Beverley (aged eleven) had been sent away from 1800–03 to attend John Strachan's Grammar School in Cornwall, Upper Canada.

The Robinson boys became major figures in early Upper Canada. Peter Robinson was a War of 1812 hero, fur trader, Family Compact government post holder, militia officer, mill owner, founder of Holland Landing, and head of an emigration scheme for the British government, which resulted in founding of Peterborough. John Beverley Robinson, a protégé of Bishop Strachan's, was a lawyer and staunch Family Compact member. He became acting attorney-general at age twenty-one when the then officeholder, Colonel John Macdonell, was killed at Queenston Heights (John Beverly had worked in his office). By the time of the 1837 Rebellion, John was chief justice of Upper Canada, and, in 1854, he became Sir John, a baronet. William Benjamin Robinson was a fur trader and businessman who, in 1828, was elected in the Family Compact interest as the first member of the Legislature from Simcoe County. He held the seat until 1857, except for one term.

North Richardson, the son of an aristocratic English family, settled in Newmarket in 1805. He was a notary public, unofficial postmaster, and provided other services to the fledgling community. He may have occupied one of those early log cabins.

Both William Laughton and Andrew Borland arrived in Newmarket in 1810, ahead of Laughton's cousin and Borland's future partner, William Roe. Laughton was a fur trader and eventually captained boats on Lake Simcoe. Borland, also a trader, moved north to establish trading posts in Muskoka and farther afield.

Newmarket was growing. In his 1820 published reminiscences, John McKay wrote, "There were three stores, one owned by Peter Robinson, which was managed by W. Sloane; one by William Roe and one by John Cawthra; one hotel (on Eagle St.), one blacksmith, John White; one saddler, S. Strogdale; one carpenter, Jacob Gill; one tailor, R. Russel; one tanner, W. Hawley; one shoemaker, Mathew Currie; one frilling and carding factory,

Eli Gorham; two flouring mills, Peter Robinson and Mordecai Millard."[5] In 1829, according to Thornhill resident Mary O'Brien's journals, Newmarket had grown to fourteen houses, three of which were stores. "It boasts a comfortable inn, a doctor's house, a blacksmith, a hatter, a shoemaker, with a mill near at hand and a small meeting house of some description."[6]

Eli Gorham, a woollen miller from Connecticut, had landed here in 1808. By 1811 he was operating a mill south of what is now Gorham Street, well to the east of the little village and the Yonge Street settlement. Hill's mill was also in operation, so Mrs. O'Brien probably missed Gorham's in her count.

Dr. Christopher Beswick, a retired British Army surgeon who had settled here in 1808, would account for the doctor's house; the inn was a successor to an Eagle Street building erected by Elisha Beman around 1822 and known as Dye's Inn (now an office building) because it was run for Beman by Daniel and Michael Dye. Records show the merchant partners Borland & Roe (Andrew Borland and William Roe) built a hotel on the southeast corner of Timothy and Main Streets in 1825. Elijah Hawley (origin not known) started a tannery in 1810. Timothy Millard arrived in 1813 from Pennsylvania — his farm ran from Yonge Street east to the Holland River. His frame home faced Main Street, north of Timothy Street.

That leaves the blacksmith, hatter, and shoemaker unaccounted for — our lost pioneers. Today, the descendants of at least three of these founding families can be found in Newmarket: the Rogers, the Millards, and the Richardsons.

## ❧ The Trading Tree ❧

THE GIANT TIMOTHY Street elm tree that, according to legend, was the original "new market" from which the town derives its name, was cut down in the last week of November 1947. Tree experts hired by town council gingerly took the old tree down piece by piece, leaving a naked bulge where the street had been paved around both sides of the tree. Council had deemed the giant unsafe to leave standing in a residential area. For years the tree had stood on a hill on the west side of the Holland

Author's collection

*This ancient elm stood on a rise of land and towered above the surrounding forest, making it a landmark for trappers paddling south on the Holland River. Fur traders William Roe and Andrew Borland established their first market under its branches — the "new market."*

River, towering above the surrounding forest and serving as a landmark for fur trappers paddling their loaded canoes south.

The legend of the "new market" is only partly true. Newmarket was but a few small houses clustered around a primitive mill and store when two energetic young men set up a fur trading post. William Roe and Andrew Borland went into business after the end of the War of 1812–14. Fur trading was big business in those days and in the spring Native trappers paddled south from the great forests of the Muskoka district and farther north to the bottom of Lake Simcoe, and then up the Holland River until they faced an arduous portage to York (Toronto) with their furs. The two men reasoned that a well-stocked post at this point (Newmarket) would attract many trappers. They spread the word that they would meet the trappers under the giant elm — a tree so tall it is said to have protruded from the forest cover, making it a landmark by which to navigate. Over 150 years later William Roe's elderly grandson told me the two brought as many brightly coloured goods as they could carry up from York, and on trading days would festoon the bushes around the elm with blankets, strings of beads, ribbons, swathes of cloth, and other items, and the trading would commence.

Borland moved on after a few years, becoming a legend in fur-trading circles in the country north of Lake Simcoe through Muskoka and the French River area,[7] but Roe stayed and prospered in Newmarket. Eventually, he built a large store and trading post at the south end of Main Street with an entrance on the street and a dock and door from the river for fur traders. In those days it was possible to bring a large canoe up the Holland River from Lake Simcoe to Newmarket. However, according to family tradition, William Roe continued to meet traders under the great elm tree for many years.

Today, the Timothy Street knoll where the great elm once stood is graced by a young maple and a plaque — and traffic still goes around it.

## Grinding the First Bushel

IN DECEMBER 1801, there must have been a celebration at Joseph Hill's mill in the little clearing in the forest that was to become Newmarket. Just imagine it! After the long arduous trek to this isolated frontier, pioneer settlers had to clear enough of the virgin forest to plant a small crop of grain between the stumps, build log cabins for the coming winter, bring in firewood, hunt for meat, and — probably last thing in the fall — dam the river, clear a mill site, and build the little mill. That first bag of flour ground from wheat carefully harvested from between the stumps must have symbolized a hard-won victory over this forbidding forest.

Joseph Hill was Newmarket's first settler and his mill — a small wooden building with two millstones between which he ground wheat — produced its first bushel of flour in the week before Christmas 1801. The gristmill was situated on the west bank of the river just south of today's Water Street. James Kinsey was the miller who did the grinding.

Hill had arrived with settlers from Vermont under the leadership of Timothy Rogers, a Quaker minister who had scouted the land in June 1800 and chose it for settlement. Rogers' goal was to create a Quaker community halfway between the Quaker settlements in Prince

Photo courtesy Newmarket Historical Society Archives.

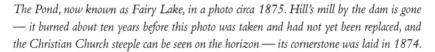

*The Pond, now known as Fairy Lake, in a photo circa 1875. Hill's mill by the dam is gone — it burned about ten years before this photo was taken and had not yet been replaced, and the Christian Church steeple can be seen on the horizon — its cornerstone was laid in 1874.*

Edward County and the Niagara district. He brought with him a group of families whose surnames are still familiar in mid-York Region — Proctor, Griffin, Crone, Clark, Howard, and Farr among them. As has already been said, Joseph Hill also built a store near the mill and to the west of that, near the present-day location of St. Andrew's Presbyterian Church, a frame house.

An ambitious man who saw the commercial potential of this site where the river converged with two great Indian trails,[8] Hill soon became a rival of another settler-entrepreneur who planned to control the "new market" and its crossroads, Elisha Beman. Beman was also an ambitious

American, originally from New York State, who had managed to get himself firmly connected by marrying a member of the powerful Family Compact ruling circle in York. Shortly after arrival in Newmarket in 1803, Beman purchased the mill, store, and house from Hill. Hill retained a sawmill on the east side of the dam. In 1804, he built a tannery on a creek crossing today's Gorham Street, but neglected to get legal title to the land. Upon discovering this, the hard-nosed Beman sensed an opportunity. He acquired the site and evicted Hill.

Hill had more bad luck in store for him. His partner Morris Lawrence (or Laurence) was a recent arrival from New York State, who turned out to have fled the U.S., leaving debts behind. His debtors from New York found him and pursued him in Upper Canadian courts, suing both partners. Although the man was not a partner in Hill's sawmill, his debtors won a judgment against it. In 1812, Hill's property was seized and auctioned. Peter Robinson, Elisha Beman's eldest stepson, acquired it all.

Hill was a ruined man and ever after bitterly claimed he had been done in by an act of judicial robbery. When war broke out in 1812 he refused to take an oath of allegiance and Newmarket's first settler left for Pennsylvania, taking his wife and family back with him.

## ℭ The 24th Regiment of Foot Often in Newmarket ℭ

TOUGH, RED-COATED soldiers of the British Army's 24th Regiment of Foot were familiar figures to the Quaker farmers and other settlers along early Yonge Street. The Quaker settlement was a good day's march from Lake Ontario and men of the unit were often billeted with residents of the area. The 24th had served in North America for many years. Initially, they had arrived in 1776 and were stationed at Montreal and Quebec during the American Revolution, then sent back to Britain. They returned to Upper and Lower Canada in 1829 and stayed for twelve years. Its troops, heading to or from the Lake Huron and western posts, regularly marched the road north from York to Holland Landing.

In September 1793, Lieutenant Governor John Graves Simcoe made his historic journey from the mouth of the Humber River to Matchedash

Bay on Lake Huron. Colonel Richard G. England of the 24th Regiment, then commanding at Detroit, wrote to Simcoe congratulating him on his return from Matchedash Bay and his account of the harbour there. He also commented on the supposition that once a fort and shipyard were built there it would likely diminish the role of the fort and the farming settlement at Detroit that he (England) had built up over the past year, but he also noted his willingness to be supportive and his assumption that all would be for the greater good.[9]

At that time, Detroit was the North West Company's chief supply base on the Great Lakes, and important to British fur trade. It was also very vulnerable to attack from the south, and since Britain was at war with France at the time, the colonel obviously relished the thought of a safer headquarters.

During the 1830s troops of the 24th Regiment were stationed at the Lake Huron base, by then called Penetanguishene. The 24th also guarded the supply transfer depot[10] at Holland Landing when necessary. The Penetang post has now been restored and reconstructed as the Historic Naval and Military Establishment, and is open to the public during the summer months. The tradition of the famous regiment has been recreated, including the nine-and-a-half-pound India pattern musket, called Brown Bess, that the guard used. The much-decorated 24th (distinctions awarded include honours for actions at the Marne, Ypres, the Somme in the First World War, and Normandy in the Second World War) traces its history back to 1689. The regiment served in a great many conflicts, including the American Revolutionary War, various conflicts in India, the Zulu War, Boer War, and two World Wars. The regiment was first posted to Canada in 1829 and stayed until 1841. Ultimately it was absorbed into the Royal Regiment of Wales in 1969; its status remains unchanged to this day.

The regiment historians say its finest day remains the Battle of Blenheim in 1704 when, under the command of the Duke of Marlborough, it participated in the capture of Blenheim, executing one of the classic and most courageous manoeuvres in military history, the line advance. In order to arrive with every man's musket loaded, and therefore able to produce the greatest possible volume of fire at the critical moment, the 24th had to march in line, under fire from guns and muskets, without returning a shot. They maintained this formation despite heavy losses, until their officers could touch the village walls with their bayonets. Only then did they fire.[11]

Although the contributions of the 24th Regiment of Foot and other units to the safety and security that allowed the Newmarket area to be cleared and settled in peace have been marked at Penetanguishene, there is nothing to commemorate the post at Holland Landing.

## Sword Led Way to Victory on Plains of Abraham

A SWORD, USED by one of the officers who led General James Wolfe's troops in the 1759 attack at the Plains of Abraham, hung on the wall of a Church Street home for many years. Wolfe's army defeated the French Army, under the leadership of Marquis de Montcalm, at Quebec City. The British forces took the fortress city and eventually the colony, ending France's colonial presence in North America except for the small St. Lawrence islands of St. Pierre and Miquelon.

Edward "Ned" Roe was a grandson of town-founder William Roe, and a great-great-grandson of one of Wolfe's young officers. William Roe's mother, Ann Laughton, was a daughter of Lieutenant John Laughton, R.N., who served with General Wolfe at the capture of Quebec, and who commanded the party that hauled the cannon up the cliff to the Plains of Abraham.

Ned Roe spent his career in William Randolph Hearst's magazine business in New York City, and returned to his hometown, Newmarket, to spend his retirement years in a family home he inherited. Lieutenant Laughton's sword came with the house and hung on the wall in Roe's upstairs bedroom until he died in October 1973. The sword was inherited by a relative living in Ottawa.

# Chapter Two

# THE REAL PIONEERS

## ❧ Beman Was a Hustler ❧

ONE OF NEWMARKET'S first pioneers was not a man you were likely to find on the business end of an axe, clearing the land. As noted, Elisha Beman was a New York entrepreneur with good political connections who had immigrated to Upper Canada. His dream was to build a business empire on the settlement road north from York (Toronto) to include mills, distilleries, wagons, ferry boats, and at least one hotel. Beman is said to have settled in the freshly cleared but not yet named Quaker settlement on Yonge Street near the Holland River in 1804. With him came his second wife, the former Esther Robinson, whom he had married in September 1802, and her six children from her first marriage. History sees him as a bit of an opportunist, since his second wife was a penniless but very well-connected widow.

Esther was the widow of Christopher Robinson, originally from Virginia, a close friend and colleague of Lieutenant Governor John Graves Simcoe. Beman had four children by a previous marriage, Esther had six, and he and Esther had a daughter, making a total of eleven children attached to the Beman household. The settlement was soon being called Beman's Corners.

Elisha Beman was a man with vision, a man willing to put aside a prosperous life in the capital, pull up stakes, and move his family to the frontier for a chance to build a commercial empire. Beman had arrived at York in 1795, opened a tavern there, and also ran a business supplying provisions and baked goods. He and a partner had tried to set up an iron foundry in the Gananoque area — Elisha indicated he had been in that business in the neighbouring states for many years — in a statement made in a written application for permission to run a foundry in York.

But he had bigger ideas for Upper Canada. Knowing the government wished to improve communications along Yonge Street, in October 1798 he proposed settling at the northern end of the portage around the rapids in the Severn River, between Lake Couchiching and Georgian Bay, build an inn, clear the land, and run a ferry on Lake Simcoe. As settlement was bound to follow, he proposed building grist- and sawmills. All he needed from the colony's administrator, Peter Russell, was a thousand-acre land grant. When the Severn River request did not work out, he settled for the portage that connected Yonge Street to Holland Landing, the location that was to become Newmarket.

The Executive Council agreed, in recognition of "his great and arduous exertions in providing the town [York] with provisions at a time when no other persons had attempted it."[1] The following spring Beman was permitted to buy an additional thousand acres at 6d. per acre, seemingly the market price at that time.

Beman acquired a number of local official positions while living in York — town assessor, surveyor of highways, and commissioner of dry measures. As tavern keepers were often appointed constables so they could keep order in their establishments, Beman was also constable in York in 1801, in the Home District (one of the political jurisdictions established in the colony predating its division into counties) in 1802, and in Whitchurch Township (Newmarket) in 1805. He was commissioned a justice of the peace for the Home District in April 1803, and was continuously re-appointed one of three magistrates along Yonge Street until March 1820.

The hustling New York-born entrepreneur (1760) was soon well on his way to his business empire. Following his marriage to Esther in 1802, he moved his family to a house built by his stepson, Peter Robinson, at Holland Landing. He next purchased property at the Newmarket site, built a gristmill on the Holland River in 1803, and, in 1804, traded that site to Joseph Hill in return for his house, store, and mill. It seems that

Courtesy of Robert Buchan

*No trace of Joseph Hill's mill built in 1801 remains, but it stood on the west side of his millpond, now called Fairy Lake, close to the dam. Today the site is a park trail, and behind it is a restaurant. To the right Cawthra House can be seen, one of the many early- and mid-nineteenth century survivors in the downtown area. Behind the mill site stands St. Andrew's Presbyterian Church.*

Hill's mill was perceived as interfering with the flow of water to Beman's mill. Beman then moved his household to Hill's house, and opened for business. In 1805, he added more land and a distillery.

As noted earlier, Joseph Hill moved east a short distance and built a tannery where the Bogart Creek crosses today's Gorham Street. He apparently didn't bother to secure title to the land, although some records show he had a lease. Beman secured a twenty–one-year lease on the land and evicted Hill, igniting a feud that lasted until Hill fled to the United States during the War of 1812. As a result some historians have accused Beman of sharp business practices.

In 1812, Peter Robinson, Esther's eldest son, acquired the balance of Hill's property, probably a small tannery and a sawmill, giving the family control of most of the business in the little community. The family soon built an ashery on the east side of the river and Peter erected a second distillery on the east side of the mill pond. In addition, Beman and Robinson were trading for furs with the Ojibwa. Thus, the Beman–Robinson enterprises were shipping furs and potash for York merchants, distilling and milling grains in Newmarket for local markets, and retailing goods obtained from wholesalers in York and Kingston. Elisha's son Eli built a mill and hotel at Holland Landing and operated boats on Lake Simcoe. Another son, Joel, managed the farms. The Bemans were once very prominent citizens of the Newmarket region, but today their surname can no longer be found in the area.

The political views of this American-raised pioneer seem not to have always found favour with his Family Compact relatives. His stepson John Beverley Robinson, by then the acting attorney-general, comments in a letter written on May 18, 1814, responding to Surveyor General Thomas Ridout's assertion that Beman, in his capacity as justice of the peace, was "not being sufficiently active, in checking seditious proceedings in his neighbourhood." Robinson acknowledged that "the observation is in my opinion just." He went on, however, to note that though Beman was "wanting in zeal, [he] is not a seditious or troublesome character, and except in his political opinions, is a good and exemplary member of Society — and in many duties of his situation as a magistrate considerably useful."[2]

As he aged, Beman transferred his business responsibilities to his sons and devoted his attention to his farms. In the autumn of 1821, his health failed and possibly he suffered a stroke. On October 7, "Being weak in body but of sound and disposing mind and memory,"[3] he made his will, dividing his land among his children. When he died a week after making his will in 1821 at age sixty, Elisha Beman — Squire Beman as he was known locally — had established himself as the area's most successful businessman. He was one of the men who laid the foundation for the "new market." He and Esther Sayre Beman are buried in the pioneer cemetery on Eagle Street.

## ❧ Teenager Saved the Colony's Gold ❧

IN 1814 WILLIAM Roe and his partner, Andrew Borland, decided that good money could be made by establishing a fur-trading post on the Holland River, one that would intercept Native trappers heading for York or other Lake Ontario posts. They spread their wares out under a huge elm on a knoll overlooking the river, and invited travellers to trade. This, according to legend, was the "new market" from which our town took its name. The

*William Roe became Newmarket's second postmaster in 1837 as a belated reward for him saving the colonial government's treasury during the War of 1812.*

two men did well and, as noted, Borland soon set off for richer fur-trapping country north of Lakes Simcoe and Couchiching to build more trading posts. Young Roe stayed and built a store on the river near the mill-pond dam. He became one of the community's most substantial citizens.

Roe came from good stock — his father Walter had served under Wolfe at the Battle of the Plains of Abraham and was one of the first lawyers in Upper Canada.[4] At age seventeen when he was sent to work in the office of the colony's Receiver-General Prideaux Selby, William Roe played a key role in saving Upper Canada's gold reserves from invading Americans when they captured York during the War of 1812. Dressed as an old woman, the teenaged Roe drove a wagon, in which the colony's treasury was hidden under a pile of vegetables, through the lines of the invading American Army. He reached safety at a friend's farm on Kingston Road, where the bags of gold and coins were buried until the invaders left.[5] Years later, as a reward for his service, Roe was made postmaster of Newmarket.

## Some Srigleys Dropped Their *H*

FEW STREET NAMES give newcomers to town as much trouble as does Srigley Street. Everybody wants to slip the sleepy *h* in and say "Shrigley" Street. Ironically, the Srigley family history shows that Shrigley is just about as correct as Srigley as far as the family is concerned.

The Newmarket street takes its name from early settler Robert Srigley, who was born in Bucks County, Pennsylvania, in 1777. About eleven years after Robert's birth his parents moved to Pelham Township in the Niagara District in Upper Canada. Robert's parents were Enoch and Mary Shrigley — with the *h*. Robert, therefore, was the first of the Canadian branch to adopt the abbreviated spelling of Srigley. He moved to York County, having purchased land for a farm east of the Holland River in the very early years of the nineteenth century. He built a home near the present site of Prince Charles Public School, and the street that bears his name was once his farm lane. A public-spirited citizen, Robert Srigley donated a corner of his farm for the community's first "public" school site, and that land, now the northeast corner of Prospect and Timothy Streets, became the location of the Alexander Muir Public School.

The Shrigley family were Quakers, and Robert and his wife, Jane Heacock, are both buried in the Quaker cemetery on Yonge Street. They had ten children, and the names of some of them show a definite leaning to historic personages both here and abroad. The first son was Elisha Beman Srigley, born in 1811, and named after the early community's most prominent businessman. Wellington Srigley was born in 1817, not too long after the Iron Duke defeated Napoleon at Waterloo. And Christopher Beswick Srigley went through life adorned with the name of Newmarket's first doctor who, according to his gravestone, died in 1839 at age 118. Today, the family history shows descendants of Robert and Jane Srigley are scattered around the world, and no wonder — they had sixty grandchildren.

If the family's favourite legend has any truth to it, somewhere in the world there may lie proof that this far-flung clan can lay claim to a vast British fortune. According to the tale, two English brothers named Stephens made a huge fortune — £82 million — trading with the East India Company. Both died, and the estate passed to a sister who was said to have married Richard Srigley, founder of the American Srigley family. Richard and his new wife emigrated to the colonies. Because the marriage of Miss Stephens could not be proven, the entire fortune went into chancery and reverted to the Bank of England.[6] No records indicate when Richard and his wife arrived in America, but there are Srigleys and Shrigleys recorded as living in Maryland as early as 1651.

## ✺ First Doctor a Mystery Man ✺

WHO WAS DR. Christopher Beswick?

He is best remembered as the man whose name was given to Beswick Park, the municipal park on William Roe Boulevard. To many of his contemporaries in the 1820s and 1830s, he was apparently as much a man of mystery then as he is to us today. Nevertheless he has several claims to fame, and some years ago Newmarket's municipal office received a query about him from the publishers of the *Guinness Book of Records*. They were trying to prove that this eighteenth-century medical man was the oldest doctor ever to serve in the British Army. Dr. Christopher Beswick died March 28, 1839.

His life's story is probably one of the most interesting of all those of the Newmarket area's pioneers, yet few of the details to fill it out have been passed down to us, and no picture of him has survived. If Dr. Beswick had joined the British Army in his twenties, he could have served in the Scottish Highlands, including the Battle of Culloden (1745), and he would have seen action in the Seven Years War (1756–62).

Dr. Beswick emigrated from England to Pennsylvania with Gabriel Lount, a Quaker and a surveyor. Records show that Lount had practised his surveying profession in Pennsylvania for twenty-five years before he and his family came to Canada in 1811 and acquired land on Yonge Street. That means that the Lounts must have arrived in America in 1786. Lount was evidently preceded to Upper Canada by his friend Beswick by a few years, because the good doctor is recorded as having built a mill in 1802 in Uxbridge.

Beswick would have been an old man in 1811 — ninety if records are accurate. The only medical man north of the Oak Ridges, he ministered to the little pioneer settlements for many years as the Newmarket area's first doctor. He practised for so many years that his friends wondered about his age, but all he would tell them was that when he died his age would be found in his Bible. Following his death the date 1721 was found carved into the inside of the leather book cover. That meant Christopher Beswick was 118 years old at his death, and that he had reached sixty-five when he sailed from Great Britain to settle in Pennsylvania in 1786.

The home he built in Newmarket stood looking down over the town from the hill where Eagle Street meets Yonge Street. He was buried in the Anglican cemetery on Eagle Street, land he had bequeathed to the church. For many years his stone stood just inside the gate. In the 1950s, most stones in this cemetery were put into two cairns.

Although little more than these bare facts are known about the life of this colourful pioneer, it may well be that we know as much about him as many of his contemporaries, for he was apparently a very private person. Since he never married, he left no descendants to keep a family history alive in this country. Accounts left by early settlers give us one more clue to the kind of man he was. It is said that he wore a wig and was regarded by others as eccentric, but his contemporaries found him to be thoroughly, and liberally, educated. They reported he took great delight in preparing the constitutions and bylaws for the various organizations that emerged in the new community.

What we don't know is if the doctor was also a practical joker. He apparently never said he was 118 years old, he just told his friends to look in his Bible after he was gone. When they found the date 1721 cut into the binding they concluded that it was his birthdate; the clue for which they were looking. We will probably never know.

## ✺ Eli Gorham Brought His Machines with Him ✺

ELI GORHAM WAS a wool miller with foresight. Before moving from Connecticut to Upper Canada in 1808, he purchased four of the revolutionary new wool carding machines. He installed two in rented space in the frame mill that had been built by Joseph Hill at the foot of Main Street, and sold the other two carders to a Dundas, Ontario, businessman, Mr. Hatt. Gorham then bought property on a stream, east of the Newmarket settlement, and built a dam, mill pond, and mill. He moved his business there in 1811. Nothing but memories remain of Newmarket's first major industry, but for the greater part of a century the Gorham mill, located on the south side of today's Gorham Street, was one of the town's greatest assets. The former site of the mill, plus the surrounding farmland, were subdivided about two decades ago and is now a residential area.

By 1836 the Gorham Woollen Mills was the little community's biggest employer. The mill had grown into a three-storey structure and employed thirty people. Renowned for its quality, the mill met the requirements of a wide territory for all-wool homespun, flannels, wool blankets, and other goods. It also furnished a market for local sheep farmers. The business was operated by two generations of the Gorham family — the pioneer Eli and his son Nelson. Both men were staunch supporters of the Reform political movement led by William Lyon Mackenzie during the 1820s and 1830s. Mackenzie was a frequent guest in the Gorham home.

Little information survives about this once-thriving pioneer business, but it seems a pretty good guess that as business grew Eli expanded the mill using brick, for in 1836 he built himself a large red-brick home (painted buff since then), overlooking his mill. The brick house, still a residence, stands today on the south side of Gorham Street at the top of the hill east of Prospect Street. The house was almost certainly Newmarket's first brick home. The pond, however, is gone. Today his farm lane is known as Gorham Street. In the early years of the nineteenth century having the woollen mill in this frontier community must have been a godsend to the pioneers clearing the land and braving the Upper Canadian winters in their log cabins. At the mill settlers could buy blankets, homespun and heavy flannels so essential to their comfort during the long cold winters.

Eli Gorham died in 1867, and in 1875 Nelson sold the mills. After the failed 1837 Rebellion Nelson was charged with high treason, convicted in absentia and attainted, thus allowing the government to seize all his property. For years he lived in exile in New York State, but was allowed to return to Newmarket in the 1840s. He took over the family business in 1859, but retired in 1873 and moved back to the United States.

Two years later the mills were sold to Messrs. Russell, Douglas & Longford. They burned in 1878, and were rebuilt as the Phoenix Mill with an added fourth storey. At its zenith in the 1880s the mill employed forty to fifty men. In the late nineteenth century the business fell on hard times, and the mills were razed in 1907. Today, all that remains of the site is a millstone resting in a garden on Prospect Street at a home that once belonged to a member of the Gorham family.

## ✑ First Settler's House Still on Eagle Street ✑

WHAT IS REPUTED to be the oldest building in Newmarket is now a six-plex on Eagle Street. The word "six-plex" would have puzzled Joseph Hill, the Quaker miller who built the boxy frame house in 1801 or 1802. It probably would also have perplexed Elisha Beman and his stepsons, Peter and William Robinson, the two subsequent owners and occupants who operated a store from it and turned the home into a warm and hospitable social centre in the woods north of York, the capital of Upper Canada.

Robinson family biographer, Julia Jarvis, writes of William Robinson:

> Most gentlemen travelling north or north-west brought with them from friends in York a note of recommendation to Mr. Robinson, whose friendly and hospitable disposition was well-known: "fast by the road his ever-open door, obliged the wealthy and relieved the poor."
>
> Governors, commodores, and commanders-in-chief were glad to find a momentary resting place at a refined domestic fireside. Here Sir John Franklin [the Arctic explorer] was entertained for some days in 1835, and at other periods the Arctic travellers, Sir John Ross and Captain Back.[7]

*William Benjamin Robinson, the middle of the three influential Robinson brothers during the Family Compact era in Upper Canada's history, grew up in Newmarket and owned businesses here and in Holland Landing. He held important government posts and militia commands.*

Author's collection

*Known as the Robinson-Beman house, this building was first the home of Joseph Hill and then, under the ownership of Elisha Beman and his Robinson stepsons, became a trading post and a social centre in the woods.*

Accounts indicate the house was built by Hill when he constructed the first mill and dam in 1801, at what is now Fairy Lake. As noted earlier, he sold both mill and home to Elisha Beman. The old building has stood for many years on the south side of Eagle Street, opposite the end of Church, but has not always been there. The house stood at Water and Main Streets, next to the location of Hill's mill, until 1855, when it was moved to make way for construction of St. Andrew's Presbyterian Church.

Squire Beman was connected to the Family Compact through his wife, the widow of a prominent United Empire Loyalist. The family stayed closely in touch with the social life of the government circles in York and, as Julia Jarvis's description of life in the Robinson house indicates, they set a high standard of refinement and culture in the backwoods community.

Those days are long gone for the old building on Eagle Street, just as the verandah that once graced its front is gone and forgotten. The fifty acres that went with it when Elisha Beman willed the property to his wife in 1820 were sold long ago and, with road widening on Eagle Street, even the front yard has disappeared.

## Peter Robinson Was a War Hero: A Family Compact Man

PETER ROBINSON WAS the eldest of three brothers who, as the stepsons of the well-connected Elisha Beman, had a profound influence on the establishment and growth of the frontier settlement that became Newmarket. The community has always claimed Robinson as a native son, although throughout his career as public-office holder, mill operator, fur trader, soldier, militia officer, and war hero, Robinson lived in many places. He was born in 1785 in New Brunswick, the eldest son of Christopher Robinson and Esther Sayre, United Empire Loyalists (UEL) from Virginia and Boston respectively.

His mother was the daughter of a renowned Anglican minister who, as a UEL, took up residence in New Brunswick. His father, Christopher, a member of a prominent Virginia family, was an officer in Lieutenant-Colonel John Graves Simcoe's Queen's Rangers during the American Revolution. His younger brothers were John Beverley (later Sir John) and William Benjamin. According to Julia Jarvis' *Three Centuries of Robinsons*, Peter died unmarried. She mentions no children. However, the *Dictionary of Canadian Biography* (*DCB*) states that Peter had at least a son and two daughters. The *DCB* cites Robinson's will as leaving a farm in Whitchurch Township to daughter Isabella, and making provision for a son, Frederick.[8] The late Whitchurch historian, Marjorie Richardson, said she found evidence the family tried to suppress the fact Peter married a North American First Nations woman.[9]

As a Loyalist, a former ranger, and Lieutenant Governor Simcoe's surveyor general of woods and forests, Christopher Robinson had left his wife and six children an established place in York society but little means to sustain it.

In 1800, at age fifteen, Peter was given a position as clerk of the Home District Court of Requests. Esther Robinson's second marriage, to Elisha Beman in 1802, introduced Peter to the world of business. In 1812, he acquired a mill in Newmarket and, in 1814, began buying lots north of the village. Over the next eighteen years he acquired eight lots on Yonge Street, including the site of the village of Holland Landing, which developed around the Red Mill, the largest gristmill in the colony at the time and built by Robinson. He invested in numerous other enterprises — an inn, a schooner on Lake Simcoe, a distillery, and more farms, but his greatest personal involvement was as a fur trader employing agents in the back country and as a merchant supplying the trade. He was associated with the Newmarket firm of Borland & Roe, which in turn was an agent for the North West Company.

At the start of the 1812 war, Robinson raised a rifle company, attached to the 1st York Militia, and was one of thirteen captains in York when that town surrendered to the Americans in April 1813. The York Militia, made up of experienced woodsmen, travelled overland to join in Major-General Isaac Brock's successful attack on Detroit in August 1812. The following year Robinson put his backwoods knowledge to use again, helping Fort Michilimackinac maintain communications with York during the American blockade. He made his way out of the fort through an American fleet of ten sailing ships.

In 1815, Peter Robinson was again living in Newmarket. After his election to the House of Assembly for York East in 1816, and for York and Simcoe in 1820, he spent more of each year in the town of York.

In 1822, Peter went to England for the first time, travelling as a tourist along with his brother, John Beverly, and his wife Emma Walker. John Beverly introduced him as an expert on backwoods settlement and the British government hired Peter to superintend an experimental emigration scheme. In 1823, Robinson sailed from Cork with 568 individuals, bound for the military and Lanark settlements in the Bathurst District of Upper Canada. In 1825, he took 2,024 Irish immigrants to the Newcastle District, where a townsite was named Peterborough in his honour. In all, he had located just under three thousand immigrants in nine townships in the Newcastle District. As a result, in July 1827 Robinson was appointed commissioner of Crown Lands (Upper Canada's first) and surveyor-general of woods. These appointments brought him into the inner circle of government, a favoured position he had not enjoyed before, first as a member of the Executive Council, and, in 1829, with a seat on the Legislative Council.

In 1836, Robinson participated as a councillor in two events that led to major controversies. Just before he left Upper Canada in January of that year, Lieutenant Governor Sir John Colborne had endowed forty-four Anglican rectories across Upper Canada with land, an action that infuriated the Reformers. It was Robinson and two fellow councillors, Joseph Wells and George Herchimer Markland, who approved the patents for the land. By March 1836, Robinson was one of the expanded council of six members who resigned to protest Colborne's replacement Sir Francis Bond Head's treatment of the council, specifically his failure to consult on state matters. Although Robinson was the presiding member, it is unlikely that he had the health or ambition to do more than follow advice, either in resigning (at the urging of Robert Baldwin and Dr. John Rolph) or in offering, along with Wells, Markland, and John Henry Dunn, to withdraw his resignation. Head refused the offer to rescind his resignation.

Robinson was still on a bad footing with the lieutenant governor when a paralytic attack on June 23, 1836, left him "deprived of the use of his left side."[10] Seeing no prospect of Robinson's recovery, Head demanded his early resignation from the Crown Lands Department, and, in order for its business to continue, offered the position to Robert Baldwin Sullivan. Robinson's will lists his lands in 1837 as more than 7,592 acres and a couple of additional properties in Toronto.

*Chapter Three*

# LANDMARKS AND OTHER ARTIFACTS

## ❧ The Pond: The Jewel Downtown ❧

MOST NEWMARKET OLD-timers still refer to it simply as "The Pond" — as people in the town have since the first dam was built by miller Joseph Hill in 1801. Officially, it is known as Wesley Brooks Conservation Area, and the lake within it as Fairy Lake, although no one seems to know the origin of the name "Fairy." It was around this little pond that Newmarket was founded, and, somehow, even in the earlier years of the twentieth century when the pond had been allowed to deteriorate into a stinking open sewer, it retained its place in the affections of the townspeople.

Mr. Hill dammed the river and built his mill slightly to the north of the former Newmarket Hydro building, which is now a restaurant. Behind it he built a store and "a fine wooden residence."[1] The mill and store long ago yielded to time, but the home, moved to Eagle Street, is still in use.

Over the first years, the five-acre pond remained the hub of Newmarket's business life as well as a good part of its social life. It was used to support sawmills, woollen mills, grain mills, and tanneries. Fur-trading posts were established below its dam, and it often witnessed brigades of fur-laden First Nations people and trappers paddling up the Holland River from the north to trade at the "new market." By the 1860s,

*Drawing by Creighton Henry*

*Joseph Hill found an excellent mill site where an Indian trail from the Rouge River to Lake Simcoe crossed the Holland River. He built a dam and created a mill pond before erecting a gristmill.*

two men with the last names of Arnott and Fox operated a sawmill facing Water Street on the east side of the pond, while their firm also had a cooper shop close to the sidewalk on the other side of the dam. The cooper shop made barrels for the Marsden flour mill, which was across the road on the site now serving as a police station parking lot.

The tannery belonging to Fred Hartry was behind the sawmill. The dock and shed behind the tannery were a popular swimming place on hot summer evenings. So was Dutchman's Bay on the other side, so named for a Mr. Bache, an immigrant from the Netherlands and the owner of a big house next to the bay during the last half of the nineteenth century. The senior's apartment building on the grounds of the Fairy Lake Gardens now occupies the site of Bach's house.

During the late 1860s and early 1870s, a floating bridge spanned the pond. It was about twelve feet wide, built of solid planks chained together, and had railings on both sides. The bridge provided a short passage for pedestrians and for cattle going to and from the meadows east of the stream. There were openings in the railing of the bridge to permit row boats to be lifted across to continue their trip upstream. Pleasure boating was a popular activity on summer evenings, and picnics were held at Cedar Point, some distance beyond the big bend at Dutchmen's Bay. Small boathouses were tucked in along the shoreline that now borders the senior citizens apartment lawns. In the winter, horse races were held on the pond's ice, as well as skating parties and curling matches.

The dam was washed out at least twice — in 1878 and 1928. During Hurricane Hazel, in 1954, the banks around it washed away but the dam held. The one previous to the present dam had a platform across it with a railing along the north side. It made an ideal bandstand, and often was used as a performance site by the Newmarket Citizens Band. The pond and its river began to deteriorate after the Second World War, and by the mid-years of that century the stench of shallow, badly polluted water on hot summer nights drove people away rather than attracting them.

The river has been cleaned up now — folks say the pond is not clean enough to swim in, but it may well be cleaner than it was behind Hartry's tannery. And a beautiful park surrounds it, once again making it the focal point of the downtown area.

*Joseph Hill's mill pond was known simply as The Pond to generations of Newmarket residents, but sometime early in the twentieth century people began calling it Fairy Lake. It is shown above in 1911 with the Office Specialty factory under construction to the north.*

## Fairy Lake and Other Local Lakes

How DID FAIRY Lake get its name? Origins of the name remain a mystery. Fairy Lake is not really a lake at all but a mill pond created at a small rapids in the Holland River. The name has stuck to the little lake for years, but nobody knows where it came from or when it was given. Local historian, George Luesby, wrote in a Newmarket Historical Society paper that it was probably bestowed by an itinerant photographer early in the twentieth century.[2] Prior to that locals simply called it "The Pond."

Central York Region is sprinkled with little lakes, most named for early settler families. Lake Wilcox, for instance, is a corruption of the lake's original name, Lake Willcocks. It was named for William Willcocks, a former mayor of Cork, Ireland, who, in 1792, followed his family's good fortune to the little colony of Upper Canada. Willcocks, a merchant in Cork, was a cousin of the Honourable Peter Russell, John Graves

Photo by the author

*Lake Wilcox is one of many small kettle lakes across York Region left by retreating glaciers. Now within the boundaries of Richmond Hill, because of its proximity to both Yonge Street and Toronto it once was a favourite place for well-off families from the capital to build country estates.*

Simcoe's successor as administrator of Upper Canada from 1796 to 1799. Willcocks arrived hoping to establish an Irish colony, and apparently through his cousin's influence was appointed a magistrate, and later York's first postmaster. His dreams of an Irish colony never materialized, but Willcocks was an active land speculator and soon owned considerable property in Upper Canada, including eight hundred acres around the lake that bears his name.

South of Oak Ridges, on Yonge Street, is another of York's kettle lakes, so-called because they were scooped out by the last departing glaciers. They are spring-fed and have no inlet or outlet rivers. This one, Bond Lake, carries the name of William Bond. In 1799, the settlement farthest north on Yonge Street was his log cabin nestled in the woods by the lake. He came to the colony, like so many others, with big dreams of empire-building. Bond planned to open a hat factory on his land around the lake and to establish homes for workers from Britain. He petitioned for more land for his project and was granted two lots east of Lake Willcocks in 1798. The plans must have collapsed quickly, or perhaps they were just a pretext for land speculation, because within months Bond had sold his land to Willcocks.

Lake St. George, a kettle lake east of Lake Wilcox now part of a conservation area, also carried the family name of an illustrious pioneer. Laurent Quetton St. George was a French army officer who arrived in Upper Canada in 1799. A refugee from the French Revolution, he and other French émigrés were settled in Whitchurch Township, south of Bond Lake. A merchant by training, St. George soon abandoned the settlement in the woods, went into business, and made a fortune trading furs and running a wholesale merchandise house. St. George returned to his family estate when the Bourbon kings were restored to the French throne, but his son Henri came back to this country years later to claim his father's holdings, and acquired the lake property in 1852 to use as a country estate.

These are but three of the pioneers whose names now mark maps of our area. Lake Simcoe, of course, was named by Lieutenant Governor John Graves Simcoe for his father, a British Navy captain.

## ❧ The Vanished Communities ❧

YORK COUNTY'S FARM-rich, gently rolling hills and their river valleys were once dotted with thriving villages. Most have now disappeared. Others, such as Sharon, Queensville, and Mount Albert, stagnated for a century or more and have only begun to grow late in the last century as the urban tide continues to press north from Toronto. Some of the earlier nineteenth-century communities aren't even dots on the map anymore, and others have been swallowed up by their larger and more successful neighbours.

Newmarket, for instance, has engulfed several of these "ghost towns" that now lie submerged within its boundaries. Armitage was a little Yonge Street community south of today's Mulock Drive. It boasted its own schoolhouse, post office (1904–71), Quaker Meeting House, cemetery, store and inn, and a tavern. Nathaniel Gamble's inn near the southwest corner of the Yonge-Mulock intersection was used for township council meetings as early as 1809 and continued to host them until 1839. As late as the 1960s the community retained its post office, and had a gas station-store and dance hall. Today, Armitage is remembered in the name of an elementary school some distance away from the community, and is the location of a secondary school opened in 2001, and named for a distinguished one-time Armitage resident, Sir William Mulock.

Armitage was the first permanent settlement in King Township, which once encompassed everything west of Yonge Street. The community took its name from its first settler, Amos Armitage, who was one of Timothy Roger's party of Quakers. However, its best-known family is undoubtedly the Mulocks. Sir William represented York North for many years in the House of Commons, was a cabinet minister, and is considered the father of penny postage. He built his estate on Yonge Street along the north side of today's Mulock Drive, then known as Gamble Road. Although most of the Mulocks' farm has been subdivided, the house and surrounding ten acres are still in family hands at time of writing.

A number of other nineteenth-century communities disappeared as Newmarket grew. Bogarttown at Mulock Drive and Leslie Street was once a thriving milling centre, and vied with Newmarket to be a stop on Upper Canada's first railway when it was built in 1853. Bogarttown lost, its mills were moved to be on the tracks, and today only the millpond remains.

Author's collection

*Poverty-stricken Irish emigrants fleeing the mid-nineteenth-century Potato Famine flooded into Upper Canada and settled in communities all along Yonge Street. Many small, inexpensive lots along Main Street, north of Newmarket, were taken up by these immigrants. They built small frame houses, planted their vegetable gardens, and worked as labourers and domestics in the nearby village. Their community became known as Paddytown, and some of their houses remain.*

Garbutt's Hill was the community on the east side of the Holland River valley — in the current Gorham and Prospect Streets area. Its stores began to fade after the river was bridged and shoppers preferred the bigger Main Street district on the Newmarket side of the river.

Paddytown, as its name implies, was settled by mid-nineteenth-century Irish immigrants fleeing the potato famine at home. It was a community of workingmen's cottages with their vegetable gardens and barns, which sprang up north of Newmarket's Huron Street (now Davis Drive) boundary along old Main Street. Some of the houses are still there, but nobody remembers Paddytown.

Two concessions east of Aurora, the communities of Petchville and White Rose, both show on nineteenth-century maps, and Glenville, west of Newmarket on Highway 9 at Dufferin Street, was once a thriving little village. Pleasantville was a crossroads community with a blacksmith shop and post office at Woodbine Avenue and Mulock Drive.

There were other crossroad communities in and around Newmarket, all of which have disappeared entirely, gone for so long that no one remembers them. Their only trace is a name visible on early nineteenth-century maps.

## ❧ Road to Uxbridge Lost ❧

NOTHING TANTALIZES STUDENTS of history like the word "lost." Tales of lost cities, lost civilizations, and lost treasures never fail to fascinate. Perhaps a "lost" road isn't in the same league with a lost civilization, but it's one of the few things that have been misplaced in this area's history.

Yonge Street is remembered as the only settlement road by which the first pioneers in the Newmarket-Aurora area reached their land grants, but, in fact, for more than the first fifty years of the nineteenth century, there was another road from Lake Ontario to Newmarket whose origins were as ancient as Yonge Street's — like Yonge, this road also followed Native trails.

The route led inland from the mouth of Duffin's Creek in Pickering Township (Region of Durham). Maps dating back as early as 1813 show this road running straight north to the townline of Uxbridge Township, then west to the townline between that township and Whitchurch. It then ran north for a short distance before forking, one branch striking off at an angle past Musselman's Lake and across Whitchurch to a point between Pleasantville and Pine Orchard. From there it ran west to Newmarket.

Undoubtedly the road was used by many settlers arriving here, probably including some of the Quakers who followed Timothy Rogers to the area. As Quaker settlements grew around what is now Uxbridge and at Newmarket, the road was well-travelled since it formed the only direct link between the two areas. W.H. Smith's map of York County in his *Canada, Past, Present and Future 1851*, showed the travelled road still striking southeast from the Pine Orchard Road past Musselman's Lake, but then turning down the 9th Concession of Whitchurch to Stouffville. This

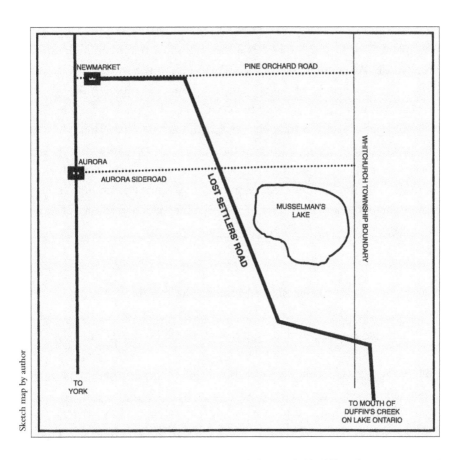

*The lost road, really just a rough wagon trail that probably followed a First Nations' footpath, brought travellers from Lake Ontario to a path that originated in Uxbridge and led to Newmarket. The sketch map shows Pine Orchard Road and Aurora Sideroad in dots as these were yet to be built.*

change was probably made by 1827, as Stauffer's Mills had already been built near the Markham townline. In 1851, travellers to Lake Ontario would take the Markham Plank Road instead of continuing on the old road to Duffin's Creek. By 1861, the concessions and sideroads in east Whitchurch had been opened and considerably improved. All that remained of the old direct road was the small stretch, still in use today, running southeast from Ballantrae along the southwest side of Musselman's Lake.

Travelled for centuries by First Nations people before being adopted to the white man's use, the old road saw many settlers loaded with all their worldly possessions, pushing northward from the lake to farms in

Whitchurch or homes in the little village of Newmarket, particularly in the years prior to the War of 1812. Records show that many residents of Whitchurch Township went to Newmarket to the justice of the peace, Elisha Beman, instead of going to see the justice in Aurora. Although the latter town was closer, the road to Newmarket was much more direct.

Today, few traces of the old road remain, and even fewer know it once existed. Some years ago, a long-time resident of the present road west from Uxbridge town pointed out where the settlers' road had run along a ridge at the back of his farm. However, he warned against bothering to climb the hill to look for it, for he said he'd looked many times and found nothing to even hint of its previous existence.

## First School Had Eight Pupils

"SCHOOL DAYS, SCHOOL days, those grand old book and rule days".

The old song goes something like that, ringing a familiar note of nostalgia for the long-gone days of the one-room schools in the country. But just how grand were those school days of a century or more ago? Compare the recollections of Newmarket's first schools to the experiences of today's

*Courtesy of Newmarket Historical Society Archives*

*In 1853, Newmarket Common School, on the northeast corner of Prospect and Timothy Streets, replaced a one-room log building constructed in 1824. The Common School, which today would be called an elementary school, served until 1891.*

*Alexander Muir Public School replaced the Common School and was named for a popular principal of that school. Originally from Scotland and the composer of "The Maple Leaf Forever," Muir taught in Leslieville, part of Toronto, from 1860 to 1870, then became principal in Newmarket in 1873 and 1874. He was the town clerk for Newmarket in 1875 and 1876, and would later return to teaching in Beaverton. Alexander Muir is buried in Mount Pleasant Cemetery, Toronto.*

students — bused to their six hours a day, five days a week education in gleaming, well-equipped buildings.

The first public school building in Newmarket was erected in 1824 on land donated by the Srigley family on the corner of their farm. A small log building that accommodated an average of eight pupils, it stood on the Prospect Street frontage of the northeast corner of today's Prospect and Timothy Streets. In the very early days, school had been taught in the basement of fur-trader William Roe's residence at the foot of Main Street, and then in part of an old distillery building on D'Arcy Street.

As attendance grew, a new twenty-four-foot-square frame schoolhouse with a metal dome was erected in 1853, and wings were added on the north and south sides in 1858. This second school building accommodated an average of 120 pupils — boys and girls — in one room and with one teacher. The first teacher was Robert Moore. The desks were built around the wall and the stove was in the centre of the room. The seats were pine slabs with the flat side up and auger holes bored through them where the legs were inserted. School was six days a week in those days, but Moore reminisced that he frequently allowed a half-holiday on Saturdays. "School was kept on Saturday in those days, but often a half-holiday was granted, depending upon how successful the pupils had been in reviews and the spelling matches," said Moore, who remained as principal until 1872 when he joined the high-school teaching staff.[3]

In 1891, the second school with its two wings had outgrown its usefulness. It was moved to a lot on Prospect Street and converted into a home. In its place a sparkling new brick building went up, which was named after one of Mr. Moore's successors as principal, Alexander Muir. This public school was demolished in 1976.

The Newmarket Grammar School was established in 1843 and was the second public secondary school in the province (the other being in Toronto). The building is still there, on the northeast corner of Millard Avenue and Raglan Street The headmaster, and only teacher for many years, was Reverend Hugh Borthwick, MA. The students were prepared for university and the law by studying bookkeeping, English grammar, Greek, French, arithmetic, geography, Canadian history, ancient and modern history, physical science, chemistry, and physiology.

By 1876 the old Grammar School was too small and the school board purchased the Newmarket High School site on Prospect Street at Pearson. The next year a brick building was erected, but it burned in 1893. A replacement building went up in 1895. It too burned in 1928 and was again rebuilt. That school, in its turn, was replaced in 1996 by a new one on a different site near Bayview Avenue and Mulock Drive. The old school was demolished in 2000.

In the early years of education in Newmarket there was no school tax. Previous to the 1862 election of school board trustees, if people wanted to send their children to school, they had to pay a fee. In 1862, the trustees decided to levy a sum of $500 on the district, which included several adjoining farms — a sum that seems miniscule when compared to today's education tax bill.

## ✧ Earliest Pioneers Buried on Eagle Street ✧

THE GRAVESTONES IN Newmarket's Eagle Street Pioneer Burying Ground read like a roll call of the town's founding families. Elisha Beman and his wife, Esther Sayre Robinson Beman, Squire Dr. John Dawson, Colonel Arthur Carthew, Dr. Christopher Beswick, fur-trader John McDonald of the North West Company and Hudson's Bay Company, William Roe and his mother, Ann Laughton Roe, wife of the last British mayor of Detroit, all lie there. Other names on stones include Irving, Townley, Gill, Allen, Boultbee, Blackstone, Richardson, Simpson, Brodie, West, and Hamilton.

Many other pioneers also lie buried there, some of their stones now lost, largely because the cemetery was badly neglected during the last years of the nineteenth century and the first half of the twentieth. These names now survive only in a dusty record book. All are pioneers, for the cemetery was little used after the public cemetery was opened on north Main Street in 1869.

Many of the names bring to mind colourful stories from the community's past. The stone in the foreground of an old drawing of the cemetery was sent to Newmarket by Lady Jane Franklin, widow of the Arctic explorer and one-time governor of the penal colony of Van Dieman's Land, Sir John Franklin. It is said to be made of Scottish granite

Author's collection

*The Eagle Street Pioneer Burying Ground was abandoned during the latter years of the nineteenth century and the first half of the twentieth. To clean it up, the surviving stones were mounted in cairns and the Newmarket Parks Department now maintains the property.*

and was sent to mark the graves of John McDonald and his wife, Marie, who died within a month of each other in 1828.

The Bemans and the Robinsons, of course, need no introductions to students of Newmarket's history. For many years, the family saw to the maintenance of the little fenced family plot in the Eagle Street cemetery.

The name Lieutenant-Colonel Arthur Carthew of Her Majesty's 64th Regiment is inscribed on one prominent stone. Around 1830, Carthew, a half-pay lieutenant, settled along the west shore of Lake Simcoe's shore near Hawkstone. Sir John Colborne had formed a preference for this beautiful part of his province when he became lieutenant governor in 1828, and recommended it to his fellow officers. Many of these gentlemen of rank soon discovered that the Lake Simcoe scenery was better than the land was for farming and they relocated. Canon Featherstone Osler, the Anglican rector at the village of Bond Head and a former navy officer, wrote in 1836:

> Mr. and Mrs. Carthew I was pleased with, and not less so from their being Cornish people. They came out seven years ago and settled in the woods. After enduring many hardships, and spending £2,000, two years since they left their land and purchased a cleared farm near Newmarket. Their first residence, Mrs. Carthew told me, was a shanty and when it rained they were obliged to hold an umbrella to keep the wet off.[4]

Carthew attended the famous meeting called by William Lyon Mackenzie in front of the North American Hotel in Newmarket during the tumultuous August of 1837. Speaker after Reform speaker harangued the crowd with anti-government rhetoric and appealed for public support for the Patriot movement.[5] At last Carthew stepped forward and, after a short speech, called on "all persons present who are against Papineau and the Canadians, let them step this way."[6] It is said that only three people, in a crowd of over six hundred, followed him.

Another character of pioneer Newmarket buried on the Eagle Street hilltop is Dr. Christopher Beswick, the town physician who was said to have been 118 years old when he died on March 28, 1839.

## 🙢 Gravestone Marks Resting Place of Renowned Fur Trader 🙠

A TALL SCOTTISH granite stone monument stands above the modest pioneer markers in the old cemetery on Eagle Street in Newmarket, but

*Author's collection*

*In 1828, Lady Jane Franklin, widow of the Arctic explorer Sir John Franklin, sent a granite stone from Scotland to mark the graves of North West Company and Hudson's Bay Company fur-trader John McDonald and his wife Marie Poitras. McDonald had aided the explorer in his search for the North West Passage. The stone can be seen from the gate.*

it bears no name. A marble plaque mounted on its face disappeared sometime in the mid-twentieth century. The monument marks the grave of John McDonald, a Scottish fur trader who was probably the only man to hold senior positions with three of the major fur-trading companies in our great Northwest

McDonald was known to his contemporaries as McDonald le Borgne, to distinguish him from McDonald of Garth and the many other members of the clan who came to America in the eighteenth century to find their fortunes in the fur trade. He deserves a greater mention than the memory of the now-missing gravestone plaque in a little Newmarket cemetery.

In 1798, the young McDonald, having served as a clerk at Lachine for seven years, became a wintering partner in the XY Company, a rival of the old North West Company formed by dissenting partners. When that rivalry ended, he was one of six wintering partners of the XY Company who became partners of the North West Company in 1804.

In 1821, on the union of the North West and Hudson's Bay Companies, many of the former's employees were forced into retirement, but McDonald became chief factor. Initially, he was in charge of the Upper Red River area. From 1823 to 1826 he was responsible for the Winnipeg River district at Fort Alexander, a very senior post. He was granted a furlough in 1827. By then he was fifty-seven and was probably ready for retirement from the taxing life of trader. He settled down on a large parcel of land he had acquired in 1825 on the north side of Kempenfelt Bay on Lake Simcoe. Along with him came his wife, the part-Native Marie Poitras, and some of their six children. Another child, a girl named Catherine, was born after they settled on Lake Simcoe.

As was often the case with the fur traders, the couple's union had not been solemnized by priest or minister since neither were readily available in fur-trading country. But there was a priest in Simcoe County, at Penetanguishene, and McDonald availed himself of the opportunity to marry Marie before their youngest daughter was born. The move was to prove catastrophic for the other children. McDonald, thrifty Scot that he was, had not retired a poor man but he died without a will. As the only legitimate child the youngest daughter, Catherine, inherited everything. His real estate alone was substantial — 6,000 acres.

McDonald and his wife, Marie, were visiting Newmarket when first Marie and then John took ill. It is not known what sort of plague or epidemic was sweeping the frontier settlements of York County that year, perhaps cholera or typhus, but whatever it was it claimed them both. As noted earlier, they both died less than a month apart, Marie died on January 15 and John on February 17, in the winter of 1828. They were buried in the cemetery up the road from Peter Robinson's inn, where they had been staying.

Because he had befriended Arctic explorer Sir John Franklin in 1825 on his overland trip, and perhaps also in 1822 and earlier, Lady Franklin sent a granite gravestone from Scotland to mark John's and Marie's resting places. The stone was delivered to the cemetery and then left lying beside McDonald's grave for many years. In 1874, chair-maker J.B. Caldwell drew school principal Alexander Muir's attention to it, and the teacher and composer organized a monument-raising bee.

The inset marble plaque with the engraving has since been stolen but the stone remains about where McDonald is buried.

*Chapter Four*

# WHO WERE THESE PEOPLE

## ❧ Area's First White Child: A Matter of Debate ❧

A CLAIM IN the obituary of Hugh D. Willson (March 14, 1887) that he was the first white child born north of the Ridges drew a heated reply in the local newspaper from the descendant of another pioneer family. Hugh Willson, the third son of David Willson, founder of the Children of Peace, the Sharon-based religious sect and builders of the Sharon Temple, died in the late nineteenth century. He was born on August 22, 1802, and is said by Emily McArthur's *History of the Children of Peace* to have been the first white child born in the Township of East Gwillimbury.[1] He moved to California in 1889 and died there.

According to Benjamin Cody, a Newmarket resident who wrote to the editor of *The Newmarket Era* on May 7, 1892, this Hugh was not the first white child born north of the Ridges. Cody said that early in 1797 his grandfather, Joseph Cody, emigrated from New York State and settled on Yonge Street, half a mile north of Aurora (now the St. Andrew's College lands). At that time he was the most northerly settler in the county. Benjamin Cody said his father often told him how before reaching their land, the settlers stopped for the night at Colonel William Graham's home, south of the present site of Aurora in the Township of Whitchurch, where they saw the Graham twins, Peter and Adam, who were about three months old at the time. He wrote, "Their births would therefore be before that of the late Hugh D. Willson."[2]

Cody added he possessed church records showing dates of births in families of some early settlers north of the Ridges and the following are all previous to the birth of Mr. Willson:

> Sarah Rogers, daughter of Isaac and Olive Rogers, King Township, born April, 1800; Ann Pearson, daughter of Benjamin and Susannah Pearson, King Township, born December, 1800; Elmsley Rogers, son of Timothy and Sarah Rogers, Whitchurch Township, born September 1800; Benjamin Wood, son of Robert and Mary Wood, Whitchurch, born June 1801; Mary Pearson, daughter of Benjamin and Susannah Pearson, King, born March, 1802; Augustus Rogers, son of Rufus and Lydia Rogers, King, born July, 1802.[3]

While Hugh D. Willson was probably the first white child born in the Township of East Gwillimbury, Cody's evidence indicates he was not the first north of the Oak Ridges. Settlement moved north from Lake Ontario following the government surveyors who laid out farm lots. Areas to the south, closer to York, were settled first; East Gwillimbury was surveyed in 1800.

## ❧ Newmarket Storekeeper Fought Bravely in War of 1812 ❧

Since Newmarket was just a gathering of a few houses and cabins, a trading post, and a gristmill in a forest clearing during the War of 1812, it is difficult to claim that any of her sons participated in that conflict. However, after the war some of the veterans did settle here and made substantial contributions to the growing frontier community. Of course, the Quaker farmers of the Yonge Street settlement refused military service but some worked on the Yonge Street supply route to the northern forts.

Yonge Street was a major military supply route to British bases on the Upper Great Lakes. Supplies such as food, ammunition, and clothing were teamed up the road to a Royal Navy storage depot at Holland Landing. From there the goods were sent on by water to the British bases at Penetanguishene on Georgian Bay, to Fort St. Joseph at the head of Lake Huron, and to the fort at Michilimackinac. Quakers were forbidden by their beliefs from joining the military or supporting it financially, and thus could not do their mandatory militia service. The government made allowance for their peace testimony, but required them to pay a fine in lieu of militia service. Many refused to pay because the money was used to support the militia and they did not wish to finance the war. These men were either jailed, or fled into the surrounding forest to hide.

British troops were often billeted in homes along Yonge Street and farmers' oxen were sometimes requisitioned to team loads up the road. Some farmers went along with their oxen, which represented a major investment for them, to ensure their animals were cared for properly. "The Friends of Yonge Street Monthly Meeting, so far as the records show, suffered more for conscience sake than any other group of Friends in Canada," wrote Arthur G. Dorland in *The Quakers in Canada*.[4]

One man, who eventually became one of Newmarket's most successful businessmen and outstanding citizens of his day, has left us stories of his adventures in the War of 1812. His name was John Cawthra. In 1820 he settled in Newmarket, built a frame house, and opened a general store at Water and Main Streets. Soon after he erected a distillery at the east end of today's Ontario Street. John was the son of prosperous York merchant Joseph Cawthra, who made his money provisioning the British Army during the War of 1812, but he was known in the colony for his lack of sympathy with the ruling Tory party, which later became the Family Compact. When hostilities threatened, young John applied for the militia commission that he felt his station in life entitled him to have. Not surprisingly, his father's anti-government politics became a factor and he was refused the commission. Instead, he joined 3rd Regiment York Militia as a private.[5]

John's son, Henry, recounting his father's tales years later, wrote, "One day General (Sir Isaac) Brock addressed the volunteers and told them he was about to undertake a very hazardous enterprise and attack the enemy in his own country — that volunteers were not obliged to leave their

*Drawing by George Luesby*

*John Cawthra, the son of a wealthy York (Toronto) wholesaler Joseph Cawthra, settled in Newmarket in 1820. He constructed this building on the site of his first trading post to serve as a store, and, in 1856, he established Newmarket's first bank known as the Royal Canadian British Bank.*

own country — and he only wished for those who chose to, to join him — that in all probability very few who did so would ever return, for he was going to attack a force superior to his own."[6] John Cawthra was said to have been the first to step forward. Many others followed, and Brock led them to one of his greatest victories, the capture of Fort Detroit on August 16, 1812.

Henry wrote:

> My father was engaged all night in getting the cannon across the Detroit River in scows ... I have heard him say that he never expected to see the next day after the guns were in position. The attack on the fort at Detroit, with their small force seemed hopeless.
>
> In the morning, all being ready, Brock sent a message to General William Hull in the fort, saying he had a large force, chiefly savage Indians, ready to attack, but for the sake of humanity he hoped General Hull would avoid bloodshed and surrender, for he feared, he, Brock, could not control his Indians after the capture, if their blood was up.

Hull sent back an indignant refusal.

Brock sent a message to say that he would attack by a certain hour unless the fort capitulated. Meantime he sent Indians into the woods — scattered all around the fort — directing them to make as great a demonstration as possible. Tecumseth accomplished this well. The Indians sounded the war whoop in all directions — the hour arrived — and one of the guns my father took across began the fight with such effect that the ball entered the room of the fort where a council of war was going on and cut in two one of General Hull's officers. The firing continued and to the surprise of the attacking force, a white flag was exhibited on the fort. A parley ensued and terms of surrender were made.[7]

After the war Hull faced a court martial for surrendering, and was sentenced to be shot. The sentence was later reprieved by President James Madison.

After taking the fort, Brock learned that a large wagon train of supplies, provisions, and materials of war, all desperately needed by his own force, was en route through Michigan to the fort. He and his men ambushed the supply train and captured it.

As summer turned to fall, Brock learned that an American regiment on the Niagara frontier was preparing an attack across the river into the very heart of his colony. He rushed his men back to meet the threat.

"My father went with him and was also at the Battle of Queenston Heights," wrote Henry. "My Uncle Jonathon was also with him (at Queenston), and a man in the front rank at Queenston, being nervous, asked Jonathon, who was in the rear rank, to exchange places with him. He did so, and almost immediately after, a round of shot took off the man's head."[8]

As the battle for control of Queenston Heights progressed, John Cawthra recognized a militia officer in scarlet tunic whom he felt was exposing himself needlessly to enemy fire. He yelled a caution as American sharpshooters were picking off the officers. The man he warned was Colonel John McDonell (MLA for Glengarry and attorney-general of Upper Canada). McDonell made a brief reply, and very soon after was shot. Cawthra called out to another soldier (Lieutenant Archibald MacLean) nearby that McDonell was falling, and the two rushed to save him. The second soldier was shot through the thigh while he and Cawthra were taking McDonell off his horse, and Cawthra and a third man carried the attorney-general to safety. Although the account does not mention it, presumably Cawthra and his comrade went back for the wounded MacLean, for MacLean lived to become a judge.

John Cawthra was entitled to prize money after the capture of Detroit, but his son claims he was too patriotic to claim it. He did, however, bring back a sword taken at the United States post, and was later awarded a medal. Although John Cawthra seldom spoke of it, his son mentions in the family memoirs that "father slept in the same tent as the Duke of Kent (Queen's Victoria's father) at Gibraltar Point (Toronto), for two nights in March of 1812, while being on guard duty with the Duke."[9] This does seem an odd thing for Henry to claim, and the Duke was not a young soldier at the time; he was forty-five years old. However, it would seem John made the claim to his son.

When John Cawthra's 1820 Main Street building burned in the mid-1830s, there was so much alcohol stored in it that farmers four miles away reported seeing the blue flames shooting skyward. He quickly replaced it with the large brick structure that served as a trading post, general store, and eventually as Newmarket's first bank. The building still stands on the corner of Main and Water. He also became involved with the milling business in Glenville, a community two-and-a-half miles west of Newmarket, at one time known as Cawthra's Mills.

John Cawthra died in 1851 at the age of sixty-two, and was buried in St. James Cemetery, Toronto. There is a plaque dedicated to the family in St. James Anglican Cathedral, Toronto. He had represented the electoral district of Simcoe in the Legislative Assembly of Upper Canada from 1828 to 1830.

## Settler Had Noble Blood

NORTH RICHARDSON, AN aristocratic young Englishman, was one of the first settlers in the little clearing around the mill pond, which eventually became Newmarket. He settled here in 1805 and became the notary public, a public officer concerned with estates, deeds, powers-of-attorney, and foreign and international business, for Newmarket and district. He also ran the first post office, which was operated in William B. Robinson's name.

Richardson had left England against the wishes of his father, Major William North Richardson of Exmouth, East Devon. It may not be a coincidence that the John Graves Simcoe family came from nearby Exeter, and owned an estate at Honiton, also in East Devon. In 1814, the adventurous young man resigned his position in Newmarket (William Roe took over Richardson's role and in 1837 was promoted to succeed Robinson as postmaster). He had heard the call to colours that lured so many young men back to Britain and into the army for the final tumultuous campaign against Napoleon Bonaparte. Richardson served in the Duke of Wellington's army, and when the smoke cleared after the Battle of Waterloo in 1815, young Richardson was there, unscathed, and holding the rank of major.

After the war Richardson returned to Newmarket, where he took up residence on Prospect Street in one of the first frame houses built in the village and resumed his role as a notary public, as well as holding other official appointments. Richardson must have married, for some years later it is recorded that his grandson, William Edwin Richardson, faced the house with brick.

Friends and neighbours called him Lord North, but, in 1933, this same grandson told local historian L.G. Jackson, then-editor of *The Newmarket Era*, that the title was honourary although there was a family connection. Seemingly, Richardson's father had disqualified him from any possible succession to the title because he was displeased with his son's decision to return in the colonies. North Richardson lived in Newmarket for the remainder of his life, and his descendants still reside in this area.

The real Lord North (Frederick North, 2nd Earl of Guilford), Richardson's grandfather, was prime minister of the United Kingdom from 1770 to 1782 — the period during which Britain managed to lose thirteen of its American colonies.[10]

##  Wellington Trained This Trooper Well

ELECTIONS IN PIONEER days were rough and tumble affairs, often lasting a week or more to give the far-flung voters a chance to get to the polling station over trails that often could only be described as roads with great generosity.

The secret ballot was a nicety not used in early elections. Voters were expected to stand up and speak out their choice. And if it happened that the other party's supporters were in the majority around the polling station at that time, it was often a case of vote your choice and take your lumps. Since many a voter had to endure considerable hardship getting from his holding to the polling place, it was not considered out of place for candidates to hold "open house" for their supporters at a neighbourhood tavern.[11]

One story has come down about a tough old settler who couldn't see the sense of eating and drinking at the expense of his friends when the opposition candidate was offering the same hospitality. In the election of July 1828, Newmarket was included in the new constituency of Simcoe County for Parliamentary purposes, and both candidates were Newmarket men. William B. Robinson was the Family Compact candidate. He had grown up in Newmarket, where his mother, Esther, and stepfather, Elisha, Beman were among the community's first settlers. His opponent was John Cawthra, who operated a trading business at what is now Main and Water Streets. George Lount, also of Newmarket, was the returning officer. The only polling place in the whole constituency was in Holland Landing.

William Robinson kept open house at Phelps' tavern, located near the Lower Landing, and Cawthra was providing hospitality in a house at Johnson's Landings, a small community at the Upper Landing near the present site of the locks.[12]

A settler, who had received a land grant somewhere back in the County for services in Wellington's peninsular campaign against Napoleon, arrived on Monday, the first day of the week of voting, and installed himself at Robinson's booth in Phelp's tavern. After feasting and drinking there all week at Robinson's expense, he set off for the polling station on Saturday morning, the final day of voting. Voting took place at a wicket approached by a small stairway leading to a platform. After casting his vote, the elector descended another stairway down the other side.

Asked which candidate he voted for, the settler replied in a loud voice, "Cawthra." There arose a fierce outcry from the gang of loafers on the ground below the wicket and the voter was in danger of being hauled down from the rostrum and mobbed. Turning to the crowd, he made the following speech: "Gintlemin! I sarved under the Jook of Wellington in the peninsoolar. Moi general larnt me to faste on moi inimies and be damned if I haven't done it." [13]

After explaining himself, the tough old veteran marched down the stairs and through the crowd untouched, then quickly set off up the lake on his way home. Cawthra won that election, the first ever held in Simcoe County, by nine votes.

## Washington Wanted to Hang This Pioneer Landowner

CAPTAIN RICHARD "HANGMAN" Lippincott (1745–1826) was one of York County's United Empire Loyalist pioneers and one of the earliest people to acquire land there. His property around Newmarket was part of a larger grant of lots that made up a total of a few thousand acres in various places, all awarded to him for his service to the king. He didn't develop his land around Newmarket or live there. Perhaps he had a rather tenuous connection to the community, but this is too good a story to pass up.

A New Jersey Loyalist, Lippincott was granted 3,000 acres of uncleared land by the Crown for his services during the American Revolution, two hundred of those acres were between Bayview Avenue and Leslie Street, south of Mulock Drive. In 1805, he sold the Newmarket land to settler Shadrick Stephens, whose family would farm it for many years. In the mid-1990s, this land was subdivided by a company called Ronto Developments, which populated the former farm with experimental high-tech homes — supposedly the first homes in Ontario to be totally wired to the internet. [14]

After the Revolution, if George Washington had had his way Lippincott would have ended his days swinging at the end of a hangman's rope instead of living contentedly with his family in what today is Richmond Hill. But Lippincott didn't earn his nickname "Hangman" because Washington wanted to string him up. He acquired it for doing some stringing up of his own. The story goes that a savage guerrilla war raged throughout 1781 and 1782 between the rebels of Connecticut and New Jersey and the Loyalist fighting units known as the Associated Loyalists. The leader of the Associated Loyalists was William Franklin, a good example of how the bitter struggles of this Civil War turned neighbour against neighbour, son against father. Franklin's father was one of the new republic's most influential figures, Benjamin Franklin.

In April 1782, the Associated Loyalists were given permission to take British prisoner of war, Captain Joshua Huddy of the New Jersey Militia, out of New York to New Jersey to exchange him for one of the Loyalists' own men being held by the rebels. The party was commanded by Captain Lippincott. Under secret orders from William Franklin, Lippincott's party took Huddy to Monmouth County, New Jersey, Lippincott's home, and against British orders hanged him from a tree. The hanging was in retaliation for the killing of a Loyalist named Philip White in the same county two weeks before.

An outraged General George Washington demanded the surrender of Lippincott. The British commander, Sir Henry Clinton, stung by the deception, had Lippincott tried for murder by a British court instead. Lippincott was acquitted because he said he was just following Franklin's orders. Lippincott emigrated with his wife (Esther Borden) to New Brunswick and settled near Richmond Hill around 1793. He had once been a member of Colonel John Graves Simcoe's Queen's Rangers and evidently came here when Simcoe was appointed lieutenant governor. A land speculator and developer, Lippincott has a street in downtown Toronto named for him — Lippincott Street.

William Franklin fled to England, never to return to the United States.

## Richest of Old Stagecoach Landlords

CAPTAIN JOSEPH HEWITT served with General Brock in the Upper Canada Militia in the War of 1812–14, and was wounded during the Battle of Lundy's Lane. Before coming to Canada he had been a captain in the Glengarry Regiment, a Scottish Roman Catholic militia unit disbanded in Glasgow in 1802. Its members were given land to settle on along the north shore of the St. Lawrence River (Glengarry County has Quebec as its easterly border). The veterans reformed their regiment as a militia unit in Upper Canada.

After leaving the militia, Hewitt settled in Newmarket. At first he worked as a guard of government supplies moving up Yonge Street. He always carried his sword with him when on duty, and, after his death, Captain Hewitt's sword was displayed in the Odd-Fellows' Hall on Lot Street, now Millard Avenue. Mysteriously it has disappeared, and some years ago a plea for its return by the editor of *The Era* went unanswered.

In 1826, Hewitt built Newmarket's first fine hotel, an establishment that was to make him famous among frontier travellers and earn him a reputation as one of the richest of the old stagecoach landlords. At least two "hotels" had preceded his on the muddy trail that was to become Main Street, but neither offered more than rudimentary overnight accommodation.

Hewitt bought property from Timothy Millard — uncleared land except for a narrow strip along the east side of the old Indian trail. It is now the northwest corner of Main and Botsford Streets. There

*Famous as a stagecoach stop on the run between York (Toronto) and Holland Landing, the North American Hotel was also the first stop on William Lyon Mackenzie's pre-rebellion meeting tour of the colony to raise support among Reformers. Located on the northwest corner of Main and Botsford Streets, the hotel was demolished in the late nineteenth century.*

he constructed a three-storey frame inn and tavern, with a broad verandah and balcony above and stables behind. He called it the North American Hotel, and the name was painted in large letters across the third storey. Hewitt and the North American played a prominent role in Newmarket's first century. The hotel was headquarters for the four-horse mail- and stagecoaches running between Toronto and the Holland Landing docks. The coaches changed horses at his inn and passengers had breakfasts and dinners there. Eventually, Hewitt became a partner in the stage company.

William Lyon Mackenzie held a huge public meeting in front of the hotel the summer before the rebellion, and the hotel grounds housed the first cattle fair held in York County. Its barroom often doubled as a local meeting place and theatre. When Samuel Morse, the inventor of the telegraph, toured the colony sometime between 1837 and 1843 to show off his invention, he stayed at the North American and ran his wire from the barroom to the stable for demonstration purposes.

Hewitt's business closed in 1898 and the building was torn down not long after. Not a trace remains of this once thriving enterprise

## ⁊ Doctor Arrived with Shipload ⁊

MANY OF YONGE Street's first settlers came to the frontier empty-handed and impoverished, looking for a chance to carve a new life out of the forest with an axe and their bare hands. But there were a fortunate few who did bring financial resources, servants, and other makings of a genteel English household. Prepared to turn their forested lands into prosperous farming "estates," these well-off settlers soon built fine manor houses in the tradition of the English landed gentry and garnered often-lucrative government positions.

Dawson Manor, a classic Georgian, red-brick home that once stood on a four-hundred-acre Yonge Street estate stretching from Bathurst Street to the Holland River, is one such manor house. This mansion was so renowned in its heyday as a fine piece of colonial architecture that, in October 1923, the *Toronto Star* sent a young reporter named Ernest Hemingway north to Newmarket to view it and write about it.

Times were tough in the British Isles during the early to mid-years of the nineteenth century. The new Industrial Age brought massive unemployment and consolidation in the farming sector caused great distress, and all of this was severely aggravated by a depression that followed the end of the Napoleonic wars. Thousands fled this poverty and unemployment, emigrating to the largely unsettled spaces of the North American colonies. Yonge Street, the government's settlement road to the vast interior — a trade route, a military road to the Upper Lakes, and most importantly, a farm road linking the rich table lands of York County to the port and market at Toronto — provided choice locations for a number of these prosperous settlers. One of them, Dr. John Dawson, built on frontage

Author's collection

*Dawson Manor, a fine Georgian manor house on a Yonge Street hill, was built by a medical doctor, Dr. John Dawson, who emigrated from England in 1832. In 1837, Ojibwa warriors camped on its lawns to protect the doctor from Mackenzie's rebels in recognition of Dawson's frequent medical treatment of First Nations people, often travelling to their encampments in response to their needs. Dawson was also well-known for his support of the Family Compact.*

on the west side of the hill about a mile west and a little north of the village of Newmarket, which lay nestled in its river valley.

A well-off Yorkshire medical man, Dr. Dawson had decided sometime in the 1820s that the future of his family lay in the New World. In 1830, he chartered a sailing vessel and in it he stowed family and servants, farm animals and implements, glass, wrought iron, and household goods. Twice the ship was turned back by weather, and, on the third attempt, was blown far off course, making port well south of its New York City destination. Undaunted, the Dawson family loaded their goods onto wagons and set out for the York County frontier. Finally arriving in York, Dr. Dawson purchased four hundred acres on Yonge Street, enough to leave one hundred to each of his four sons, and set off up the muddy wagon road.

Once there, family and servants set to work constructing a log cabin that would serve as home until a proper manor house could be built. It would take until 1837 to finish the elaborate building. Bricks for the fourteen-inch thick walls and three chimneys were made from clay found on the property and baked in a nearby kiln. Enoch Rogers, a Newmarket builder, did the carpentry work. The house was probably the first in the area to have central heating — a wood-burning furnace was installed during construction.

Dr. Dawson not only offered medical care but filled his own prescriptions from a dispensary he ran from his home. A staunch government man, he was named a justice of the peace and performed many a wedding in the days when preachers were scarce on the frontier. His neighbours soon started calling this multi-talented landowner and physician Squire Dawson. Dr. Dawson often ministered to First Nations people of the area and was well-liked and admired by them.

Newmarket was a centre of rebel activity. During the 1837 Rebellion, when word reached his Native patients that their friend might be in danger, an Ojibwa war party came south down Yonge Street and pitched their teepees on the lawns at Dawson Manor, serving notice that the family was under its protection.

Squire Dawson died in 1851, but his manor remained in the family until 1988. Joy Hughes was the last Dawson descendant to live there. Dawson Manor was moved from its hilltop to make way for a Canadian Tire store. At its new location, a block away, it was converted into a spa.

*Chapter Five*

# THINGS HAPPEN

## ❧ The War of 1812 Created Prosperity ❧

THE WAR OF 1812 was good for the Newmarket area — it created a market for farm produce, forced development of Yonge Street as a military and settlement road, brought businessmen and settlers into the area, and created jobs. Troops passing up and down Yonge Street spent money along the way. Best of all, no battles were fought around Newmarket and the invading American troops who captured York in 1813 didn't go north of Oak Ridges looking for loot and food.

The war drove produce prices up and the army paid in hard cash — a very scarce commodity on the frontier — so farmers prospered. Local men found work moving supplies and armaments up the trail from York to the upper lakes military base at Penetanguishene. A storehouse and some log huts built at Soldiers' Bay, north of Holland Landing on the Holland River, served as a transfer point on the route north. In winter, part of the traffic was carried on sleighs by way of Newmarket and across the Lake Simcoe ice from Roches Point on the southeast shore, but most of the heavy traffic was teamed up Yonge Street to the Landing and carried over water to Kempenfelt Bay.

The war brought prosperity to the area's farmers and traders in other ways as the Yonge Street trail was forced into heavier use. It became dangerous to sail Lake Ontario and Lake Erie where American warships prowled and forts at Detroit and Niagara guarded key passages. Yonge Street was the safest route for soldiers and traders heading to the British posts at Penetanguishene and Michilimackinac on Lakes Michigan and Superior, and in the west and northwest.

Around this time great numbers of First Nations people began coming to Newmarket to trade. Consequently, voyageurs from Drummond Island (the British post at the west end of Lake Huron) and beyond brought furs all the way to Newmarket for sale. This, of course, was all to the benefit of Elisha Beman and his stepson, Peter Robinson, and their trading post, and to William Roe and Andrew Borland with their post established at the close of the war. The Cawthra family would become involved in the Newmarket fur trade about 1820.

The northwest traffic up Yonge increased before the Royal Navy achieved control of Lake Erie in 1813. During 1814–15 a very large quantity of stores passed up to the military warehouses at Holland Landing on its way northwest. These included heavy goods like cannon balls, other ammunition, and food supplies for the dockyard at Penetanguishene as well as cannon for arming the vessels and protecting the post. The *Upper Holland Conservation Report* points out that the resources of the district around Yonge Street and the landings on the Holland River must have been strained to provide teams for hauling this transport. The annoyance to settlers of having oxen and horses commandeered at inconvenient times would sometimes be compensated for by payment in hard money for food, lodging, and fodder. However, they were often given government certificates, which may or may not have been redeemed later for cash.

It must have been disturbing for the quiet Quaker families to have troops billeted in their homes, men who drank, smoked, and swore, and were notoriously careless with fire. As noted, Quakers not only refused to serve in the military, but would not pay the resulting fines. Often their young men were jailed or forced to hide in the bush. They would not accept payment from the military either for billeting or supplies requisitioned, because that was interpreted as aiding the war effort. In this regard, those Quakers families located in the vicinity of Yonge Street were the most severely tested in the colony.

*Author's collection*

*A Royal Navy work party was hauling this giant anchor to a shipyard in Penetanguishene when word arrived that the War of 1812 was over. The teamsters abandoned the anchor at the Royal Navy Holland Landing Depot and headed for the taverns of York. The anchor can still be seen at East Gwillimbury's Anchor Park on Doane Road.*

The war left a monument in the form of a great forged anchor that still lies in a Holland Landing park near the old landing places. Made in England for a large frigate under construction at the mouth of the Nottawasaga River and intended for use on the upper lakes, the huge anchor had been hauled up Yonge Street with great difficulty by teams of oxen and men. They were almost at the Landing Place when, according to the story, a horseman overtook the teamsters with the news that peace had been declared. With a cheer the men abandoned their charge where it lay and headed back down Yonge Street to celebrate. Years later the historic relic was moved to its present location at Anchor Park in Holland Landing.

## ❧ Booze to Blame for Town's First Homicide ❧

NEWMARKET'S FIRST HOMICIDE apparently went unpunished except, as the brother of the victim said, by "the Great Judge of all things, which will, no doubt, punish the murderer sooner or later."[1] The shooting was an accident, the result of an excess of alcohol-induced exuberance during a chivaree (a noisy, mock-serenade to newlyweds, usually followed by a party) in the fall of 1818 at an early hotel and tavern. Very little was recorded or survived in records of the event and most of what we know comes from a letter Thomas Selby of Sharon wrote in May 1819, about the death of his brother Robert at the tavern.

It would appear that Robert Selby and Thomas Webb were riding past the tavern when one of the celebrants inside, David Cummings, stepped to the door and began firing a weapon. Selby was killed and Webb wounded. When Thomas wrote his letter, months later, he told how it aggravated him to see the killer of his brother still in the community, implying that the colonial authorities didn't press charges.[2]

The hotel itself was the frontier inn erected by Elisha Beman on land across Eagle Street from today's senior citizens apartments. The second building on this site, also erected as a roadhouse, still stands there. It dates to 1822, making it one of the oldest surviving structures in town.

Beman is thought to have built the first tavern shortly after his arrival. Daniel Dye operated it for him and by 1822 he and brother, Michael Dye, apparently owned it. It was in that year that they built the Georgian frame

Author's collection

*Dye's Inn is shown as it looked in its earlier days, circa 1885. Today it is missing the two-storey verandah and is used as an office for a publishing company.*

structure that still graces the site. The expenditure was too much for them and the pair went bankrupt shortly after the building was completed. However, it continued to be operated as a tavern until about 1840, when it was purchased by John Cawthra and made into a private residence. It remained such until the fall of 1985 when it was converted to commercial and office uses. It is still known locally as Dye's Inn.

## How Agnes Defeated the Ghost

Agnes Pretty purchased Dyes' Inn in the 1980s and renovated it for use as both home and real estate office. She replaced all the windows, redid the old floors, had the wiring redone, put in a high-efficiency gas furnace, insulated and put new siding on the outer walls, cut a door into the hall from the small room behind the west-side living room, turned the attic into a den, the lawns into a parking lot, and put in a new kitchen

One night, not long after Agnes Pretty first moved her business in, she was sitting alone in her office looking out over Eagle Street when the calculator on her desk suddenly started to run. She turned it off. It came on again. She pulled the plug, deciding there must be a short-circuit somewhere, and sat back again to read. A few minutes later the calculator started operating again. Totally baffled, she left the room. At 7:00 a.m. the next morning she was on the telephone to the electrician, demanding he get right over there and find out what the problem was with the electrical system. He came — but couldn't find a problem. She next called Newmarket Hydro in to check, but their experts couldn't find any problem either.

The mystery never was solved, and strange things kept happening. Dishes rattled for no reason, footsteps and other noises were heard when no one was there, doors slammed. There was an unexplainable cold spot partway up the main staircase. People in the inn often simply had the feeling they were being watched by an unseen presence.

However, Agnes said nothing to her employees. About three months after the episode with the adding machine, a secretary at her real estate firm, which was housed in the building, said she too had had strange experiences. "There's something in this house, Agnes," she said.[3] The woman had a friend who worked for the Ontario Science Centre and she invited him up to investigate. He brought a meter that detects energy levels, one that is often used in searches for ghosts. At the cold spot on the stairs the needle went off the chart.

*Dye's Inn, at the corner where Water Street meets Eagle Street, is one of Newmarket's oldest buildings. It is also the location of the community's first homicide. No one knows whose playful little ghost annoyed Newmarket realtor Agnes Pretty after she turned the building into her office in the mid-1980s, but the ghost met its match!*

Drawing by Creighton Henry

The ghost was never trouble, said Agnes, it just continued to make its presence felt with annoying pranks. Finally, late one evening when the calculator was going on and off while Agnes, a peppery Scottish woman, was trying to work, she decided she'd had enough. She blew up at the ghost and told it off. "I have to run a business in this house and I have thirty-five sales people I have a great interest in keeping busy selling houses and that can't be done if these distractions continue," she angrily told her unseen visitor. "If you keep this up there's going to be a battle, and I can assure you it's not going to turn out well for you."

"After that night," said Agnes, "I've had no problems. The ghost just doesn't bother me anymore. I'm very comfortable with it. In fact, when strangers come into the house, they often comment on what a 'nice feeling' they get."[4]

## Murder Rare in Quaker Community

"MURDER MOST FOUL" — it happened even in the most peaceful of Quaker pioneer settlements.

One of the best documented crimes from the early days of settlement in this area is the murder of eighteen-year-old Isaac James on the bush road between Newmarket and Uxbridge. Poor Isaac was done in by his father's hired man so the murderer could steal the James's prized span of dappled grey mares. It happened in the autumn of 1828.

Ezekiel James, the father, had hired an Irishman named Michael Christie to help with the harvest on his farm near Uxbridge. Part of the compensation agreed upon was that James would transport Christie, his wife, and children to York after the work was done. When the day came, Ezekiel was ill and Isaac had to embark on what was then a four-day return journey. The only way from Uxbridge to York was via the old settlement road to Newmarket, and then down Yonge Street. Between Uxbridge and Newmarket there were twelve miles of solid bush with the road merely brushed out around the trees.

The night after they left, Isaac's mother had a horrible dream. She saw her son wounded, bruised and bloody, and groaning in pain. A good Quaker woman who was by no means superstitious, Mrs. James returned to sleep, but the dream was repeated. She became so alarmed she woke up the whole household, and wanted to set out immediately to follow Isaac. However, her husband was still very sick and more than a little skeptical, and decided to wait until the four days it would take Isaac to make the trip had passed. But Isaac did not arrive as expected, and the alarm was given to the neighbours, who had already heard of Mrs. James' dream. A search was organized, led by Mrs. James, along the road to Newmarket. Every thicket and swamp was scrutinized, but nothing found. At one point, within a mile of being through the twelve miles of woods, the horses became frightened. They sniffed and snorted, and shied off as they passed a log-heap beside the track. At the time it was assumed a small animal hidden in the stack had frightened them.

The search party continued until it reached the farm of Isaac Lundy, Mrs. James' brother, near Yonge Street, but there was no news of young Isaac or the team there. Mr. Lundy checked with a Yonge Street blacksmith who had often shod the horses. He reported the team was seen passing his shop the same day it left the James' farm and that a strange man was driving, and a woman and child or two with him, but no Isaac. That night, tossing and turning in bed at her brother's home, Mrs. James heard a voice in her room say distinctly three times, "In the woods, in the woods, in the woods." Startled, she immediately woke up her brother, and yielding to her entreaties, he sent horsemen to alarm settlers in Whitchurch and East Gwillimbury to turn out and search the woods on both sides of the road for a distance of forty rods.

Again Mrs. James led the Whitchurch party. They had proceeded only a little beyond a mile along the wooded trail when, pointing to a log heap on the right-hand side of the road, she told the party "search there." This was the spot where the horses had shied on her earlier journey. There the body of the missing Isaac was found. He had been shot through the head and then beaten with the gunstock until it was broken. The boy had obviously lived for several days after being left for dead. An inquest returned a verdict of willful murder, and the government of Upper Canada offered a $400 reward for Christie's arrest.

But the murderer had fled with the horses and wagon. Going around York, he succeeded in reaching the head of Lake Ontario and crossed the border, stopping at Troy, New York. However, William Reid of Sharon, a high-spirited young man, was among those who set off in pursuit. Enquiries at Hamilton put him on the track, and by racing at full speed on horseback, he caught up with the culprit at Troy. Christie was returned to the authorities in Upper Canada, made a full confession, was tried, convicted, and hanged.

## Switch for Oxen Grew into a Giant Willow

THE FARM IN the Yonge Street Quaker settlement first settled by Ebenezer and Elizabeth Doan was noteworthy for many years for two huge Lombardy willow trees — one on each side of its gate. In 1808 their farm was on the west side of Yonge Street, north of Green Lane. About 1820 the family sold and then moved to a farm north of Sharon. The Doan family had been farmers and cabinetmakers for generations, and Ebenezer is remembered as the master builder of the Sharon Temple.

Ebenezer's son Abraham often told the story of how those unusual willow trees came to be growing at the end of a Yonge Street farm lane. The Doans had emigrated in 1808 from Bucks County, Pennsylvania, where Abraham had been born six years earlier. Their long and arduous journey to Upper Canada, travelling in wagons covered by stretched canvas and pulled by oxen, took a month. Their route for moving all their household goods (including a cow), took them through the town of Bethlehem and over the Allegheny Mountains in the north part of the state.

After Abraham's death in 1892 a friend wrote in *The Newmarket Era* that he often heard him relate this story:

> My father cut a limb from one of our willow trees in Bucks County the morning we started for Canada, to use for the double purpose of a whip and cane. We drove a cow along with us, which we milked night and morning, and churned [butter] once by the roadside too. Well, when we got settled in our new home on Yonge St., I asked father to give me leave to plant the whip, to see if it would grow. He did not think it would, but [said] I might do so.

I did, and in a short time it really did begin to bud, and grew nicely that summer. The next spring I took a branch from it and put it the other side of the "bars" that were there at that time, and that is the way the trees first came here.[5]

Abraham Doan lived all his life in the Sharon area. He married Elizabeth Reid, daughter of another Sharon family, and they had six children. There are still Doans in the area, and their family association periodically holds a reunion at Sharon Temple. The trees are long gone, victims of road widening.

## Gifts to First Nations Distributed at Holland Landing

EARLY SETTLERS TO this area knew of two main landings on the Holland River — the Upper or Canoe Landing, and the Lower or Steamboat Landing. Little trace of either exists today, just as nothing remains of the British naval supply base at the Lower Landing, or the fur trading posts of Newmarket firms that flourished there for some years. The Upper Landing was the ancient place of embarkation of Native hunting and war parties. After the white man came, the landing continued to be used for canoes and lighter craft. About a mile and a half above the Upper Landing arose the village of Holland Landing.

When regular navigation opened on Lake Simcoe, the steamboat landing about one-and-a half miles north of the Upper Landing came into use. At this place the river was about twenty-five yards wide, its banks low and marshy and thickly wooded with tamarack. It was at this uninviting place that Yonge Street, the great colonization highway, terminated and merged into the water course across Lake Simcoe. A surviving description of the Lower (Steamboat) Landing depicts it as a clear space in the woods, where some long, low buildings of log stood, with strong shutters on the windows that usually were closed.[6] These buildings were the government depositories of naval and military stores.

The gifts were treaty payments given annually, and sometimes semi-annually, by the government to First Nations people when on their way to

Penetanguishene. The clearing was used as a camping ground by both the Natives and fur traders. Here, as an early account states, large numbers of Natives, often from very remote districts on the upper lakes could be seen encamped at all seasons of the year: "Many of these came several times a year for the purpose of bartering their furs at Holland Landing, which was a sort of emporium for a large part of the northern country."[7]

During these early years of the nineteenth century, a number of Newmarket businessmen, such as William Roe and partner Andrew Borland, Elisha Beman and the Robinson brothers, and the Cawthras, operated fur trading posts at the landing. Here too the annual distribution of presents to the First Nations people was made. An interesting description of one of these treaty days at Holland Landing has been left us by Captain Basil Hall of the Royal Navy, who happened to be passing through the area in July 1827 and had made a digression to Holland Landing to watch the July 27th distribution. He reported:

> On July 19th, instead of proceeding, as we had intended, straight along the great road to the eastward, we made a sharp turn to the left, and travelled for some 30 miles directly north towards Lake Simcoe, one of those numerous sheets of water with which Upper Canada is covered; and destined, no doubt in after times, to afford the means of much valuable intercourse from place to place, when their banks are peopled and cultivated. Our present object, however, was to witness the annual distribution of presents, as they are called, made by government to the Indians; the regular payment, in short, of the annuities, in consideration of which, the Indians have agreed to relinquish their title to lands in certain parts of the country.
>
> The scene at Holland Landing was amusing enough, for there collected about three hundred Indians, with their squaws and papooses, as the women and children are called. Some of the party were encamped under the bush wood, in birch-bark wigwams, or huts, but the greater number, having paddled down Lake

Simcoe in the morning, had merely drawn up their canoes on the grass, ready to start again as soon as the ceremonies of the day were over. The Indian agent seemed to have hard work to arrange the party to his mind; but at length the men and women were placed in separate lines, while the children lay sprawling and bawling in the middle. Many of the males as well as the females, wore enormous earrings, some of which I found, upon admeasurment, to be six inches in length; and others carried round their necks silver ornaments, from the size of a watch, to that of a soup-plate. Sundry damsels, I suppose at the top of the fashion, had strung over them more than a dozen of necklaces of variously stained glass beads.

One man, I observed, was ornamented with a set of bones, described to me as the celebrated wampum, of which everyone has heard; and this personage with four or five others, and a few of the women, were wired in the nose like pigs, with rings which dangled against their lips. Such of the papooses as were not old enough to run about and take care of themselves, were strapped up in boxes, with nothing exposed but their heads and toes. So that when the mothers were too busy to attend to their offspring the little animals might be hooked up out of the way, upon the nearest branch of a tree, or placed against a wall, like a hat or pair of boots, and left there to squall away to their hearts content.[8]

The annual distribution of presents in compensation for the First Nations surrender of lands in the area took place at Holland Landing until 1828, then at Orillia, and then at Present Island near Penetanguishene until 1835. In 1836 it was moved to Manitoulin Island.[9] Payment originally was the equivalent of five dollars per treaty Indian. However, some treaties, including the Manitoulin Island Treaty of 1868, agreed to invest income from First Nations land sales in annuities for their benefit.

Today, treaty annuity payments are paid annually on a national basis to registered status Indians who are entitled to treaty annuities through membership in bands that have signed historic treaties with the Crown, according to the federal Indian and Northern Affairs Canada ministry.

## ❧ Stories of Local 1837 Rebels ❧

THE STORIES OF the Newmarket-area men who fought in the Rebellion of 1837 are seldom told, and now after 150 years many of these accounts are lost to history.

When the rebellion failed and government supporters among the rebels' neighbours launched a campaign against those who had marched with Mackenzie or were even suspected of sympathizing with him, many rebels hoped by lying low they could weather the storm without being hauled off to prison. They didn't want their stories told. Others actually joined in the hunt in the hope their actions would throw suspicion from

*Construction had barely been completed in 1837 on this Presbyterian Kirk on the northeast corner of Timothy and Church Streets when it was commandeered for use as a jail for captured rebels. The prisoners, chained together, were eventually marched to Toronto. As it took two days for the party to reach Toronto, they slept overnight in an unheated barn near Thornhill.*

themselves. Some succeeded in staying quiet and unnoticed, and some of their stories came out years or even generations later.

Others, like J.B. Caldwell the Newmarket chair maker, were so respected in the community they were put on parole and left alone. Caldwell, a friend and supporter of Mackenzie's, had drawn the line at armed rebellion and refused to take part. However, when the rebel prisoners were locked up in the Timothy Street Presbyterian Kirk behind Liberty Hall, Caldwell's Botsford Street home, he and his wife took hot food over the fence to the men and pushed it through the kirk windows. Many of the rebels were taken from their homes, locked up in the unheated church, and then chained together and force-marched through the mid-winter cold to Toronto. Some reported later that among their guards on that march were men who had been with them a few weeks earlier in the Reform cause.

Luther Elton, a Newmarket tailor, and Joseph Brammar and Robert Moore of Sharon, were three who were marched on the chain to Toronto. Peter Rowen, a Sharon blacksmith, is said to have made pikes for the Mackenzie supporters, but may not have been arrested, for his name does not appear on the list of those jailed. Elton, a Vermonter born in 1800 or 1801 who came to Canada in 1833, was known as an outspoken radical during the tumultuous summer of 1837. Active throughout the rebellion, he was arrested a few days after the final battle and kept in jail until the following May, when he petitioned for a pardon. Instead of the pardon that was granted to so many who played only minor roles in the rebellion, Elton was sentenced to three years in the Kingston penitentiary and then to banishment. He was pardoned in January 1839 along with several other rebels who were imprisoned at the time. In the 1840s Elton was naturalized and bought a lot in Newmarket — a small part of Lot 91, Concession 1, Whitchurch Township, probably to return to his trade as a tailor.

Joseph Brammar, a Yorkshireman born in 1809, emigrated as a young man and first worked at his trade as a wheelwright in Hogg's Hollow. He married Ellen Lundy in 1833 and settled in Sharon. He was a strong supporter of Mackenzie who particularly took issue with the government over its refusal to secularize the Clergy Reserve. Brammar marched with the Sharon men to Montgomery's Tavern and took part in the battle. A few days later when the lieutenant governor, Sir Francis Bond Head, offered an amnesty to all who had taken up arms if they returned peaceably to their homes, Brammar and Robert Moore of Sharon decided to take advantage of the offer. They came out of hiding and started the trek north. Fearing bands of loyalist cavalry out hunting rebel fugitives, the two men travelled through the woods and on more than one occasion walked backwards for a concession or two along a muddy road so their tracks might give the impression they were southbound. The trip took several days. Shortly after reaching home, Brammar was arrested by local militia and locked up in the Timothy Street Kirk. The same thing probably happened to Moore. After being marched to Toronto, the prisoners were incarcerated in the King Street market buildings, and later in the old Front Street Parliament Buildings.

Shortly after Brammar watched his friends Samuel Lount and Peter Matthews being hanged in the courtyard of the King Street Gaol, the Grand Jury brought in a true bill against Brammar for high treason. Upon being arraigned and asked to plead, Brammer replied, "Your Lordship, I am an Englishman. I have a heart as true and loyal to the Queen and to Britain as any British subject in the country, but if you mean disloyal to the Family Compact and the men who are robbing this country, I am guilty."[10]

Strangely, after making his plea he was never tried. Several days later when some fellow inmates were being freed, Brammar and Moore walked out with them. Both men fled to Buffalo, where they stayed in exile until it was safe to return to Sharon. Brammar was a member of the Children of Peace and helped build the Sharon Temple.

## Wellington Veterans Saved Lount Home

SAMUEL LOUNT WAS hanged for high treason following the Rebellion of 1837, but to many of his neighbours he remained a hero. He was a hard-working Quaker settler, a generous storekeeper, a blacksmith, and a popular politician whom they had sent to represent them in the Legislative Assembly of the colony.

The very fact that there were thousands of petitioners for his pardon, surely is an indicator of the kind of man he was. One story showing Lount's generous spirit has come down to us. After the battle at Montgomery's Tavern, government loyalists declared open season on rebels and reformers. One day a drunken mob set off up Yonge Street to burn the Lount home near Holland Landing where Mrs. Lount and their seven children lived. Warned by a neighbour, Mrs. Lount loaded what possessions she could into a sleigh and sent them away. As it turned out the sleigh was stopped and its cargo confiscated.

However, the home was saved by a grateful neighbour. The story goes that when Moses Hayter and his family emigrated from England to the Holland Landing area in 1832, they faced starvation when their first crop failed. Hayter appealed to the kindly Quaker blacksmith and storekeeper at Holland Landing for a barrel of flour to keep his family from starving. He received two barrels. Lount and Hayter became lifelong friends after that.

In 1837, Hayter was returning from York on foot and arrived at the Lount house on the night a "drunken, roistering mob came in procession up Yonge St., with flambeaux, mingled oaths and fearful imprecations and threats to burn the home of Mrs. Lount and her children."[11]

About midnight, the mob arrived and Moses Hayter stepped forward.

> Do you call yourselves Englishmen? I am an Englishman from London. I was usher to the Duke of Wellington. I was taught to know no fear in a just cause, and I declare you shall not enter this house with the intention of burning it over the heads of this defenceless woman and her children. You shall have to walk over the body of a dead Englishman. He once saved my life and that of my family from starvation when that fate stared me and them in the face: and hundreds can testify that he has reached out a helping hand to those in great need. He saved my dear ones and I shall save his![12]

The mob, defeated by the bravery of one man, quietly dispersed and went home. Hayter later worked tirelessly gathering signatures on petitions asking the governor to spare Lount's life after Lount was sentenced to death for his part in the rebellion. Friends of Lount gathered thousands of signatures on petitions asking Lieutenant Governor Sir George Arthur (who had replaced Bond Head) not to execute Lount and

Matthews, but Arthur decided an example was needed, and ordered them hanged. The government minimized the number of signatures gathered, and Reformers probably inflated the number.[13]

Moses Hayter became Barrie's first jailer in 1842 after the Lake Simcoe community built a county courthouse and jail. He served there for ten years. After Lount's conviction for treason, the government seized all his property. Mrs. Lount moved her family to a new frontier in Michigan.

## ❧ Salt Well Boon to Pioneers ❧

THERE USED TO be a deer lick in the old Bogart woods at Bogarttown, a pioneer milling community to the east, which today is part of Newmarket. More precisely, the old community was located at Leslie Street and Mulock Drive.

When John Bogart Sr. brought his family from Pennsylvania and settled land in the area in 1802, he found that wild deer came to a certain spot in the woods to lick the natural salt found on the ground. During the War of 1812, salt became a rare commodity, and Bogart sank a well from which salt water was taken and boiled down to obtain salt for ordinary purposes.

This salt well was cribbed with pine slabs and eighty-eight years later (1895), a Bogarttown resident named Sterling Chappell reported to *The Newmarket Era* that he had discovered the old well, and that the slabs were as good as the day they were put down.

## ❧ Fire Brought Renewal to Colonial Main Street ❧

NEWMARKET'S FIRE DEPARTMENT, with its up-to-date stations on each side of town and its array of modern equipment, gives little hint of its disastrous mid-nineteenth-century beginnings.

Fire was a mixed blessing in early Ontario towns. Raging out of control through the often flimsy wooden buildings thrown up in frontier days and still in use decades later, it wrought havoc and destruction of the most complete kind. But out of the ashes usually grew bigger, better, more modern brick buildings that contributed substantially to the development and prosperity of the community in future years.

Newmarket was incorporated by the government of the colonies of Upper and Lower Canada in May 1857. The village council took office January 1, 1858, and one of its first resolutions was to establish a fire brigade. It took three years to accomplish, but finally a ten-man volunteer brigade was set up and equipped. Water tanks with 5,000 gallon capacity each were constructed at main intersections, and the village purchased a horse-drawn steam-power fire engine and pump, as well as buckets, hoses, and ladders. All this was a considerable expense for a village of a few hundred residents, but people considered it a good investment, for fire was the most feared word in colonial Newmarket — probably in most colonial communities. When a fire started it could be devastating, claiming whole blocks and sometimes whole neighbourhoods. Protection was usually limited to neighbours who formed bucket brigades to the nearest wells or pond and fought to keep the fire from spreading.

So it was with the Great Fire of 1862 that wiped out a large chunk of Newmarket's Main Street. But for the valiant efforts of every able-bodied man who could be mustered on that cold December night, it might have swept away the whole south end of the village. No one ever knew what started the fire, but it was first spotted about 3:00 a.m. on a bitterly cold December 6th in a wooden tenement occupied by a watchmaker named Dieterlie. The building was located about halfway up the hill on the east side of Main Street. A strong wind was blowing from the north and the flames spread rapidly southward through the wooden buildings. Although the village's volunteer fire department was called almost immediately, it took it an hour to get into action and by then several buildings were in flames.

The delay brought bitter recriminations, especially when it was learned that the newly acquired and expensive fire engine the village was so proud of could not be brought into action during that first crucial hour because someone had allowed the water in its boiler to freeze in the December night. Before the fire was under control it wiped out all the buildings on the east side of Main Street from the Central Hotel (opposite Park Avenue) to halfway between Timothy and Water Streets. Among the businesses burned out were Henderson's Grocery, Lee the shoemaker, and a bakery run by another Lee family member, Wallis' Saddlery and Harness Shop, the Caldwell Chair Factory, and Saxton's Jewellery.

Mr. Wallis's store stood on the north side of the laneway opposite the end of Botsford Street (site of the former IDA drug store and a law office early in the twenty-first century). His home was behind his store and behind his home he ran a tannery. All three were burned down. The chair factory was in a wooden building on the south side of the laneway — at the beginning of the twenty-first century the site of Cassidy's Flowers. South of it was Joseph Millard's furniture factory, which boasted the first planing mill north of Toronto (the machine was put on rollers and pushed out of the burning building).

Arriving amid this devastation, the Hook and Ladder Company tried to pull down buildings before they caught fire, but with little success. Sparks from the burning tannery carried across Main Street and ignited fires on the roof of the frame North American Hotel at Botsford and

Courtesy of Richard MacLeod

*This early Newmarket fire pumper was a successor to the first unit, which had a large steam boiler that froze on the night of the great Main Street fire. Firefighting was hard work in those days. A gang of volunteers pumped this apparatus by hand, throwing a spray on the burning building.*

Main, and volunteers fought to save that building. By 7:00 a.m., the fire had been subdued, but much of Main Street was a smoulding ruin and the village was organizing relief for the homeless, establishing salvage efforts, and appointing a watch to stand guard over piles of furniture and other belongings saved from the fire. It must have seemed a dark day for the little village. Yet the pioneer spirit was strong and in less than two years, rebuilding was complete.

Joseph Millard erected a much-expanded workshop and installed a powerful new steam engine, as well as two brick stores, both three-storeys tall. New brick stores went up north of Timothy Street, and J.B. Caldwell built a three-storey chair factory and warehouse on his site. Both Saxton and Wallis rebuilt and modernized and the owner of the Commercial Hotel replaced the sheds and driving houses he lost. Main Street was whole again. Many of those new buildings were built of brick and still serve today.

# Chapter Six

# IN VICTORIA'S REIGN

## ✦ Bogarttown: Rival for Newmarket? ✦

"On Bogart Pond … free trees, lake and fresh air with every purchase," read the big real estate advertisements running in the summer of 1999. "A charming enclave … set on the hillside, creekside and pondside of 25 acres of environmentally precious and incredibly beautiful land, surrounding an historic 5-acre mill pond."[1]

One wonders what John Bogart, the builder of that mill pond nearly two hundred years ago, would think of the developer's description of the area where he and his family cleared the forests and his pioneer community sprang up. In all likelihood he would be pleased, for John Bogart was an entrepreneur.

At one point the community of Bogarttown, which grew up around his mill and other enterprises, was a thriving centre, and one guesses there were some who thought it might grow to rival Newmarket, its neighbour. However, in 1853, when the colony's first railway chose to run tracks through Newmarket and Aurora and bypassed communities such as Bogarttown, the settlement began to fade. Today all that's left of a once thriving milling community is the pond and John's now-ancient home. Bogarttown now lies within Newmarket's municipal boundaries.

Of Dutch descent, the Bogart family had been pioneering in North America for two centuries when John decided to take advantage of Lieutenant Governor John Graves Simcoe's offer of free land in Upper Canada for experienced settlers. The family had settled in Bedford (now Brooklyn, New York) in 1663. Bogart probably came north to look for land sometime in 1801. He returned in 1802 with a caravan of thirty-one family members and friends to settle four hundred acres he had purchased in the area of today's Leslie Street and Mulock Drive; apparently, if you wanted to choose your land, you had to pay for it. With the family came horses, cattle, sheep, and poultry, and generations of experience in clearing the land, home and mill building, and farming.

They arrived on their heavily-forested land on October 29, 1802. The closest settlement, Newmarket, was three log huts set in a clearing, and York was but a hamlet. By 1805 a home had been built, the river dammed, and a sawmill was in operation. During the next year a gristmill was added. John Sr. was able to leave his eighteen-by-twenty-foot log cabin in 1811 and move into a new two-storey frame home. Basically unchanged, it still stands today facing Leslie Street, east of his pond. The bedstone of this pioneer gristmill was preserved for many years in the Prospect Street

*John Bogart built this frame home for his family in 1811, and the two-hundred-year-old structure, shown above, is still in use as a residence.*

garden of E.A. Bogart, John's great-grandson, and continues to grace a garden in Newmarket.

## ❧ Mud-Brick Mansion Boasted of Wine Cellar ❧

A COLONIAL MANSION of mud bricks built by an eccentric ex-British Army officer once graced the hollow at Woodbine Avenue and Mulock Drive where the Ontario Society for Prevention of Cruelty to Animals (OSPCA) has its sprawling headquarters. Colonel W.H. Beresford purchased Lots 30 and 31 in the 3rd Concession of Whitchurch Township during the 1830s. The lots are north and south of Mulock Drive (formerly the Vivian-Bogarttown Road) on the west side of Woodbine Avenue. By 1853 his many-peaked mansion had been built on the southerly side of the two lots.

The mansion must have been a wonder to the residents of colonial York County. It had eighteen rooms, seven fireplaces, a ballroom, and an extensive wine cellar. It stood on the banks of a little stream that passes

Author's collection

*Colonel W.H. Beresford's sprawling mud-brick home on Woodbine Avenue, near Mulock Drive, boasted of a wine cellar and a ballroom. After his death it fell into disuse and slowly disintegrated. No trace of this once grand mansion remains.*

through the property. The walls of this house, made of mud and pea straw, were three feet thick and the building is said to have measured about eighty feet by forty feet. Within there were forty-five doors.

Not much is known of the colonel's life, his army service, or why he chose to settle at a rural crossroads east of Newmarket. However, his house may have been his magnificent obsession, for it is said the cost ruined him. The mansion eventually fell into decay, and today no trace of it remains. The surviving photograph shows two distinct peaked wings, joined by a centre structure with twin peaked dormers. All three portions had their own verandahs.

An earlier Beresford house, built of more conventional clay brick, has survived. It is on the northwest corner of the same intersection. Built in 1840 and known as Pleasantville House, it appears to be a modest single-storey structure, but does have rooms on a second floor. Its most outstanding feature is an elliptical fan light over the front door.

Colonel Beresford was a member of St. Paul's Anglican Church in Newmarket, and his name occasionally can be found on lists of other Newmarket organizations of the period. He died alone.

## Butcher's Fair Made Main Street a Cowtown

A "BUTCHER'S FAIR" operated for many years on Newmarket's Main Street when the community was but a struggling village. The fair is said to have been one of the major factors in Newmarket's emergence as the economic centre of the area, but it must have given the dusty little village, then not many years beyond its frontier stage, the look of a Grade B-western movie Texas cowtown.

A newspaper advertisement from 1855 provides an early reference to the fair. It states, "The butchers of Toronto will hold their Fairs this year in Newmarket on the first Monday of each month."[2] Cattle and sheep were herded into pens in the centre of the village's downtown by area farmers, where the animals were inspected, prodded and poked, bid for, and haggled over by the Toronto butchers and their buyers who undoubtedly came up for the occasion on the recently (1853) completed railway.

*Author's collection*

*The farmer's market on Market Square was a focus of Newmarket's Saturdays. Farmers from all over the area came to town to sell their produce, butter, and other goods, while both locals and wholesalers from Toronto came to purchase. This photo shows the south side of Market Square crowded with buggies on market day, circa 1910.*

Both the Forsyth House, at Timothy and Main, and the North American Hotel, at Botsford and Main, were thronged with hungry, thirsty farmers and buyers, and the hotel yards became jammed with livestock. As the fair grew, the hotel yards were no longer adequate for use as stockyards, thus a vacant space two lots south of Forsyth House was also set up for cattle pens. The fairs continued to be held until 1867, and their success made it obvious to villagers there was a need for a full farmers' market. As early as 1857 people began to talk of the need, but it wasn't until a decade passed that there was action. In May 1867, a public meeting was called and a committee appointed to work with village council.

Not much happened until April 1869, when the committee decided to purchase property for a market building. It bought a parcel of land between Timothy and Botsford Streets, 130 feet west of Main Street (the present Market Square), and erected a shed on the west side. The land cost taxpayers $1,275; the expenditure raised a storm of protest from villagers. But the business community argued the market should be given a fair trial. This view did prevail, but work on the market was delayed until the crop on the newly acquired land could be harvested.

Things literally bogged down for another year when, in the spring of 1870, the roads in the area were so bad no market could be held. It wasn't until May of the following year that a notice was published announcing "a public market would open after the First of June."[3] Soon Saturdays were firmly established as market days in Newmarket, and long lines of farmers in buggies, democrats, and assorted wagons loaded with produce, became a familiar sight jogging along the dusty roads into the village. Extra space was soon needed for the market and the adjacent two lots on Main Street were leased. Later another building was put up on Botsford Street. By the early 1880s Newmarket's business community was again concerned about maintaining the commercial edge it had established, and many foresaw the need for a substantial new market building with improved facilities.

After much debate, a combination market building, auditorium, and town hall was constructed on Market Square and opened in July 1883. It cost $6,000 to build and is the structure we now call the Old Town Hall. It was completely renovated in 1983, including the replacement of the ornate bell tower that had been removed for safety reasons years before.

In 2009, the Old Town Hall temporarily closed its doors for major renovations to restore the cultural landmark to its former glory. These renovations were made possible by a $3.4 million grant received from the Building Canada Fund. The work is expected to be completed in early 2011.

## Water Street at the Foot of Main: An Early Industrial Area

THROUGHOUT NEWMARKET'S HISTORY the Water Street property at the foot of Main Street has frequently been the site of new construction. As recently as the early 1990s St. Andrew's Presbyterian Church built a modern addition eastward from its venerable old building onto the site.

Some of old Newmarket's biggest businesses have stood there. Joseph Hill's mill, store, and home, Newmarket's first buildings, were on the west side of the pond. The mill burned in 1860 and the home was moved to an Eagle Street location to make way for the Presbyterian church.

*Donald Sutherland became a wealthy mid-nineteenth-century miller and merchant. A Scottish miller and farmer who had settled in Schomberg in 1840, Sutherland moved to Newmarket in 1848 and established his milling operation there. He later acquired a general store, and, with a partner, established a flourishing business. During the 1860s he was reeve of the village of Newmarket. Sutherland died in 1881 and is buried in the Newmarket Cemetery.*

In 1853, builder Robert Brodie put up a building on the site for W.A. Clarke who opened a store there for the sale of factory cloths, tweeds, woollen blankets, yarns, and similar goods manufactured at local mills he controlled. It was the year after the arrival of the Ontario, Simcoe & Huron Railway in Newmarket and the new mill store helped to put the village on the map.

Clarke later added groceries to his stock. A year later he sold the store and nearby Cotter Gristmill to an affluent miller, Donald Sutherland, who had emigrated to Upper Canada from Scotland in 1840, initially settling in Schomberg. Sutherland expanded the business into a general store. Later, he took William McMaster Jr., nephew of William McMaster, the wealthy Toronto merchant and banker, into partnership. McMaster & Sutherland claimed to be the biggest store north of Toronto.

McMaster eventually took over the operation but later moved his enterprise to the Millard Block on the east side of Main Street, opposite the end of Botsford Street. As for Sutherland, he had taken on a new partner and opened a store in the Millard Block before McMaster moved there.

The Water Street store was next occupied by John Ashworth's hat factory. In 1884 it was employing forty people. Still later the building was occupied by the Novelty Company, a toy maker. It was demolished in the spring of 1895 to make way for a substantial Victorian home, which in its turn was torn down when the church expanded in 1992.

## Fur Trader Brought Seven Hundred to Party

A YOUNG FRENCH fur trader made his mark on the frontier "north of Yonge Street" in the early days of the colony. Francis Gaudaur, the son of a French trader, had helped his father develop an extensive trade with the First Nations in the north country as far away as Lake Superior. During this period, he developed a positive relationship with the First Nations people, and was often employed by the government as an interpreter at Rama Reserve, established in 1830 on Lake Couchiching.

Although only eighteen years old during the Rebellion of 1837, Francis was already a seasoned frontiersman, and was selected to convey government dispatches down Yonge Street from Newmarket to Toronto, and later from Holland Landing to the British garrison at Penetanguishene.

Mackenzie's rebellion had come to a head and fizzled out at the battle of Montgomery's Tavern early in December 1837. On New Year's Day 1838, young Francis Gaudaur surprised the residents of Newmarket, most of whom had been strong supporters of Mackenzie, by showing up for the day's festivities with seven hundred Native men, women, and children. He was given a rousing reception by the militia volunteers and loyal residents of the community, but supporters of the defeated Reform party were much more subdued.

The former Canadian Football League Commissioner Jake Gaudaur Jr. and Jake Gaudaur Sr. (1858–1937), a world-class rower, are both descendants of Francis Gaudaur.

## Mansion House: A Meeting Place for Rebels

A LONG-FORGOTTEN Newmarket hotel seems to have been a meeting place for Mackenzie sympathizers during the summer before the 1837 Rebellion. The Mansion House stood on the west side of Main Street near its south end, right next door to the Cawthra house. The hotel is known to have been a two-storey building, probably frame, and that the innkeeper from the early 1830s until sometime after 1861 was Thomas Mosier.

Mosier's wife, whose maiden name was Nancy Ann McNulty, was probably a sister of Eleanor McNulty Hewitt, who, with husband Joseph, operated the North American Hotel at Main and Botsford Streets, according to Susan MacDonald who compiled the Mosier family genealogy.

In his memoir, Henry Cawthra, son of the Cawthra store proprietor John Cawthra, said that as a boy of seven or eight his close friend was next-door neighbour Jack Mosier. The boys were in and out of the hotel on a daily basis. One day in the summer of 1837, they saw people in the Mosier kitchen spreading butter on long loaves of bread and wondered what was going on. Later the same day, they heard of a "training" to take place in a field to the west of Newmarket, so they went to see. There they saw these same loaves of buttered bread stuck on the end of

*Drawing by Creighton Henry*

*Sir Francis Bond Head, governor of Upper Canada from 1835 to 1838, refused to believe a rebellion was imminent in 1837, saying settlers knew too well which side their bread was buttered on to rebel. In reply, disgruntled settlers used loaves of buttered bread stuck on pikes for target practice.*

a pole firmly placed in the ground. Small platoons of men with rifles marched towards the pole, rank on rank, and fired at the bread. After each platoon had several shots, the order to retreat was given. Other manoeuvres followed. Reaching home, they told their parents what they saw. John and Will Cawthra, Reform supporters but not rebels, left immediately for Toronto to inform Lieutenant Governor Sir Francis Bond Head what was going on in Newmarket. Head refused to take them seriously.[4]

Henry Cawthra said it was years later when he finally understood the meaning of the buttered loaves being used as a target. A few days before the incident, when warned of dangerous developments in the colony, the governor said, "They know too well which side their bread is buttered on to attempt rebellion."[5]

Was Thomas Mosier, about fifty at the time, a supporter of rebellion, and were other meetings held at his inn? "It seems likely," said Susan MacDonald.[6] Was he at the Battle of Montgomery's Tavern? Probably not, as his name does not show up in lists of participants. However, evidence is inconclusive, as no complete list of participants has been found. John J. McNulty of Queensville, probably his brother-in-law, was at the battle, and then took part in the Short Hills raid on the Niagara frontier. He was captured, sentenced to exile in Van Dieman's Land, and died there.

On the other side of the coin, Thomas' brother, Captain John Mosier, played a prominent role on the government side. He claimed to be a key player in the burning of the *Caroline*.[7] Thomas Mosier and his wife seem to have arrived in Newmarket in the 1830s, perhaps at the invitation of the Hewitts, who may have had more business than they could handle. In 1830, they were farming in Clarke Township, but do not show up in the 1831 census. They may have founded the Mansion House as early as 1831. It was still appearing in the 1861 census, but is gone by 1871, when Thomas, by then eighty-four years of age, is listed as a baker.

Nancy Mosier died in February 1875, and Thomas followed in December of the same year. The name Mosier can no longer be found in the Newmarket area.

## ✑ Riding Key to Fight for Responsible Government ✑

IN NOVEMBER, 1931 a statue was unveiled in Montreal dedicated to a great French-Canadian leader whose political career was saved by the people of York County. The statue is of Sir Louis-Hippolyte LaFontaine, a key figure in the long fight for responsible government in Canada. It is a largely forgotten fact of Canadian history that this great parliamentarian twice sat in the colonial legislature for the York County constituency centered on Newmarket (Fourth Riding of York) and is one of those behind York County's claim to be "the birthplace of responsible government."

The story of how LaFontaine, a unilingual French-Canadian lawyer and dedicated nationalist from Montreal, came to be elected member of Parliament in 1841 for the Fourth Riding of York is the story of how the farmers and villagers of this county remained steadfast to the principles of Reform despite the setbacks their movement sustained in the Rebellion of 1837. Lafontaine defeated William Roe, one of Newmarket's founders, who was the Tory candidate.

Robert Baldwin, leader of the Reform movement in Upper Canada and a man who had represented North York County for some years, was determined that government rule by responsible party cabinet should replace Governor Sydenham's (Charles Poulett Thomson, 1st Baron Sydenham) system of rule by governor's coalition. Baldwin and LaFontaine shared a vision of a united Canada where French and English could live together on equal terms and govern according to the will of the people. When plans for uniting Upper and Lower Canada were announced, Baldwin wrote to LaFontaine suggesting a partnership between their two political parties. LaFontaine agreed. In the first election for the new united Canadian Parliament in March 1841, the new Reform Party won a majority of seats in both Canada East and Canada West.

Baldwin won the Fourth Riding of York and a seat in Hastings County, but Hippolyte LaFontaine withdrew from his re-election race in Terrebonne, charging that the governor of Quebec had fixed it after a Tory mob refused to allow his supporters access to the polling booths. However, Baldwin, who needed LaFontaine in Parliament, informed the Fourth Riding electors meeting in Newmarket he would sit for Hastings, and proposed they accept LaFontaine to run in the by-election. They

Author's collection

*Built as an architectural testament to the vision of the Children of Peace, a split-off group from the Yonge Street Quaker Meeting, Sharon Temple was completed in 1832. David Willson, the group's charismatic leader, held such sway that he was able to deliver a block of votes from his followers to Reform candidates over the years, ensuring their election. These included William Lyon Mackenzie, Robert Baldwin, and Louis-Hippolyte LaFontaine, the latter two both fathers of responsible government.*

did, and in September the candidate paid his first visit to the riding. Significantly, he arrived on the evening of September 4, 1841, the night the Children of Peace at Sharon held their Illumination Ceremony, when a lighted candle is placed in every window of the Sharon Temple to illuminate all 2,952 panes of glass. This thanksgiving service, attended by all members, creates a spectacular sight as darkness falls. The ceremony is one that the Temple Society continues to this day.

Sect leader David Willson was a firm friend of Baldwin's and regularly turned out a solid Reform vote. Baldwin, in endorsing the French-Canadian lawyer, told the Fourth Riding electors, "It will be satisfactory to you to know that the manner in which your nomination of Mr. LaFontaine has been received by the Lower Canadians proves the correctness of the views which had led you to the nomination. It is not too much to say that it has been received from one end of Lower Canada to the other as a pledge of sympathy and closer union between the Reformers of both sections of the Province."[8] LaFontaine's opponent William Roe was a former fur trader who had become a prosperous merchant and the village postmaster. LaFontaine won handily by a majority of 186–52.[9]

In 1842, LaFontaine was appointed as attorney-general east and Baldwin as attorney-general west. It was then a British tradition that such appointments be confirmed by a by-election. LaFontaine was easily returned in Fourth York, again defeating William Roe. However, Baldwin lost in Hastings. It was LaFontaine's turn to demonstrate the unity of Reform. He found his friend a safe seat in Rimouski County, an all-French speaking constituency along the south shore of the St. Lawrence River, east of Quebec City, which in early 1843 acclaimed the unilingual English-speaking Baldwin. This time, the two men again became attorneys-general, and the government at Kingston had a French-Canadian attorney-general for Lower Canada representing an English-speaking riding in the heart of Upper Canada, and an English-Canadian attorney-general for Upper Canada sitting for the Rimouski riding deep in Quebec.

In 1848, LaFontaine was called upon by Lord Elgin to form a government, becoming the first prime minister of Canada in the modern sense of the term. Baldwin and LaFontaine continued to dominate Canadian politics through the 1850s. The LaFontaine-Baldwin ministry became the first to take office in direct consequence of its party majority in Parliament. Responsible government was established.

By then, Baldwin was back representing the Fourth York, and LaFontaine sat for Terrebonne once again. Historians say neither man could have prevailed alone in the fight to establish responsible government but as a team they won the day. However, without the loyalty of the people of York County to the principles of Reform and responsible government, there would have been no team. That's why old York County is called the birthplace of responsible government.


## Friends and Colleagues Until Chips Are Down

DOCTOR HUNTER AND lawyer Boultbee had been what are called "friends and colleagues" for a long time, but that didn't mean they liked each other. Of course they always said they did, but events would prove otherwise.

*Alfred Boultbee was the first solicitor for the Village of Newmarket. The family had deep roots in the area. Alfred's brother, William, married Marion Mulock, sister of Sir William Mulock, and after graduating from law school, young William Mulock articled in Boultbee's law office.*

Newmarket in the 1860s had about 2,000 people and in a village that size, politics had to be as much "you-scratch-my-back-and-I'll-scratch-yours" as "knife-between-the-shoulder-blades." When the campaign opened for the Confederation year elections of 1867, the doctor's and the lawyer's true colours began to show.

Dr. James Hunter and Alfred Boultbee had been sitting on the village council since Newmarket was incorporated as a village in 1857. Of the nine years that had passed, Dr. Hunter had been reeve and chief magistrate for two, 1859 and 1861, and lawyer Boultbee for four, 1863 through 1866. Confederation year was the first time a general election was to be held for the position of reeve. Other years the post was filled by the village council electing one of its own. But 1867 was the prize. Hunter may have been disappointed ten years before at not being the first reeve (that honour went to merchant and mill owner Donald Sutherland), but to be reeve in the first year of the Dominion would make up for it. It was his chance to leave a mark on history and he was willing to give up a lot for victory.

Dr. Hunter had been away to Chicago that fall to buy a medical practice in the big city. But he showed up again before election time, arriving back in town by train. Then the dickering among the Reformers — for everybody in village politics in those days belonged to the Reform Party — got underway.

Nominations were held on a cold, snowy December 28, 1866, in the Mechanics' Hall on Timothy Street. A crowd came out, and most of the property owners who were eligible to vote were there. Nominations were held, both men's names were entered, and then Alfred Boultbee spoke. He told the crowd he had been reeve for the past few years and had done a good job. He said if electors were satisfied, they wouldn't want to see things changed. He pointed out that during his term as reeve a place for the Agricultural Society Fair has been assured, a "neat and commodious engine house" had been erected for the fire department, and sidewalks had been kept in repair — all without a tax increase. Then Dr. Hunter arose and after a short review of his service on council, offered an explanation of why he was opposing "a man who had been a long-time friend." Boultbee, he said, had asked him to run and promised not to oppose him — and the silence in Mechanics' Hall was deafening.[10]

Hunter said he had therefore dropped plans to move to the United States, although he had already bought and furnished a house in Chicago, and decided to run. Then, he said, Boultbee changed his mind, explaining he planned to run for the Legislature some day and felt he should keep his name before the people. The doctor said he had called a meeting of his supporters from previous elections and tried to back out in favour of his friend, but they would have none of it. Consequently, at his meeting of Reformers it was decided that two mutual friends from each of the candidates' camps, plus a fifth chosen by the first four, would select the candidate.

Dr. Hunter told the nomination meeting that the Boultbee party had agreed to this, and set Monday night, December 28th, for the meeting at the Forsyth House. But Monday morning, Hunter charged, Boultbee issued a flyer announcing his candidacy.

"Such a betrayal of confidence I could not account for. All that could be done had been done to avoid the necessity of this contest," he lamented. "I even offered to give way if Mr. Boultbee would, and let a third friend be chosen. In fact, I was prepared to pursue any honourable course to avoid a personal conflict with that gentleman."[11]

Hunter's speech raised quite a ruckus in the little hall, and no sooner had Dr. Hunter regained his seat than Alfred Boultbee was on his feet demanding an opportunity for rebuttal. Clerk E.P. Irwin, chairman of the meeting, granted it, and Boultbee said this much was true, he had met Hunter upon the doctor's return from the United States and he had asked him if he planned to be a candidate for reeve. Hunter, said the lawyer, told him he had no intention of standing as he had already furnished the house in Chicago and planned to move there immediately. Boultbee's friends then advised him to run and he decided he would, he said, and the day after that he again met Hunter and told him so. Hunter replied he had changed his mind and wanted to run too.

And as for the meeting of "friends," said lawyer Boultbee, "It was rigged."[12] From his perspective, the four were new to the Reform Party and could not be considered as any indication of the views or feelings of the party. He wanted no part of that compromise.

So the fat was in the fire. Both men stood for election. Voting day was January 7, 1867, and that election campaign continued the whole nine days the way it had started.

"It was perhaps the most exciting election ever held in Newmarket," wrote *Era* editor Erasmus Jackson, who was himself one of the four elected village councillors:

> There was much angry feeling displaying itself, while friendships and ties of years of intimacy, and even business relations, were ruthlessly severed.
>
> Stories the most wicked and slanderous, the most reprehensible, were invented regarding the candidates for reeveship. Bribery and coercion, we have been led to believe, followed in their train.[13]

Dr. Hunter won, polling 120 votes to Mr. Boultbee's 101, and what had turned the tables on the incumbent reeve was an election-morning surprise. Hunter had been found early that day on Timothy Street, lying dazed in a snowbank, smeared with blood.

"The attempt on the morning of the polling, by some cowardly swine, to take Dr. Hunter's life, largely arousing the sympathy of the public, gave an advantage to the friends of the latter that contributed in no small degree to decide this controversy," reported editor Jackson.[14]

The villagers were shocked, angered, and incredulous. Rumours began to fly — nasty rumours. Dr. Hunter hired a detective from the attorney-general's office to hunt his assailant and offered $100 reward for information. On January 18 the village council, with Alfred Boultbee in the chair for the last time, voted unanimously to pay the detective's bill and doubled the reward. The detective's report came to council the next week and for Dr. Hunter, who by then was reeve, it backfired. He took strong exception to its implication that the assault had been a fraud, and asked council to appoint the three village magistrates, Donald Sutherland, John Bentley, and R.H. Smith, as a committee of enquiry before the report was made public. The reeve said he could prove the detective's report incorrect. The magistrates declined to act unless they were given the detective's report to work with, but council refused. The committee was dissolved. It looked like the whole thing was ready to fizzle out at last.

Then the bombshell landed. Two provincial detectives arrived in town from Toronto and arrested one John Mosier. Mosier, a man Dr. Hunter had known since boyhood and an employee of one of Hunter's staunchest supporters, was charged with the assault. At the trial, it came out that three doctors had been called that election morning by panicky neighbours to examine the blood-besmirched Dr. Hunter. All who had examined "the victim" found no injury, but on hearing his explanation accepted the story that he had been struck across the back of the neck. Hunter himself testified he could not identify Mosier as his assailant, and knew of no reason why the man should strike him, but did little else to clear him.

The trial dragged on day after day in the Mechanics' Hall before the truth came out. Mosier had nothing to do with the event. Another citizen had killed several chickens early that election morning and allowed the blood to drip along Timothy Street as he carried them downtown. He met Hunter. It was about 6:00 a.m. and they were alone on the street. A passing remark turned into a conspiracy when the doctor willingly lay down in the snow while his supposed assailant smeared him with chicken blood.

Although the matter was allowed to die, it was not forgotten. No further criminal charges were pressed and Dr. James Hunter retained his reeveship. Although he was never re-elected to the post, he continued to live in Newmarket. Years later, during a hearing of a protest being held in the Mechanics' Hall against the election of A.H. Dymond as member of Parliament for North York, Dr. Hunter was called to give evidence. Just as he was about to take the oath, a chicken was thrown from the audience and dropped at his feet.

## 🌿 Gold on That Thar Creek 🌿

THERE ARE TWO legends of hidden treasure in Newmarket.

One is that a horde of gold coins was buried near Gorham's mill pond by a wary Reform sympathizer after the failure of William Lyon Mackenzie's 1837 Rebellion. A May 1886 newspaper report that a certain citizen named Charles Edmundson had been told of the lost treasure by his grandfather set off a gold rush in Newmarket. Rebellion records do indeed show one William Edmundson was the rebel courier who on December 2, 1837, carried the message to Samuel Lount in Holland Landing to start his men marching to Montgomery's Tavern.

The Gorham family was noted for its Reform Party sympathies, and their friends and neighbours had good reason to fear government retaliation. So having obtained the secret location from his grandfather, Charlie Edmundson raised some money, hired four men, and started digging. As far as anyone knows today, they came up empty-handed.

The second legend, the story of a hoard of French gold, is equally intriguing and apparently linked to the same location near the former site of Gorham's mill. According to this tale, French Army regulars were stationed on the height of land between the Lake Simcoe and Lake Ontario watersheds (south of Oak Ridges). Over the watershed went the two main Native trails: the Rouge Trail, which ran northward from the mouth of the Rouge River to Lake Simcoe (a branch of it became Newmarket's Main Street); and the Humber Trail (Carrying Place Trail), which ran from the Humber River through King Township to the west branch of the Holland River and thus to Lake Simcoe.

In October 1749, Marquis de la Jonquière, the governor of New France, wrote to the French minister of marine proposing construction of a trading post and fort at Toronto to intercept First Nations traders coming south with furs on these two trails. Traditionally, they would cross Lake Ontario to trade with the English at Oswego.

"Too much care cannot be taken to prevent the said Indians from continuing their trade with the English and to see that they find at this post all that they need as cheaply as at Chouaguen [Oswego, New York]," wrote the marquis.[15] In due time, Fort Rouillé was built at Toronto, and it seems most likely, as the legend relates, that its commandant would have stationed some of his men at the height of land to direct the First Nations traders to the new installation.

According to the legend, a pay packet of gold arrived for the Toronto garrison after its commander, Captain Alexandre Douville, had been ordered by his superior, the commander of Fort Niagara, to burn the fort and retreat to Montreal. The British Colonial Army, under Sir William Johnson, had Niagara under siege and the dispatch to Toronto went out hurriedly as the fort was about to capitulate. The courier found the post on Toronto Bay burned and the troops at the lookout gone. He decided that taking the gold back to Montreal through what by then may have been British-held territory was too risky. He is said to have buried the gold on the old Rouge Trail.

The legend could be true. Niagara fell quickly, being attacked on July 6, 1759, and capitulating on July 23, leaving little time to warn Montreal to recall the pay detail.

"Those who concealed the gold were unable to locate the spot where it had been buried," wrote Ethel Trewhella in the *History of Newmarket*. She said it was "believed to have been on the land many years later acquired by Eli Gorham on Gorham Street. This would be on the Rouge trail."[16]

Maybe they found it and maybe they didn't. Maybe it's still there.

##  Newmarket's Fair: Biggest in the County

As YORK COUNTY emerged from its frontier phase, farmers and village manufacturers started country fairs to display their accomplishments.

The Sutton Agricultural Society, founded in 1855, holds its "Georgina's County Fair," the Sutton Fair and Horse Show, in early August. The Schomberg Agricultural Fair, still featuring livestock competitions, homecrafts, and school work, marked its 150th year in 2000. The Aurora Fair and Horse Show only dates back to 1922 when Aemilius Jarvis opened his estate, Hazelburn Farm, at the south end of town, for a horse show. Today it is run by the Aurora Agricultural Society in a municipal park.

The area's largest county fair for many years was the York North Agricultural Fair in Newmarket, and became one of the factors in

Newmarket's success as a market town. Started in the mid-nineteenth century to bring farmers to Newmarket, by the beginning of the new century it had grown into a major commercial and industrial showcase for north York County. Founded 1852 as a fall exhibition of livestock, produce, and implements, it was held at Newmarket's Railway Hotel. There were about two hundred entries that year and about one hundred people sat down to dinner at the hotel, then went to an auction of goods shown at the fair. By 1905 the Fair was long-established on its own fairgrounds at the east end of Timothy Street, with fine exhibition buildings, a half-mile track for horse racing, a grandstand, and a midway.

Farm produce and livestock remained a feature of the Fair, but by 1900 business had moved in, in a big way, reflecting the increasing industrialization of the area. Davis Leather Co., Gardners Foundry, Roadhouse Furniture, Cane's Woodworking, and Office Specialty Co. all had large displays of their products. There were 3,558 exhibits that year, including livestock and poultry, fancy horses and race horses, grains, seeds and roots, vegetables, plants and flowers, cut flowers, domestic products, dairy produce, sewing, crocheting, baking, fine arts, photography, and

Author's collection

*The elegant York North Fair Palace was built in 1866 at the cost of $2,000. The architect was John T. Stokes of Sharon. As the main exhibition building for the annual fall fair in Newmarket, it stood in today's Fairgrounds Park. The structure was demolished, probably in 1939 when the fair wound up.*

the many large displays of manufacturing products — and, of course, a midway. The fair had grown in less than fifty years from a small agricultural exhibition to a three-day farm-and-trade show that drew thousands of visitors to the town. At the turn of the century, the Radial Street Railway brought in trainloads of fair visitors. It was reported that over 7,000 visitors came over the three days. Not bad for a little town with a population barely over 3,000.

The three-day fair was always held in mid-September and the whole town took on a festive air. Decked out in flags and bunting, Main Street businesses displayed their best with goods often overflowing onto sidewalks. The streets were thronged with farmers and their families, strangers from nearby towns, and Toronto visitors arriving on the train and the radial railway. Schools were closed for the first day of the fair, known as School Children's Day. All the children joined a parade and were admitted free. The fair was at its zenith in the first two decades of the twentieth century. Horse races were held each day on the track, there was a midway of up to thirty sideshows, flags fluttered from exhibitors' tents, and a beautiful grandstand drew big name entertainers. The Palace, the fair's major exhibition hall, was jammed.

As the 1920s drew to a close, the fair began its decline. The directors found themselves competing with new forms of entertainment and transportation, and attendance was dropping. At the same time, farmers and manufacturers were marketing farther afield and it was becoming harder to attract quality exhibitors. By 1927 directors were talking about switching the date to July 1st weekend to stimulate attendance, which happened in 1935. For a time it seemed racing might be the answer. A new race track was built in 1935, and after the old grandstand burned down a grandstand and stabling for forty horses were purchased from the village of Agincourt. It was reassembled in Newmarket in time for the July 1st festivities in 1938, when motorcycle racing was planned.

Two years later the Second World War put an end to the fair. Closed "for the duration" and its grounds converted to an army basic training camp, it never reopened. Today all that remains is the municipal Fairgrounds Park. The north York County's own exhibition had served the area well for more than eighty years as a showcase for the county's produce and prosperity. The fair closed permanently in 1939.

## May 24th Just Isn't What it Used to Be

IN THE DAYS before the sun (that was never to set) finally went down on the British Empire, and Victoria was queen and empress, the queen's birthday was one of the biggest annual holidays celebrated in the colony of Upper Canada. If the reminiscences that have come down to us through many years are any indication, the biggest and best of all the queen's birthday celebrations ever held in Newmarket was the one which took place in 1862, twenty-five years after Victoria ascended to the throne.

In those days, Newmarket was a village of fewer than 2,000 residents living and working in a cluster of homes and businesses along the Main Street and up on Garbutt's Hill (now the Timothy-Prospect-Water Street area). In that year, May 24th fell on a Saturday, and Saturdays were always special days in market communities like Newmarket. It was the day farmers quit the fields, loaded the wagons, and came to town to buy, sell, visit, and often enjoy a little leisure in one of several saloons.

On May 24, 1862, celebrations began shortly after sunrise with the booming of cannon and the discharge of small arms into the air. Thus aroused, the citizenry was soon thronging the streets. Arches of evergreen boughs had been constructed across Main Street and vibrant red, white, and blue bunting fluttered from numerous flagstaffs and windows. Shortly after 9:00 a.m. the town band, accompanied by the Hook and Ladder Company in full uniform, marched off from the village's principal public building, the Mechanic's Hall on Timothy Street. They proceeded up the street to the home of Dr. James Hunter, the village reeve, where Mrs. Hunter presented the band with a superb silk flag.

By then followed by hundreds of citizens and new arrivals from the country, the whole entourage proceeded to Eagle Street, where a procession was formed. Shortly after ten o'clock the band struck up a lively march and — preceded by the parade marshal who was followed by the year-old fire engine, the hose, and the Hook and Ladder Companies — it marched up Main Street, then returned to the cricket grounds where a day of field sports got underway. There were jumping contests, races, football matches (country versus village), throwing the 56-pound weight for distance, putting the stone, and other feats of strength. In the evening there was a giant bonfire, followed by a

*Civic occasions in nineteenth- and early-twentieth-century Newmarket almost always included a parade. This military band marched to its concert on May 24, 1914. It is shown passing the church at the top of the Main Street hill. Little did Newmarket realize that in less than four months, Canada would be at war.*

fireworks display. A promenade concert back at the Mechanics' Hall wound up the day's festivities.

Today the 24th of May is still a statutory holiday, and some still call it Victoria Day, but most folks don't realize that it originally was a celebration of that queen's birthday. Victoria reigned for more than sixty years, and the longer she was on the throne the bigger the celebrations of her birthday seemed to get. The one described above marked the silver anniversary of her reign.

### ❧ Everybody Skated on the Pond ❧

SKATING WAS A popular winter activity for young and old in mid-nineteenth-century Newmarket. The Pond (Fairy Lake) became such a popular place that in 1863 a proper rink was built on the ice and named the Royal Rink. In 1864, it was the scene of a skating carnival which attracted three hundred people. The Sharon Brass Band supplied the music.

On Christmas Day, hundreds of citizens turned out with their skates at the Pond, and according to *The Newmarket Era* a good time was had from early morning until late in the evening. Sometimes as many as one hundred people were on the ice at a time.

During the 1870s, a skating rink was built on the north side of Timothy Street east of the railway tracks. It was about 90-feet long, and a flight of about ten steps led down the embankment from the street. Skaters raced along the frozen river to the dam and back. During the summer a floor was laid down for roller skating.

The area was filled and paved in 1973. Part of it is now a parking lot for the apartments in the former Office Specialty furniture manufacturing building, and part is a park featuring a playground and a walking trail following the river.

## Stranger at Station Sets Off Fenian Scare

ONE DAY IN 1866 a large, plain box and a mysterious stranger arrived at the Newmarket railway depot, and a flood of rumour and suspicion swept through the village.

Canada had been living under the gun for the past several years as two of the most powerful armies in the world battled out the Civil War to the south. When hostilities ended in 1865, many believed the battle-hardened Union forces would be turned north to complete what the War of 1812 had started. Adding fuel to this speculation was a group of Irish-Americans known as Fenians who were boasting they would separate Ireland from England by invading Canada. Rumour that day had it that the stranger in town was a Fenian, and that the box carried arms for Irish sympathizers in this area. The poor man must have wondered what he had stepped into once getting off the train, for both he and the box were thoroughly investigated. It was determined he had no connection with the Fenians, and there were no arms in the box.

However, the rumours and the search indicate the atmosphere of suspicion and fear that permeated the village, and indeed the whole colony, in the year preceding Confederation. Rumours that a Fenian raid was planned on St. Patrick's Day in March 1866 resulted in 10,000 Canadian militia volunteers being ordered to the frontier border with the United States. The raid came in June at Black Rock, when about 900 Fenians captured Fort Erie and marched on to Ridgeway, where they were defeated by the Canadians. Further attempts at invasion failed and finally authorities in Washington, who until then had reacted with indifferent contempt to the Canadian and British protests, closed the border to the Fenians. The invasions were probably as effective a weapon as any John A. Macdonald had in his campaign to garner support for Confederation. Citizens of the colonies were deeply incensed at the intrusions.

In Newmarket, for instance, village flags were left at half-mast to honour those killed at Fort Erie and Ridgeway, and militia units were quickly organized. A troop of cavalry was formed, a second volunteer company of militia recruited to augment the existing company, and the Home Guards organized. The village must have looked like an armed camp on drill nights. In September, all the militia units were ordered to Camp Thorold in the Niagara Peninsula for training, and the whole town turned out to see the soldiers off by train. Bands played, bunting and flags were flown, and a large crowd gathered at the railway station.

It was during this September that the various volunteer companies were organized into York County's 12th Battalion, York Volunteers. The unit, one of the predecessors of the Queen's York Rangers squadron now stationed in Aurora, made its headquarters at Newmarket until 1873.

## Citizens Opposed Riel

CONFEDERATION WAS RUNG in July 1, 1867, and then the citizens of the new Dominion began speculating about the future of the vast lonely land lying west of the Great Lakes. The Hudson's Bay Company, the owners of much of the territory then known as Rupert's Land, relinquished their claims to the British government for £300,000 and other considerations. London then transferred the territory to Canada. The arrangements were finalized during 1869, but the new federal government in Ottawa did little during that time to reassure the 10,000 residents of the area that their rights and property would be protected. Most of these "new Canadians" were Métis, many uneducated, some being farmers and some nomadic fur traders, but all with little experience of or faith in British tradition or government.

Rumours began to spread. Land-surveying parties at work in the area fuelled fears of property loss, and when the French-speaking Métis consulted Louis Riel, one of the few of their neighbours who had formal education, they ultimately found themselves led into armed rebellion. The first military execution in Rupert's Land was carried out by Riel who had a young rabble-rouser, twenty-one-year-old Thomas Scott, shot.[17] Riel's provisional government ultimately negotiated the terms under which the modern Province of Manitoba entered the Canadian Confederation, but because of Scott's execution Riel was forced into exile.

In Newmarket, a large and vocal meeting convened in the Mechanics' Hall on Millard Avenue on April 22, 1870. Reeve Nelson Gorham was in the chair. By then he was a prosperous mill owner, but immediately following the 1837 Rebellion he had been a fugitive with a price on his head, charged with high treason for being a rebellion leader. In 1842 he had been pardoned along with other leaders of the rebellion, and allowed to return from exile in New York State. Gorham opened the meeting with a speech reminding his audience of the satisfaction the acquisition of the Red River country afforded Canadians. He went on to speak of the bungling and mismanagement by government and of the pain experienced because lawful authority had been resisted and a ruthless murder committed.

Canon S.P. Ramsay of St. Paul's Anglican Church, who had known young Thomas Scott's family back in Yorkshire, brought the western tragedy home to people of Newmarket when he spoke. He wound up by proposing the following resolution:

> That we, the residents of Newmarket, having learned with extreme regret that Thomas Scott, a loyal Canadian subject, resident in the Red River Territory, has been brutally murdered by a band of rebels in that Territory, and by mark of our abhorrence of such an atrocious

outrage, we respectfully and firmly demand that prompt and decisive means be speedily taken by the proper authorities to bring the murderous conspirators to justice, who justly deserve the condemnation of the whole civilized world.[18]

This and other resolutions were carried by the meeting, among them one by Reverend A.A. Smith of the Wesleyan Methodist Church, seconded by George Lount, calling on the government to protect the lives and liberty of Canadian citizens in the territory, and another moved by *Era* publisher Erastus Jackson and seconded by E.G. Campbell, expressing "disapprobation of the dilatory course pursued by the government."[19]

It wasn't long before Canon Ramsay, Reverend Smith, and Messrs. Lount and Jackson, got their wish. The government announced it was sending troops west, and within a week of the meeting the call went out for thirty-five volunteers from the 12th Battalion, York, to join the 4th Brigade Division for North-West duty — the Wolseley Expedition.

*Chapter Seven*

# FASCINATING FOLKS

## ❧ Buffalo Bill: Almost a Newmarket Boy ❧

BUFFALO BILL CODY, folk hero of the American west, was almost born a Canadian. His grandfather, Philip Cody, migrated from the United States to Canada in 1800 and settled near Newmarket. He had followed his brother Joseph here, and among the properties the two brothers owned and farmed was the land now occupied by St. Andrew's College in Aurora. Although the Cody brothers arrived at about the same time that Timothy Rogers' first wave of Quaker settlers was homesteading along Yonge Street, they apparently were not part of Roger's group. However, they were Quakers and there are Codys buried in the pioneer burial ground next to the Quaker Meeting House on Yonge Street.

Philip's son Isaac was born in 1811 in what is now Peel County, where his father had moved in 1806. Isaac was the father of Colonel William "Buffalo Bill" Cody. Philip moved his family to Cleveland, Ohio District, in 1829 when Isaac was eighteen. A few years later Isaac moved on to Kansas, the true "Wild West" of his day. Isaac was murdered there for his anti-slavery activities.[1] His son, William, enlisted in the Union Army when the Civil War broke out, some said to avenge his father's death on the field of battle.

Cody family members are descendants of French Huguenots who fled persecution on their native land and settled in Massachusetts in 1698. In 1939, Codys from all over North America held a reunion in Newmarket. It was a gathering of the Cody Family Association, a group first suggested by Colonel William "Buffalo Bill" Frederick Cody (1846–1917) to his niece, Mrs. Mary Allen, who founded the organization in 1925. At that time there were said to be between six and seven hundred Cody families living in Canada and the United States, all descendants of those seventeenth-century French Protestant immigrants.

## First Lawyer Had Famous Name

HENRY WILLIAM BLACKSTONE, the first lawyer to practise in Newmarket, carried one of the most famous names in British jurisprudence. The grandson of Sir William Blackstone (1723–80), famous for his book *Commentaries on the Laws of England*, was a judge and professor at Oxford University. One of the brilliant legal minds of his age, young Henry had little opportunity to prove what kind of a mind he possessed — he was killed in a barroom brawl in Holland Landing before he got the chance. However, a historian of the period wrote that "his conspicuous talents gave promise of an eminence in his profession not unworthy of the name he bore."[2] Sir William wrote his *Commentaries* in 1765, which remain familiar to students of the British legal system today.

The younger Blackstone grew up in Quebec where family influence secured a number of lucrative posts for his father, also Henry Blackstone. Henry Jr. moved to Upper Canada in 1831, attended Osgoode Hall law school, was called to the bar and enrolled in the Upper Canada Law Society in 1837. He first established his practice in Holland Landing, where a large brick house known as the Blackstone House still stands. However, before long he opened an office in Newmarket as well. In those days before the arrival of the railway, Holland Landing was a busy port on the water route north and seemed to have a brighter future than little Newmarket.

Details of Blackstone's death are sketchy. Toronto historian John Ross Robertson writes that he died as a result of injuries received in a squabble with some itinerant workmen known as shantymen, the *History of East Gwillimbury* adds that the brawl happened in a tavern, a Simcoe County history puts the date at about 1850, and yet another book refers to a gambling debt as the cause of the fight.

The mystery remains. What brought this scion of a famous British legal family to practise law in the rowdy Upper Canadian frontier village of Holland Landing when a far more lucrative career must have beckoned in York? How did a lawyer and eminent member of the community come to die in a brawl with shantymen?

## Holland River Named for Dutch Surveyor

MANY PEOPLE THINK the Holland River was given its name because it winds through the Holland Marsh, an area drained and settled by Dutch settlers. But as the old song says, it simply isn't so. The river was named after a native of Holland who left his mark on early Canada long before the marsh settlers arrived, a colonial officer whose name also happened to be Holland. And the marsh, in turn, is named after the river. Although Major Samuel Johannes Holland was one of colonial America's most distinguished surveyors and mapmakers, he probably never set eyes on the little river that bears his name today.

Holland was surveyor-general of Quebec, and for a time before the American Revolution he was surveyor-general of northern district of North America, which included all British possessions north of the Potomac River. It was for his work as a surveyor that he was commemorated in the name of the river, circa 1792.

Holland, however, was much more than a surveyor in colonial America. He was an army officer, military engineer, office holder, politician, and major landowner during the continent's most turbulent years. A young Dutch artillery officer during the War of the Austrian Succession, Holland decided a brighter future awaited him under the British flag. He was probably under the protection of the Duke of Richmond who Holland met during that war (1740–48) when the Netherlands and Britain were allies. In 1754, he moved to England, and with the Duke's aid was commissioned an officer in the Royal Americans.

This was a regiment that had the Earl of Loudoun (John Campbell) as colonel-in-chief and Frederick Haldimand as lieutenant-colonel when it was shipped to America in 1756. Both officers rose to high command in North America, a connection that did no harm to the career of the young Dutch officer. Holland saw lots of action. He was assistant engineer in the expedition against Louisburg under General James Wolfe and was commended by Wolfe for his bravery and technical competence. That winter he and his new survey pupil, James Cook (later captain), charted the St. Lawrence in preparation for the attack on Quebec. Holland also surveyed plans for Halifax and supervised construction of Fort Frederick (Saint John, New Brunswick). He was a captain when he served at the Battle of the Plains of Abraham and was wounded, but was back in action at the Battle of Sainte-Foy the following spring. After the French defeat he surveyed the settled part of the St. Lawrence Valley, and drew up plans for a new citadel at Quebec. Appointed surveyor-general in 1764, he was also named to the newly established civil authority, the Council of Quebec.

His first chore was to survey St. John's Island (Prince Edward Island). He divided it into counties, parishes, and townships, established sites of towns, including the capital, which he named Charlottetown. Today, he is considered one of that province's founding fathers. That done, he moved on to Îles de la Madeline and Cape Breton Island, and by the late 1760s Holland and his crews were working down both shores of the St. Lawrence.

By 1770, he was directing survey parties in the enormous task of mapping Atlantic coastal lands from the Saint John River (New Brunswick) to New York City — a chore the British wanted done in anticipation of the troubles brewing in their colonies. During the early 1770s Holland the surveyor helped establish the boundaries of New Hampshire and served on the New York–New Jersey boundary commission. He was also the New York representative on a commission to settle its boundary with Pennsylvania.

The outbreak of rebellion in 1776 found the Holland family living in Perth Amboy, New Jersey, and the proprietors of 3,000 acres in New Hampshire and 24,000 in Vermont. Holland came under great pressure to join the revolutionaries but refused. He sent his family into hiding and fled to Great Britain. Commissioned an army major, he returned as a British aide-de-camp to a Hessian mercenary commander and appears to have seen action near New York City. In 1777, he organized a colonial unit, and the following year was called to Quebec by his old friend Frederick Haldimand, by this time the governor. He re-united with his family and settled there.

The British decision to settle Loyalists in Upper and Lower Canada after the revolution put a premium on Holland's much-needed skills, and his recommendations resulted in large-scale surveying on the upper St. Lawrence, the north shore of Lake Ontario westward from Cataraqui (Kingston), the Niagara Peninsula, and land along the Detroit River. Although Holland visited these sites in late 1783 and the spring and summer of 1784, his health was deteriorating, and he apparently never returned to this area. In subsequent years he began relinquishing posts and responsibilities.

Samuel Holland died at his Quebec City home in December 1801. According to the *Canadian Dictionary of Biography*, "The topographic name Holland in several provinces is a reminder of the prominent role he played in the shaping of this country."[2]

Samuel Holland had a colourful and successful career and the high standards of accuracy in mapping and land measurement he set have given him an important place in Canada's history.

## Bishop's Throne Now in Museum

AN ELEGANT VICTORIAN parlour chair that had been a prized possession of pioneer William Roe is now in the collection of Newmarket artifacts housed in the museum on Main Street. William Roe's grandson, Ned, told me years ago that the chair was known in the Roe family as the "Bishop's Throne."

When the patriarch of colonial Upper Canada, Anglican Bishop John Strachan, visited St. Paul's Church in Newmarket, he usually stayed at the nearby Roe house. The portly bishop apparently found the chair exceedingly comfortable and so had it moved to the church for his use during the Sunday services at which he officiated. Thus, within the Roe family the chair was known as the Bishop's Throne and the name stuck through the generations. The chair bears no markings to indicate where or when it was made, but Ned Roe told me he did not think it locally made. He said he had been told that his grandfather purchased it in either Montreal or New York on one of his trips to purchase goods for his store and fur trading post.

The Roe family home, a large white frame building, stood on the east side of Main Street's south end. The Roe business was next to it at the corner of Main and Water Streets. And the town's early post office was attached to its north side, for William Roe was appointed postmaster in 1837.

Ned Roe, the last of the immediate family to live in Newmarket, arranged for the chair to stay in Newmarket after his death, although at the time there was no museum. He also left a number of other artifacts. Among them is the Roe family pew table from the first little-frame St. Paul's Church, and a framed plate on which a member of the family had painted a picture of the early church.

Old St. Paul's stood on the same site as the present St. Paul's. It was built in 1834, and church historian Reverend Arthur Patstone describes it as being of an unusual design for an Anglican church. It had a high pulpit against the north wall in the centre, with steps to it on the east side. The prayer desk and

Author's collection

*This chair from William Roe's living room was so comfortable that the rotund Bishop John Strachan had it taken over to St. Paul's Anglican Church for his use when he was invited to conduct a service in Newmarket. It is now in the town museum. The Roe family named it the "Bishop's Throne."*

Author's collection

*Old St. Paul's Anglican Church, built in 1835, was demolished in 1882 to make way for construction of today's stone church in 1883–84. The new church is at the corner of Church and D'Arcy Streets. Bishop Strachan was often a guest and would conduct the service at Old St. Paul's.*

lectern were at the side of the pulpit facing the congregation. The holy table was below and in front of the pulpit, with a kneeler and rail both in front and at the sides of the platform that constituted the sanctuary. The pews were of the traditional English style, sometimes referred to as horse-box pews. They had seats all around with a door that opened to the aisle. There was often a small table at the centre for books, mittens, or fans, or even milady's smelling salts, Patstone suggests. It is this little table from the Roe family pew, roughly made of pine and, according to Ned Roe, dating back to the first days of the little church his grandfather helped found, which is now in our community museum.

## "Fleetfoot" Corbiére: Fastest Mailman on the Frontier

ELI CORBIÉRE WAS a pioneer mailman who must have had one of the longest routes in history. His route went from the end of the stagecoach run in Newmarket to the British military garrisons at Holland Landing and Penetanguishene. As there was no road north of Holland Landing, he had to carry his load by foot to the settlements that became Barrie and Orillia and to points farther north, all the way to Penetanguishene.

Lean and strong and possessed with great endurance, Corbiére covered the frontier forest trails at a steady trot, and it is recorded that on at least one occasion he covered the sixty miles between Holland Landing and the fort at Penetanguishene between sun up and sun down. But eventually even Corbiére's fine physic was worn down by the terrible

Drawing by Creighton Henry

*Eli "Fleetfoot" Corbiére was the first mail carrier to transport the mail from the end of the stage route at Newmarket to the first post office to the north, the military station of Penetanguishene, when no road existed north of Holland Landing. He delivered the mail over forest trails to remote outposts, exact dates not known.*

punishment that climate and unsettled terrain inflicted on the frontier mailman. In his later years, the man who was known across the Upper Canadian frontier as "Fleetfoot" became quite lame. He settled down in Holland Landing where he became a cobbler. He lived just west of and quite close to the railway tracks in his later years, close to the road that now leads to Bradford.

"Fleetfoot" Corbiére, as might be guessed from his name, spoke fluent French, as well as having acquired facility in several Indian dialects. He served for many years as a clerk in the Holland Landing-based fur-trading firm of Borland & Roe. As a mail carrier, he pioneered much of the service in this area. When a few log cabins broke the wilderness where Barrie now stands, "Fleetfoot" Corbiére was the man who set out over a stretch of more than thirty miles of unblazed trails through woods and over bogs to deliver the mail there. When Orillia and Penetanguishene applied for mail service volunteers were sought to challenge the wilderness and Fleetfoot applied.

His son, christened Carlos Corbiére, anglicized his name when he grew up to Charles Kirby. He moved to Newmarket and lived out his life there. Eli "Fleetfoot" Corbiére, along with other members of his family, is buried in the pioneer Methodist cemetery on the hill north of the village of Sharon.

## Pioneer Colonel Was Canadian-Born

JOSEPH HILL, BORN at Fort Niagara where his father was stationed with the British Army, was a Canadian officer in the British Army's 69th Regiment of Foot. He had attained the rank of captain when he retired in 1835 after having seen service at the Battle of Waterloo, in India, and in Ireland. He bought seventy-five acres in Newmarket, and shortly afterwards was made a lieutenant-colonel in the local militia. Hill was one of the few government loyalists in Newmarket to stand up to William Lyon Mackenzie and his sympathizers during the troubles of 1837, and his home became a rallying point for government supporters.

After the rebels were dispersed at the Battle of Montgomery's Tavern north of Toronto (Yonge and Eglinton area), government supporters suddenly became more plentiful in the area. A group from Holland Landing-Newmarket was raised to march to the aid of Toronto and Hill assumed command. He died in 1854 and is buried in the pioneer cemetery on Eagle Street.

## Heroes Risked All to Fight Plague

OUR PIONEER HEROES and heroines are often lost in the mists of time. But now and again a memory, a written line, or a family legend revive — if ever so sketchily — the deeds of one of these brave souls of the frontier days. Such are the brief tales of Hannah Kinsey Curry and Wright Burkett. During the first decades of the nineteenth century, when hardy men and women were struggling to clear the land in the upper Holland River area, build homes and communities, and create a prosperous life, sickness was their greatest scourge.

In 1809–10, typhus ravaged the colony, leaving few families untouched. Five children in the family of Newmarket pioneer Timothy Rogers, for instance, died within a few days of each other. In 1832, the immigrant flood from Europe into Canada peaked, with 51,185 people arriving at Quebec City that year. With the new arrivals came a dread disease — Asiatic cholera.[3] The plague swept the St. Lawrence Valley, arriving in Kingston on June 20th and in York on June 21st. Within days it spread up Yonge Street. Hundreds died. York, with a population of 5,500, had almost 600 deaths.

Plague struck again in 1847, this time it was typhus brought by shiploads of starving Irish and Scottish immigrants fleeing the ravages of the great potato famine and Scottish immigrants searching for a better future after the Highland Clearances. Called "Irish Immigrant Fever" by the settlers on the frontiers who were to suffer so severely, the typhus raged through the colony in epidemic proportions.

Small settlements like Newmarket and its surrounding communities had little medical expertise to fall back on, and virtually no facilities. During the 1847 epidemic those stricken with typhus were segregated in an abandoned brewery situated a little west of Water Street on Boulton Street (now D'Arcy Street), and a call went out for volunteers to care for them. Probably a small frame building, the derelict brewery was no doubt dank and dusty and smelled of hops. Equipped with makeshift beds, it would have had little in the way of sanitary facilities, and of course no kitchen or fireplaces to ward off an evening chill.

We know at least three people came forward to act as angels of mercy in what was probably Newmarket's first hospital. One was Hannah Curry, the daughter of an early settler, James Kinsey, who arrived with the first wave of Quakers in 1801. Along with Joseph Hill, Kinsey had built a mill on what is now Fairy Lake. Hannah may well have been one of the first children born in the new settlement. Having been brought up in true pioneer fashion, she was familiar with the medicinal value of all the herbs and trees in the district. Hannah worked in the little hospital, visited the sick in their homes, and, miraculously, came through the experience unscathed.

Two other volunteers were not so fortunate. Wright Burkett and a harness-maker named William Wallis also responded to the call. Both contracted the disease. Burkett died, while Wallis recovered. All three risked death, without hope of any reward save the gratitude of their neighbours. They deserve to be remembered.

## Samuel Morse and His New Telegraph

IT WAS A cold and blustery winter evening when chair-maker James Caldwell bundled up his little girl, Sarah Jane, and carried her down the Botsford Street hill from his home at the top to see history being made at the North American Hotel on Main Street. A famous artist turned inventor, the renowned New York City portrait painter Samuel Morse (1791–1872) was staying at the hotel. He had promised the citizens of the little village a demonstration of his new invention called the telegraph, which he claimed could send messages along wires.

Years later Sarah Jane recalled for her children how Morse coiled his long line around the hotel parlour, then ran it into the barn, which stood back of the hotel on the north side of Botsford Street. Morse stationed an assistant in the barn to tap out the message, and before the eyes of the assembled villagers he received that message in the hotel parlour.

Author's collection

*James Caldwell operated a chair-making business on Main Street for half a century and lived on Botsford Street, a few hundred feet west of his shop. He is shown above in old age, with his wife, Rosanna. As a young man, he carried his little daughter Sarah Jane down to the North American Hotel at Botsford and Main Streets one evening so she could watch the famous American artist and inventor, Samuel Morse, demonstrate his invention, the telegraph.*

We have no date for Samuel Morse's demonstration here, but it must have been sometime between 1837, when he took out a patent on the telegraph, and 1843, when the United States government finally acknowledged that maybe he had invented something more than a toy and set up an experimental line from Washington to Baltimore.[5]

Those were bitter years for the artist turned inventor who, legend says, developed the telegraph after his family could not reach him to tell him his wife was dying.

Morse studied painting at London's Royal Academy from 1811 to 1815. He became a successful portrait artist in Charleston, South Carolina, and New York City, though he didn't become rich from it. On his way back from a trip to Europe in 1832, a shipboard conversation inspired him to develop the concept of an electromagnetic recording telegraph for the rapid transmission of intelligence. The family tragedy spurred him on to perfect his idea and develop a system of communication, the Morse Code.

No one took his invention too seriously at first, and Morse evidently had to take to the road on a selling job. Perhaps that's why, on a cold winter night, he found himself giving a demonstration in a rambling frame hotel on the Main Street of a little village of a few hundred people in Upper Canada.

The story has a happy ending for Samuel Morse. Despite the success of the test line in 1843, the government in Washington continued to neglect his invention, so Morse took on a business manager and continued to develop it himself, ultimately becoming a very rich man.

## Reeve Gorham Had Faced Treason Charge

CHRISTMAS 1837 FOUND Nelson Gorham, the idealistic son of wealthy Newmarket woollen-mill owner Eli Gorham, stranded on the American side of Lake Ontario, a price on his head, and the charge of high treason against his name. Gorham, then about twenty-five and well-educated (his family had sent him to school in New York), must have known this was the possible outcome of his actions when he helped plan an armed uprising against the government of the new queen, eighteen-year-old Victoria.

Both Nelson and Eli were strong supporters of William Lyon Mackenzie, the firebrand politician who represented this area as an opposition member of the Legislature for many years. Nelson worked closely with Mackenzie throughout the period of political turmoil leading up to the summer of 1837, when Mackenzie stumped the province setting up a "vigilance committee" structure capable of being turned into an instrument of revolt. His father, Eli Gorham, remained in the background. On August 3, 1837, the first public meeting of the campaign was held in Newmarket, and most prominent among the seven Newmarket men named to that committee of vigilance was Nelson Gorham.

Throughout the fall things moved rapidly towards Mackenzie's goal of open rebellion. Military drills by committee supporters, led by former army Sergeant Anthony Anderson of King Township, were reported on the outskirts of the village at night. Rifle practice was underway. When the rebels marched down Yonge Street early in December, Gorham was a leader. William Babcock Crew of Richmond Hill later swore in court that when he was taken prisoner by the heavily-armed rebels on Yonge Street, in order to prevent him riding into the city to warn authorities, Nelson Gorham was one of the rebel leaders and told Crew they were marching to overturn the government.

Mackenzie dispatched his trusted friend Gorham to the London district with messages for Dr. Charles Duncombe, a rebel leader who was to lead an attack on Hamilton. Roads were bad and it took several days to reach Duncombe, thus Gorham missed the Battle of Montgomery's Tavern. Learning of the rebel defeat, he fled to New York State. When Mackenzie set up a government-in-exile on Navy Island in the Niagara River, Gorham was one of eleven chosen for a cabinet post. He also headed up recruiting for the new "Patriot" army, but the invasion that was to return the rebels to Upper Canada never took place, and Gorham seems sensibly to have retreated from the field to take up farming in upstate New York.

In 1843, he and four other leaders were pardoned. Gorham returned to his home and family business in Newmarket (on Gorham Street). He couldn't stay out of politics, however. He retained his loyalty to the Reform movement, sat on the Newmarket village council for many years, and was elected reeve in 1863, 1870, and 1871. He held militia commands and many other civic posts before finally retiring back to New York State, where he died at a very old age.

Reform stalwarts like the Gorhams kept the cause of change and the hope of responsible government alive in York County during the years after Mackenzie's foolish failure. Eventually, York County was the key — making it possible for Louis-Hippolyte LaFontaine, the Reform leader in Lower Canada, to win a Parliamentary seat here in the Fourth Riding of York, defeating William Roe of Newmarket, the Tory candidate. The seat had been long held by Robert Baldwin, the Reform leader in Upper Canada, who switched ridings to open York for his Quebec ally. In 1849, as principal ministers, the two Reformers presided over the introduction of responsible government.

## Her Church Bell First Rang Her Own Funeral

BROOK WAKEFIELD, WHO settled a farm on North Main Street very early in the nineteenth century, left $10,000 to the Christian Society to build a church in Newmarket. Lord Dufferin, the governor general, laid the cornerstone of this building, and the church stands today at the top of Main Street hill. Alexander Muir, then principal of the village school, had the school choir sing the first public performance of his new anthem, "The Maple Leaf Forever."[6]

Wakefield's daughter, Mrs. Brook (Amelia) Howard, gave $2,000 to purchase a bell for this church. Its first service was to toll her own funeral, which took place before the bell had been raised to position in the steeple.

## Farm Boy Became Renowned Artist

WHEN HE WAS a boy growing up on his father's farm in Newmarket during the 1840s, young Benoni Irwin took art lessons from his older brother, Daniel. By the time he died in a freak drowning accident at his summer home on Lake Wangumbaug, South Coventry, Connecticut, the Newmarket farm boy had become one of America's most prominent portrait artists. By age fifty-six, Irwin had established himself as an artist who had the wealthy and the famous of cities from New York to San Francisco tendering him commissions.

Said the *Louisville Courier* (Kentucky) in reporting his death, "His polished manner and noble bearing gave him entrance into the best families in both Europe and American."[7]

Benoni Irwin was one of seven children born to Jared Irwin and his wife, Lydia Kennedy Irwin (1807–71). Jared was a brother of E.P. Irwin, the first clerk of the village of Newmarket. Benoni's grandfather, Charles Irwin, settled here in 1810, and according to family tradition farmed the land now occupied by Pickering College and the residential area to its east. Jared joined Samuel Lount and William Lyon Mackenzie in 1837 and after the debacle at Montgomery's Tavern was imprisoned for a time.

After finishing an honours degree at the University of Toronto, the young Benoni left for Europe where he studied under noted artists in France, Italy, and Germany before recrossing the Atlantic to settle in New York City. There he quickly became much sought-after for his portrait work. He later lived for periods in Baltimore and San Francisco, and about every two years visited two brothers, who had settled in Louisville, where he would hold exhibitions of his works and accept commissions.

Irwin married twice. According to the *New York Times*, October 18, 1867, his first wife, Lizzie B. Bunner of New York City, died at age twenty-two. In 1873, while in California, Irwin married Adelaide Vellejo Curtis (1853–1932) and they had two daughters, Edith and Constance. Six-

*Benoni Irwin was a Newmarket farm boy who grew up on the farm later occupied by Pickering College, where his family had settled in 1810. After study here, in the United States, and abroad, he became a world-renowned portrait artist. He painted this portrait of Mary Cawthra Mulock, the mother of Sir William Mulock, in 1866.*

feet tall and weighing over 200 pounds, Benoni Irwin was described as distinguished looking, with classic features and a wealth of iron-grey hair.

His end came unexpectedly. He was standing in a small round-bottom boat in which he had set up a camera to take pictures of the sunset — in the 1890s cameras were large cumbersome affairs and had massive tripods — when the whole works upset, dumping Irwin and his camera into eight feet of water. Although he was said to be an expert swimmer, the postmortem revealed he drowned after being knocked out by hitting his head on the edge of the boat as he fell. Benoni Irwin is buried with his wife, Adela, and daughter, Edith, in Coventry, Connecticut.

Although portraits by Benoni Irwin still hang in many a mansion and museum south of the border, there are only a few known to be in this area.

*Chapter Eight*

# GROWING INTO A TOWN

DURING THE NINETEENTH century, the militia in York County was organized and re-organized several times. The militia became active on a number of occasions before the end of the century. The first was during the War of 1812 when it served under General Brock at the capture of Detroit and Queenston. Few, however, saw action after the capture and burning of the town of York in 1813.

The next occasion was the Upper Canada Rebellion of 1837. That year saw a new militia regiment, named the Queen's Rangers, organized in York. When Samuel Lount led a rebel march down Yonge Street from Newmarket, meeting William Lyon Mackenzie at Montgomery's Tavern, the Queen's Rangers responded, confronted, and dispersed the rebels. The 12th York Battalion of Infantry, the lineal descendant of those Queen's Rangers and ancestor of the present Queen's York Rangers, was formed in September 1866 from five independent companies: the Aurora Rifle Company, organized in 1862; the Lloydtown Infantry Company, organized in 1862; the King Infantry Company, organized in 1863; the Newmarket Infantry Company, organized in 1866; and the Scarborough Rifle Company, organized in 1862.

When formed, the 12th York Battalion was headquartered in

Newmarket but moved to Aurora in 1873 when a new drill hall was built. The newly formed Newmarket Company was one of those called out to repel the Fenian aggression of that summer (1866), and spent time on guard duty on the Niagara frontier.

In 1885, four companies of the 12th Battalion (now also titled York Rangers) were called out for service in the North-West Rebellion of Louis Riel. They served in a composite unit, the York-Simcoe battalion, made up of men from the 12th and the Simcoe Foresters. Officers detailed for service include Major J. Wayling, in command of Newmarket and Sharon; Captain L.L.F. Smith, in command of Aurora and Sutton; Lieutenant W.J. Fleury of Aurora; and Lieutenant J.A.W. Allan of Newmarket. Men were selected for service from throughout the regiment. Lieutenant Allan and Major Wayling both later commanded the regiment.

When war broke out in South Africa between Great Britain and the Boer republics, the Rangers' commanding officer, Lieutenant-Colonel Thomas H. Lloyd, offered the services of the regiment. Although no action was taken on the offer, when Ottawa finally did decide to send 1,000 troops quite a number of Rangers were selected.

In the First World War the Rangers were kept in Canada as a recruiting regiment, forming and sending overseas the 20th, 127th, and the 220th battalions. At the outbreak of the Second World War the regiment was not mobilized for active duty overseas, but instead trained recruits for service in other regiments. In 1942, the regiment was assigned to Canadian Territorial Defence, while continuing to train soldiers for duty in Europe. By the end of the war, the Queen's York Rangers had supplied 124 officers and 1,891 other ranks.

In 1947, following the Second World War, the regiment was given a new name and a new role, becoming the 25th Armoured Regiment (Queen's York Rangers) and equipped with Sherman tanks. The regiment has used its current name since 1958 and has been an armoured reconnaissance regiment since 1965.

The militias of York County have a long and colourful history. Today's Queen's York Rangers, a militia unit made up of citizen-soldiers, is not unlike its earliest predecessor, Roger's Rangers, a company of New England frontiersmen raised to serve with the British Army in the Seven Years War (1755–63). In recent years, Rangers have served with regular force regiments in Cyprus, Namibia, the former Yugoslavia, Somalia, and Rwanda.

The regiment's illustrious history includes participation in the capture of Louisbourg in 1758 and service with General Wolfe at the Plains of Abraham. In the American Revolution, Robert Rogers raised a Loyalist battalion called the Queen's Rangers, a unit that was commanded by John Graves Simcoe later in the war. In May 1779, as a mark of favour, five Loyalist units were designated "American Regiments." Simcoe's Queen's Rangers were given the place of pride as the "1st American Regiment," a designation their successors still carry. Dispersed as a regiment at the end of the American War of Independence, it was reformed in Upper Canada by Simcoe with many of his same officers and sergeants after he was named governor. One of its tasks was to build Yonge Street to open York County for settlement.

## Village Clerk Predicted Boom Times

NEWMARKET'S FIRST BIG boom came in the early 1850s when the Ontario, Simcoe & Huron Railway chose the village as a terminal and drove its tracks through on their way to Collingwood and the Great Lakes. That was in 1852, when the community was a struggling village of between four hundred and five hundred people. It had so few citizens who could read that the first newspaper publisher, G.S. Porter of *The New Era*, gave up after a year because he saw no future in the newspaper and printing business in such a backward community.[1]

A few years later, boom times changed all that. An accurate picture of the village in 1861 has been left us by its clerk, Edwin P. Irwin, who was appointed enumerator for the Canadian census that year. By 1861, the village had 1,388 residents living in an impressive collection of homes. Irwin tells us most were more than one-storey buildings, with ninety-one being a storey-and-a-half, seventy-eight two storeys, and eight with two-and-a-half storeys. Only seventy-five were single storey and there were only twenty log cabins left from the village's frontier days. Most homes, 199 in all, were of frame construction or frame and rough cast. Only thirteen were brick.

Although the village had a variety of small industries, well into the twentieth century its major interest was furniture-making. There were three furniture and cabinet manufacturers listed, the largest a well-equipped shop boasting lathes, boring, planing, and mortising machines, all powered by steam. The two smaller shops used horses to power their machinery. The village's two flour mills drew an extensive trade to the community from the surrounding rich farmlands. The largest mill, water-powered with four run of stones[2] and a capacity of one hundred barrels of flour a day, was set on a mill race running from Fairy Lake on the east side of the railway tracks south of Timothy Street.

The second mill was steam-powered and was on the west side of the tracks north of Huron Street (now Davis Drive). The only sawmill was next to this second mill and powered by the same steam engine. Irwin noted it didn't do much business though, as most of the surrounding land had been completely cleared of timber by 1861.

Several other industries figured in the village's commercial life. Gorham's woollen mill was a large brick building equipped with spinning machines, a power loom, and draping machinery, all run with water power obtained from Bogart Creek just south of Gorham Street. Two iron foundries and machine shops turned out threshing machines, plough castings, steam engines, and mill gearing. One of the community's unusual industries was a sewing-machine factory that had started in 1859. It built about two hundred machines a year, which were called the Canadian Family Sewing Machine. There was also a small Newmarket brewery, located at the bottom of Superior Street, a carriage and wagonmaker, blacksmith, shoemaker, tailor, tinsmith, and a saddle-and-harness-making business.

The village was served by three schools and seven churches: Anglican, Roman Catholic, Presbyterian, Congregational, Wesleyan Methodist, Episcopal Methodist, and Christian. The large common school, replete with teacher's apartment and library, stood on the northeast corner of Prospect and Timothy Streets. It's the same site later occupied by the Alexander Muir Public School, and later still by a seniors' residence named for Muir. The grammar or secondary school was on Lot Street, now Millard Avenue, and a separate school was located in the basement of the Catholic church.

Edwin Irwin has left us a picture of Newmarket that has largely disappeared due to multiple demolitions, numerous fires, and lost records. But this astute man's final prediction for the community held true: "The agricultural part of the community is increasing rapidly in population and wealth and the capabilities of supporting a much larger population of manufacturers than the county contains at present is perfectly obvious."[3]

Irwin, the son of Quaker settlers who had cleared their land, was obviously pleased with the progress "his" town was making. His prediction that someday Newmarket would support a large number of manufacturers took much longer than he probably envisioned. The town was dominated from the late nineteenth century to the mid-twentieth century by three large manufacturers, Office Specialty Manufacturing Company Limited, which made office supplies and furniture; Davis Leather Company, a tannery that shipped their fine leather all over the world; and Cane Woodworking, which eventually became Dixon Pencil Company. It wasn't until late in the 1900s, more than a century after Irwin wrote his report, that industries began knocking on Newmarket's door. Industrial areas were laid out on the east side of town in the late 1970s (prevailing winds are from the west), and by the end of the century had filled up with gleaming new plants.

## The Era: Most Enduring of Newmarket's Newspapers

ON A SUNNY June day in 1853, two enterprising young newspapermen stepped off a train at the Newmarket station and walked into the town's history. Twenty-four-year-old Erastus Jackson and his friend and partner, E.R. Henderson, had been newspapermen on the *Toronto North American*. They came to Newmarket to buy the floundering newspaper business established in February 1852 by English immigrant printer G.S. Porter.

Porter later described his publishing efforts as inopportune because of the scarcity of money in the area and the meagre education of potential readers. In those days Newmarket was a hamlet of fewer than five hundred people. Most homes were grouped around the south end of Main Street. From the top of Main Street hill sizable patches of virgin forest could be seen to the north and west.

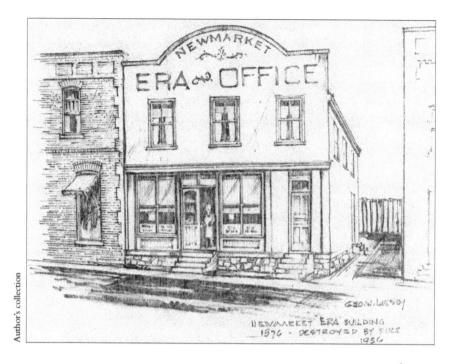

*Author's collection*

*The Era has been published under a number of names and from a number of locations. In 1876, owner Erastus Jackson built this structure for his newspaper and printing business on the east side of Main Street, near the top of the hill. The building burned in 1956. The newspaper plant moved to Charles Street, and the neighbouring funeral home of Roadhouse & Rose Funeral Service built on the site.*

*The New Era*, then the only newspaper between Toronto and Barrie, was a slender four pages weekly, which specialized in long, dull articles on agriculture, literature, and science that Porter reprinted from other publications. Its headquarters, a single-hand press and stationery store, were in a small frame building on the east side of Main Street opposite the end of Park Avenue. In the fall of 1853 the partners moved the business to a new building on the southwest corner of Main and Mill (Queen) Streets. Sometime during the first five years, the partnership split up and Henderson moved on. In later years, Jackson said, "During the first years of *The Era's* history the grammar and public schools had not long been established to exercise a potent influence of developing newspaper readers — hence the first 10 years were a hard struggle to make two ends meet."[4]

Jackson never left any doubt about where he and his newspaper stood on political issues. *The Newmarket Era* was a Reform publication and Jackson was ever ready to tackle the Conservative side in his columns. In those years newspaper editors did not aspire to impartiality and objectivity in their reporting as is done today. Jackson was involved in his political party, served on its executive and on more than one occasion was its candidate. He took a prominent part in nearly all the Reform-Liberal party conventions and was a friend and supporter of George Brown from 1858 until after Confederation. As a reward, Jackson was appointed coroner and issuer of marriage licences during the Sandfield-Dorion administration of Old Canada (1862–64), posts he held until 1878.

Erastus Jackson was born in Merrickville, Upper Canada, in 1829 and said his parents gave him all the advantages of education obtainable in those early times. When he was sixteen his father apprenticed him to a Cobourg printers, and three years later he followed his employer to Toronto. In 1850 he joined a Guelph newspaper and two years later returned to Toronto on the staff of the Honourable William McDougall's *Toronto North American*. His first decade as publisher in Newmarket was a hard struggle to make ends meet, but by the 1860s the business was flourishing, occupying a new building on Main Street.

Erastus was into politics. He held a village council seat for many years and served as reeve (the village had no mayor) from 1871 to 1876, and again from 1877 to 1881. After Newmarket was incorporated as a town, he continued as reeve and was elected to two terms as mayor, 1890 and 1891. He also served a term as warden of York County (chair of County Council, which was made up of local council members).

The Jacksons were staunch Methodists, and he held a number of church posts as well as community positions. He was secretary-treasurer of the North York Agricultural Society for twenty years, and is credited with arranging the purchase of Newmarket Fairgrounds (now Fairgrounds Park), and the erection there of one of the best exhibition halls in the province. He was president of the Newmarket Mechanics' Institute, which later evolved into a public library, and served for many years on the executive of the Canadian Press Association.

On top of all that, Erastus Jackson was a pretty colourful writer. Take this example of his retaliation in *The Newmarket Era* for comments made in the *Aurora Banner*, which opposed Newmarket's bid to obtain town status.

Something must have gone wrong with poor Horace's digestion [Horace was the offending *Banner* editor]. His ravings about the presumption of Newmarket aspiring to the dignity of a town gives unmistakable evidence of one of two things — either his Thanksgiving Dinner was too much for his stomach, or he displays an amount of pitiful jealousy not at all creditable to his head and heart.

And then a memory of the past, combined with a painfully realizing sense of the estimation of his own worth by the community in which he lives, nearly upset his equilibrium. Wonder and amazement seized his imagination and jealousy completely unmanned him. After saying something which he no doubt fancied peculiarly smart, in regard to Newmarket, he added "Wonder if they will have the Governor-General up to assist in the inauguration; if they do, perhaps Erastus will get to wearing his white kids, and enter the governor's carriage before the Governor, as he did on a previous occasion." Well now, this may all be — stranger things than this have transpired; but it isn't everybody who can wear white kid gloves and be invited by a Governor-General to step into carriage and ride with him.

At any rate we have a sort of undefinable impression that it will be a long time before Horace can boast of enjoying the confidence of his neighbours to such an extent as will entitle him to be recognized by a Governor-General, let his kids be never so white; when he does, it will be time enough for him to speak despairingly of others who have already attained that distinction.

The action favouring the incorporation of Newmarket as a town arose at a public meeting of the people, and the council carried out their wishes. They were, perhaps, wrong in not asking Horace about the matter before doing so, but it is too late now. We hope, however, he will survive the shock to his dignity.[5]

On July 19, 1861, *The New Era* changed its name to *The Newmarket Era*. In 1875, *The Newmarket Era* moved to a new location again, this time to within steps of its original home. Jackson built his new plant near the top of Main Street hill. That building burned in June 1956, and the business moved to Charles Street. In 1982, it moved to larger premises on Steven Court in the industrial south end of town.

Erastus Jackson retained sole control of *The Newmarket Era* for thirty years. In February 1883, his son, Lyman, took over and continued as publisher until March 1931, when he sold to Arthur Hawkes and his daughter, Evelyn Crickmore. But those were the Depression years, and Lyman was obliged to buy the business back and return to active management in May 1932. In August 1934, Colonel W.P. Mulock and Andrew Hebb became joint owners, with Hebb as editor and publisher. This continued until 1946 when a John Meyer bought out Hebb and succeeded him as editor.

In 1952, C.A. "Tiny" Cathers purchased the newspaper, and he sold to Major James Baxter in 1958. During that time Cathers was the Progressive Conservative member of Parliament. In May 1965, the *Toronto Telegram* purchased *The Era* and established Inland Publishing Company to operate its weekly newspapers. Inland in turn was acquired by Torstar Inc., the *Toronto Star*'s owners, and became part of its Metroland chain. At that point the name became simply *The Era*. Later in the 1980s the paper was amalgamated with the *Aurora Banner* to become *The Era-Banner*. Still later the two were separated and it again became known as *The Era*.

Throughout *The Era*'s long business success there have been few years when it did not have at least one competitor. First to appear was the *North York Sentinel,* founded December 1855 by Dr. James Hunter, Alfred Boultbee, Benjamin Pearson, and George Hughes. It was Reform in politics and disappeared after less than a year. In December 1867, the first Conservative newspaper appeared, the *Newmarket Courier*. G.M. Binns was editor. The *Courier* turned Liberal as early as 1873 after a local doctor, Dr. Playter, acquired control in 1871. Two years later he sold to George H. Fox. In 1876, the *North York Reformer,* a Reform paper, bought the *Courier.*

The *Reformer* was founded that August by a group of Reform politicians who had a falling out with Jackson because he refused to endorse the party's official candidate, Newmarket lawyer Alfred Boultbee.

Although never nominally leaving the Reform fold, during this period *The Era* took an "independent Reform" stance, and eventually Erastus Jackson himself ran for the Legislature on that ticket. He lost. In 1880, his newspaper still contended it was a Reform paper, but "not slavishly partisan." Thus, the official Reform paper remained the *North York Reformer*, and it published well into the 1880s.

Other newspapers cropped up along the way. The *North York Intelligencer & Advertiser* had been absorbed by *The Newmarket Era* about 1870, and in the 1890s the *Newmarket Express & Advertiser* was on the scene as a Conservative publication. In 1901, the *Express & Advertiser* purchased the *West Sutton Herald* and became the *Express-Herald*, E.W. Burnham publisher. He was succeeded by J.D. McKay, W.E. Wiley, J.F. Harvey, J.W. Bowman, and Angus West. In 1942, West sold to Mulock and Hebb, thus creating *The Newmarket Era & Express*. Its name soon changed to *The Era*. In 1961, the Jones-Poirier Publishing Co. put out the *Newmarket Post*. Eight years later it was taken over by *The Era* and disappeared. In the early 1980s, the *Newmarket News* made its appearance and survived about a decade under various ownerships.

## Three Generations of Canes Were Mayors

THREE GENERATIONS OF the Cane family were mayors of Newmarket and under their leadership momentous changes occurred.

William Cane, son of Irish immigrants from Antrim County, moved his woodenware manufacturing business to Newmarket from Queensville in 1872, and built it into the town's largest employer. While living in East Gwillimbury, William had served as reeve, deputy reeve, and for fourteen years as a school trustee. He was elected warden of York County in 1874. His fitness for municipal office was soon recognized in Newmarket and he was elected to village council. He pushed for a change in the village's status to town, and when Newmarket was incorporated as a town in 1880 he was acclaimed its first mayor. He was re-elected nine successive times.

Mainly through his efforts, the town hall and market building was constructed, a move that ensured the new town's position as the commercial centre of the district.

William's eldest son, Henry Stiles Cane, served twenty-seven years as a town councillor and reeve before being elected mayor in 1897. He was mayor until 1904, and again in 1915 and 1916. He is said to be the mayor that brought Newmarket into the twentieth century. Through his leadership a municipal waterworks system was built, a modern fire department organized, electricity brought to the town, and a telephone system inaugurated. He is also credited with attracting the Davis Leather Company, the Office Specialty Manufacturing Company, and Pickering College to Newmarket.

W.H.S. Cane, known as "Howard," was William's grandson and the eldest son of Henry. He spent his career with the family woodenware company and, in 1920, installed machinery for the manufacture of lead pencils — the first in Canada. Following in the family footsteps, Howard served as a town councillor for many years and was mayor from 1922 to 1924. He left town politics when appointed deputy sheriff of York County, and went on to become the sheriff in 1935.

*Author's collection*

*William Cane built up a large woodenware manufacturing business that made clothes pins, wooden buckets, and other household implements in Newmarket. The town's largest employer, he became Newmarket's first mayor in 1881, following its incorporation as a town.*

## ⚭ Photo May Be One of Cane's Former Slaves ⚭

AN OLD PHOTO of an elderly gentleman of African ancestry was given to me along with a handful of other photos many years ago. Apparently these had been found in the attic of a house under renovation in Newmarket. The only identifiers on the Black man's photo are the legend, "A North York Old Boy," and the name of the photo studio, "Smith Bros., Newmarket, Ont." The photo has always puzzled me. It would seem to date to the late nineteenth century or early twentieth. It's the only photo by Smith Bros. I've ever come across, so I don't know when they were in business here. Racial attitudes were much different one hundred years ago, and I wondered if that label was somebody's poor attempt at humour, or if this gentleman was a well-known figure in Newmarket in the nineteenth century.

A little further research revealed that the latter could well have been the case. The story starts with William Cane, one of Newmarket's foremost citizens of the nineteenth century, the town's first mayor, and owner of one of its largest industries. Slavery ended in Upper Canada in 1834 with the passing of the Slavery Abolition Act abolishing slavery in most of the British Empire, but was not ended south of the border until 1865. In the interval our colony became a haven for escaped slaves. Cane, at that time, was operating a sawmill on the 5th Concession (today Kennedy Road) of East Gwillimbury, turning the timber from the surrounding hills into lumber and wood products. Fire at that mill forced him to move his business to Newmarket in 1874.

As he was always short of labourers to work in the woods, Cane brought in a number of former slaves to help supply his mill. He probably hired them at a stop on the Underground Railroad run by Quakers, a farm near Aurora on the west side of Woodbine Avenue south of Wellington Street. A Black settlement developed near the mill, and by 1882 about fifty men lived there with their families. As the forest was pushed back and work at the mill tapered off, then ceased in 1874 when the business moved to Newmarket, many members of this African-Canadian community found other employment.

The settlement's founding members were Henry Hisson and his wife Sarah Jane, Taylor Tamar, and Edward Provost, all of whom escaped

*Slaves escaping from the United States were hidden by Quakers at a camp located near Newmarket on a farm on the east side of Leslie Street (in the vicinity of present-day Wellington Street and Woodbine Avenue) until they could be safely settled. Many found work at William Cane's mill on the 5th Concession of East Gwillimbury, east of Queensville, and stayed in the area. Although unidentified, this North York "Old Boy" may have been one of these men employed by Cane.*

to Upper Canada prior to the American Civil War. Old newspaper files reveal that Tamar was known as "Darkey" Taylor and that his back carried the whipmarks of the lashings by his slavemasters. He married an Irish woman, built a log cabin on his land, and his home was used by the Black lumbermen for Sunday services and political gatherings.

Hisson, Tamar, and Provost were the first to purchase land from Cane, Hisson buying twelve acres, Taylor ten, and Provost sixty. The York County map of 1878 shows William Cane, and William Cane & Sons Ltd., owning considerable land in the 5th Concession of East Gwillimbury. The three lots purchased by Hisson, Tamar, and Provost are marked only by their initials and are found a concession north of Davis Drive. A sawmill and pond are shown two concessions north of that in the 5th Concession, adjoining Cane land. This was probably the Cane mill.

Henry Hisson turned to charcoal-making on his land, hauling his product to Toronto to sell. He had a horse, wagon, and barn, and was said to be the most affluent Black living in the area. His son Edward John Hisson (1881–1949) moved to Guelph and found work making stoves.[6] Two of Henry's other sons, Samuel and Israel, followed him. Other members of this little East Gwillimbury community probably moved to Newmarket looking for work, and the gentleman in the photo could well be one of them.


## ❧ Charcoal-Maker Had Found Freedom in Upper Canada ❧

THE DIRTIEST JOB on the colonial frontier was that of the charcoal-maker, and, in this district, the only charcoal-maker on record was an escaped slave who plied the trade near Sharon. As indicated in the previous story, Henry Hisson and his wife, Sarah Jane, settled on the 5th Concession of East Gwillimbury, and Henry went to work in the lumbering business of William Cane. Eventually, he acquired sixty acres from Cane — property that is now part of the Pheasant Run Golf Club — and soon after turned to making charcoal and hauling it by wagon to sell in Toronto, Newmarket, and other local communities.

During the 1800s charcoal was a common household commodity

put to many uses. People cleaned their teeth with it, and although initial results might have looked ghastly, it actually worked very well. It was used to calm upset stomachs, to sweeten breath, to purify water, and to remove offensive odours from just about anything. Charcoal also had many industrial uses. It was utilized in the making of iron, ice was stored in charcoal, gunpowder and printer's ink were made from it, as well as black paint and medicines.

Each charcoal man had his own recipe for building the mound of wood to be charred. And as recently as 1979 the remains of some of Henry Hisson's mounds could still be found just north of Newmarket, but they have now disappeared with the grading of the golf course. The time required to char a small mound varied from one to two weeks, but a large mound of thirty feet around or more, as Hisson evidently used, could take a month. During that time, through every kind of weather, Hisson had to live with his mound, sleeping only in short dozes for fear a flame might start and explode into a full fire, which would demolish the mound. There was no time for washing and seldom any more shelter than a bark lean-to. And there were so many things to watch for in a "live mound" that the man became almost part of it.

At first lighting, a heavy, dark smoke poured from holes in the middle of the mound. This was quickly smothered until a blue haze arose. Hisson had to keep the smouldering fire within the mound alight by constantly smothering any flames with moist charcoal power. Then there was the "sweating period" when the mound emitted a yellowish smoke. Moist charcoal or mud would be quickly applied until the smoke turned grey. Until the heat subsided, the mound never stopped "working" and neither did the man. Knowing how and when to walk on the mound was an art in itself, and many a man fell though into the furnace-like heat.

However, the charcoal business was apparently good to the Hisson family, for long after emancipation in the United States, when many former slaves returned to the Republic, the Hissons were living and raising their large family on their land in East Gwillimbury. Having a horse, wagon, and barn, Henry Hisson became the most affluent Black in the small African-Canadian community that had grown up around Cane's lumbering operation and mill. Remembered as a well-mannered gentleman, it is not hard to imagine Henry Hisson slowly driving his wagon through the streets of villages such as Newmarket, calling out the charcoal man's traditional chant:

> Charcoal by the bushel,
> Charcoal by the peck,
> Charcoal by the frying pan
> Or any way you lek!

## Citizens Band Founded in 1872

THE BRASS BAND founded by sixteen-year-old Walter Roe in Newmarket in 1872 is Canada's oldest continually-operating community concert band. The Newmarket Citizens Band was founded by young Mr. Roe with the help of eleven of his friends, who circulated a petition appealing for funds from their elders. It read:

> Whereas we, the undersigned, think it a disgrace to the inhabitants of Newmarket that they should have, on all festive occasions, to send to the small villages of Aurora or Sharon for a band, we have determined, with the consent and assistance of our fellow-townsmen, to form one of our own.[7]

Walter Roe, writer of the appeal, was the eldest son of William Roe, pioneer merchant and postmaster of Newmarket. The original teenage sponsors of the plan, all of whom subscribed five dollars, were: Walter W. Roe, George Hackett, George Dolan, John Hughes, William Hutchcroft, James Harrison, Thomas Gain, Frederick Saxton, Albert E. Roe, Frederick Roe, Robert Rest, and Frederick Raper. Sixty-nine other citizens, a large proportion of the village's senior population, signed up and contributed an additional $219. Among them appear such names as John Joseph Cawthra, later a leading financial figure in Toronto, and Robert Simpson, founder of the Simpsons department store empire. The petition for funds

Author's collection

*The Newmarket Citizens Band has been entertaining the community since 1872, making it the oldest continually operating community concert band in Canada. Above, members of the band pose for a photograph in 1883.*

Author's collection

*The Citizens Band is shown marching in a parade up Main Street in 1953. It is led by renowned bandmaster Bill Greig.*

Even as a teenager, Walter Roe was acknowledged as one of the village's most accomplished musicians. At the time, he was organist at the Christian Church (now Christian Baptist Church). He had won the post because the organist's post at his own church, St. Paul's Anglican, was filled. Three years after the founding of the band — on May 31, 1875 — both Walter and Fred Roe were drowned while on a fishing trip on Lake Simcoe. Walter was nineteen, and Fred fifteen. Their bodies were not recovered from the weeds of Cook's Bay until June 21.

Those three weeks were a period of deep strain and concern, not only for the grieving family but for the entire village, and particularly for the remaining band members, as a member of the Roe family would note later. A long poem of lamentation signed by band members was published in *The Era*. Old St. Paul's Church was crowded for the funeral and the new band accompanied the cortege to the family plot in the cemetery on Eagle Street, playing the "Dead March" and other funeral music. The Newmarket Citizens Band's two young founders still lie buried in the little pioneer cemetery.

## Pomp and Ceremony Greeted the Governor General

PEOPLE TOOK GOVERNORS general much more seriously a hundred years ago than they do today. When Governor General Ed Schreyer arrived in a cavalcade of limousines in November 1982 to lay the cornerstone for a new building at Pickering College, he wore a business suit, carried out his duty expeditiously, shook a few hands, and was off again. No pomp, very little ceremony.

When Governor General Lord Dufferin came to town more than one hundred years earlier to perform the same duty at Main Street's Christian Church (now Christian Baptist Church), the pace was more leisurely and there was pomp and ceremony aplenty. The governor general and his party arrived on a special train on July 25, 1874. It stopped at a decorated temporary platform at the Water Street crossing. Members of both town and county councils greeted the visitors and then, preceded by the Newmarket Citizens Band and two bands from outside town, the vice-regal party was conveyed in carriages up Main Street hill to the church site. Accounts leave

Author's collection

*Main Street was bedecked with arches made of evergreen boughs for the progress of Governor General Lord Dufferin and his wife when the couple visited Newmarket in 1874. The arch above was located near the juncture of Botsford and Main Streets.*

An honour guard of one hundred volunteers of the 12th Battalion, York Rangers, awaited him. During the ceremony they fired a royal salute. There were floral tributes to Lady Dufferin and a second highlight of the day came when children from the town school, uniformed as British sailors in brass-buttoned, double-breasted jackets of blue with white trousers, sang "The Maple Leaf Forever." They were under the direction of their principal, Alexander Muir, the anthem's author. This is believed to be the first occasion on which "The Maple Leaf Forever" was sung in public by a chorus, according to *The Newmarket Era* of July 24, 1874. Lord Dufferin shook hands with Mr. Muir and complimented him.

The cornerstone-laying ceremonies over, the entourage reformed, and proceeded north in stately procession along a splendidly decorated Main Street and Huron Street (now Davis Drive) to the railway station, where the governor-general reboarded his train. It is said that six triumphal evergreen arches were erected over Main Street for the occasion. After the train pulled out of the station, the village of Newmarket entertained the volunteers and the bands at the Royal Hotel, while refreshments were served to the public by members of the Christian Church in the Mechanics' Hall, around the corner from the church on Millard Avenue.

Although Schreyer's visit was only the third time a governor general had paid an official visit to Newmarket, the town has had three royal visits and one near miss. The near miss came in 1939 when King George VI and Queen Elizabeth toured Canada. Their train travelled the line east of Newmarket, stopping briefly in Pine Orchard, a hamlet about three miles east of Newmarket. Albert Edward, Prince of Wales, was the first member of the British royal family to visit, arriving with his entourage by train on September 10, 1860. In 1881, the Marquis of Lorne, then governor general, and his wife Princess Louise came, and in October 1901 the Duke of York, later King George V, and his duchess, later Queen Mary, paid a visit. All travelled by special train, stopping briefly at the

*The Governor General, the Marquis of Lorne, and his wife, Princess Louise, were welcomed in 1881 by this crowd at the railway station.*

depots in Aurora, Newmarket, and Bradford, during which time the local civic leaders made their formal presentations.

## Stickwood Brick Built Old Newmarket

CREAMY BUFF BRICK was the building material of choice for many of Newmarket's lovely late nineteenth-century buildings, and there's a good reason for that. Those bricks were made right here in Newmarket. Examples include the Trinity United Church on Main Street and the Old Town Hall on Botsford Street.

The Stickwood Brickyard operated on the north side of Srigley Street, just east of Bogart Creek, from 1860 until after 1910. Practically all the brick buildings erected in Newmarket during that period are built of Stickwood brick.

Isaac Stickwood, his wife, and family came to America from Cambridgeshire, England, in the spring of 1857. Their sailing ship landed in New York, and they made their way to Toronto. Isaac spent two years working in the Davisville Brickyard, near Davisville and Yonge Streets, before purchasing the Srigley Street property and going into business for himself. He made his first bricks in 1860 and continued until 1871, when his son William took over.

In 1890 William turned the business over to his younger brother, Charles, who carried on until 1917 when a scarcity of hardwood to fire the kilns forced a decision to close. During its years of operation, the brickyard turned out a variety of products. Baked white brick was its most common, but a creamy or pink tone resulted from some of the clay deposits on the property. Yellow and red bricks were also made by adding yellow oxide of lead or red oxide of iron before baking.

The Stickwood family home, which stood near the present site of Prince Charles Public School, was a large two-and-a-half storey red-brick house with a verandah, set well back from Srigley Street. Fuel for the kilns was cut from the hardwood bush that covered the area on both sides of the 3rd Concession (Leslie Street) east of the brickyard. The men who worked the brickyard six or seven months each year spent the winter cutting wood.

Room and board came with the job. The men stayed in the huge Stickwood farmhouse and ate at a long table in the dining room. Servant girls under the supervision of Mrs. Stickwood prepared and served meals. This whole operation was very self-sufficient. The women baked their own breads and pastries, cured their own pork, and raised their own beef, as well growing and storing their own vegetables.

Newmarket is fortunate that so much of its first century's built heritage is of Stickwood brick.

## Strange Societies Appeared on Great Occasions

GREAT OCCASIONS IN Newmarket's history seem always to have spawned strange and colourful organizations bent on civic improvement and entertainment. The evolution of a group of Kanataites[8] determined to perpetuate the fun and games of the 1980 town centennial follows a long and honourable Newmarket tradition.

Does anybody remember, for instance, the Newmarket Canoe Club and Camel Corps (NCC&CC)? A group of livewire citizens with an affinity for conviviality, they had neither canoes nor camels, but somebody in the organization did own a pith helmet. The group evolved during an earlier centennial celebration — the one in 1957 that marked the one hundredth anniversary of Newmarket's incorporation as a village. The NCC&CC's major accomplishment that year was the cleaning of the face of Fairy Lake dam, which, to mark the centennial occasion, was scrubbed, refaced, and floodlit with coloured lights.

A much earlier example of this organizational phenomenon appears in the records of Newmarket's celebrations for Queen Victoria's birthday during the lead-up to the first Dominion Day. A day of parades, sporting events, and musicals was organized and the highlight was the high jinks of the Phantazmagoria Society. Its members claimed to be representatives of the "old original Calithumpians." In fact, their 3:00 p.m. appearance on the Main Street hill proved so exciting that *The Newmarket Era* reporter of the day had a hard time finding words to describe it. Here's what he wrote:

At three o'clock the Phantazmagoria Society made their appearance; and although from what was previously announced much was expected the reality exceeded all preconceived opinions.

From the Marshal, down to the lumber train of an apparent fatiguing party which brought up the rear, they exceeded any former demonstration ever attempted in this part of the country and completely distanced anything ever witnessed in either of the surrounding villages.

By this time, the throng had increased to such numbers as to completely block up Main St. the whole length of the procession — and was variously estimated at between 3,500 and 4,500.

Anything like a clear description of the dress, regalia or antics of these representatives of the "old original Calithumpians" is out of the question: suffice to say they beat all creation and astonished the natives.[9]

And Calithumpians? A name used by folks who staged satirical presentations, lampooned pompous visitors, held parades, and other spectacles during the Prince of Wales' 1860 visits to colonial towns and probably long before.

*Chapter Nine*

# MORE LIFE IN THE NINETEENTH CENTURY

## ❧ Artesian Well Went Wild ☙

A GUSHER OF water erupting at the bottom of Main Street in March 1891 surprised the whole town, including waterworks engineer Stephen Warren. At that time the town's water supply came from a series of artesian wells along the shores of Fairy Lake.

Everything had been working well until one evening when Mrs. Warren noticed the water from her tap was "riley." Her husband went to the pumps at the municipal wells and saw they were not working smoothly. He found the water coming from the ground was dirty but cleared by the time it reached the upper reservoir on Prospect Street. He decided one of the wells had caved in at the bottom. To move the concrete cap from the well he first had to shift three cords of firewood. By the time the cap came off it was 10:00 p.m., and a gusher of muddy water burst forth. It continued all night.

By Saturday there was great excitement throughout the town. The flow was found to be 172,000 gallons every twenty-four hours, and chunks of soapstone clay as large as goose eggs, as well as gravel and sand, were coming up with it. Even though this 250-foot-deep well was in a group of four within fifty feet of each other, the other wells were not affected.

On Monday morning four men were speculating on the power of the gusher. They put a plank over the pipe and all four stood on it. It threw the plank right off, but the water was badly riled by the stunt and the flow weakened.

The decision was made to drain the well, but the pump got stuck, buried in fifteen to twenty feet of fine gravel. When it was finally freed, more water than ever before poured out of the well.

Finally, after two weeks of work to no avail, the well cured itself. It was soon producing 200,000 gallons of crystal clear water; evidently the spring water filtered though gravel. It became the town's largest artesian well.

These wells were closed many years ago. Today, the Regional Municipality of York manages a region-wide water distribution system with thirty-nine production wells. Most of Newmarket's water comes from four wells in the Queensville area. A small amount — about 10 percent — is added from Toronto.

## Early Railway Could Have Had Its Own Lottery

CONSTRUCTION OF THE railway, which arrived in Newmarket in 1853, guaranteeing the community's position as the commercial centre of north York County, was nearly dependent on a lottery — and that was more than a century before Lotto 6/49.

The story of the railway that made Newmarket begins August 29, 1849, when the Toronto, Sarnia & Lake Huron Railway Company was chartered with a capital of £500,000 in £5 shares. The road was to run from the city of Toronto to some point on the southern shore of Lake Huron, touching at the town of Barrie on the way. Plans were to complete a survey within three years and build the line in ten. The company was authorized to raise the amount of the stock either by subscription or lottery. The lottery scheme, however, was never put into practice.

The name of the rail line was changed to the Ontario, Simcoe & Huron Railway Company (OS&HR), known locally as the Oats, Straw and Hay Railway, and its tracks reached Newmarket in June 1853 and Barrie by October, with a branch to Bell Ewart, then a steamboat port on Lake Simcoe. Its northern terminus was built at Collingwood by the end of 1854. This was the third railway to be built in the colonies north of the American border and the first outside Quebec.

With a view to controlling the navigation on Lake Simcoe, the railway directors purchased the steamer *Morning* and the wharves at Orillia and Bradford. They also built the steamer *J.C. Morrison* to ply the lake. In 1855 they contracted for a tri-weekly line of steamers between Collingwood and Chicago and the other Lake Michigan ports, and a weekly run to Green Bay. The construction contract for the OS&HR totalled £579,175 and locomotives, rolling stock, way station service, the terminal depot, harbour service, and steamboat service brought the total up to £702,560.

Revenue during the early years was estimated at £136,000 per annum. Between 1850 and 1859 the railway made money in all years except 1857 and 1858, but it wasn't enough. As so many businesses then and now have done, the railway directors dipped into the taxpayers' pockets. The government loaned it £475,000. The company never got around to paying back anything but the interest, and as soon as this capital account was exhausted it stopped paying that too. As a result, the government took a lien out against the tracks, buildings, land, and equipment. In 1858, the government moved to foreclose and sell the company to regain its investment. However, no buyers could be found. Having decided it couldn't afford to be in the railway business itself, the government contented itself with a reorganization and refinancing.

That same year, the name of the railway was changed to the Northern Railway Company of Canada. In 1888 it, in turn, was taken over by the Grand Trunk Railway Company. Through amalgamation, in 1922 it became part of the Canadian National Railway.

The railway had a tremendous impact on the communities it passed through, ensuring growth and prosperity for those touched by its tracks and decline for those that were not. The first train to travel from Toronto to Aurora consisted of two boxcars, one car (half baggage and half passenger), and one coach devoted to passenger service. Pulled by the steam engine "Toronto," it arrived at Machell's Corners (now Aurora) to be greeted by virtually the whole population of the community — about one hundred people. Industry soon followed the tracks, and by 1863 Aurora was incorporated as a village and became a town in 1888. Newmarket became a village in 1857 and a town in 1880.

Rail travel not only made it easier and cheaper for farmers to ship produce, it was "fast" service for the mid-nineteenth century. In the 1850s passenger trains on the line hit speeds of up to twenty-four miles-per-hour and averaged twenty miles-per-hour when stops were included. Express trains ran five miles-per-hour faster. Freights hit fifteen miles-per-hour and averaged twelve. It's interesting to note that when a new and more business-like managing director, Frederick Cumberland, was appointed in 1859, he discovered all the railway's profits were being made on local traffic and wiped out by the through traffic. He immediately began to build sidings and upgrade local facilities to attract more business from the rail communities. It's also interesting that the company's president was none other than that one-time Newmarket boy and Family Compact star, the Honourable John Beverley Robinson.

## ᖇᑎᕈ Oldest Companies Started in the Mid-Nineteenth Century ᖇᑎᕈ

TWO PILLARS OF Newmarket's business community trace their roots back well over a century and a half. Roadhouse & Rose Funeral Service counts its start as 1842, and *The Era* was founded as *The New Era* in 1852. The *Aurora Banner* began in 1864.

At age fourteen, Samuel Roadhouse moved from Peel County to Newmarket and became an apprentice in the Main Street shop of John Botsford, a cabinetmaker. He established his own cabinetmaking and undertaking business when Botsford died in 1842. Roadhouse remained at the original location at Main and Botsford Streets until 1853, when he built his own home and woodworking factory on the northeast corner of Main and Queen Streets. At the time most cabinetmakers offered funeral services as the manufacturing of caskets was an important part of their business.

Another substantial brick building on the east side of Main Street near the top of the hill, built in 1866 by Joseph Millard, was sold to the Watson and Hall Funeral Home in 1918. Three years later it was purchased by Samuel's son, John Roadhouse. He discontinued the cabinetmaking and moved the undertaking business there from his father's original site. Funeral services and furniture retailing continued.

John's son-in-law, Lyman Rose, joined him and the partnership continued until John's death in 1932, when the firm assumed its current name, Roadhouse & Rose. In 1953 the business was taken over by Rodney Ecobichon, Wray Playter, and Lyman Rose's son, Donald Rose. The retailing of furniture was discontinued in 1969, allowing them to concentrate on the funeral end of the business and to increase the size of the funeral home. Rod Ecobichon retired in 1974, followed by Donald Rose in 1984. Glenn Playter, a nephew of Wray's, along with his wife, Jackie, became owners. They have now turned ownership over to their son, Wesley.

As noted in an earlier story, *The Era* has published continuously since 1852 when a storekeeper and printer named George S. Porter launched *The New Era*, a four-page weekly "devoted to news, agriculture, science, morality and amusement." In 1853, Porter sold out to two newcomers to town, Erastus Jackson and A.E.R. Henderson, and left for Australia. Porter was reported to have said later of his Newmarket venture, "It was not a very wise thing to do. They were not a literary people and they never paid."[1]

In 1854, Jackson became sole proprietor, and the weekly remained in family hands until 1934. After passing through several ownerships in the 1940s, 1950s, and 1960s, it was purchased by John Bassett and the *Toronto Telegram* interests. Some years after the demise of the *Telegram*, Bassett's community newspaper company, Inland Publishing Company, was acquired by Torstar, owner of the *Toronto Star*, and amalgamated with its community newspaper company to form Metroland Publishing Company, the current owners.

## ⤳ Telephones Came Early ⤳

JUST THREE YEARS after Alexander Graham Bell transmitted voice sounds over a wire strung between Brantford and Paris, Ontario, in 1876, the first telephones were operating in Newmarket. In October 1879, S.A. Russell & Company, successors to the Gorham Woollen Mills business, leased a pair of telephones for use on a private line between its offices and mill buildings. The mill system was linked to the Montreal Telegraph Company's office on Main Street, giving it access to lines outside the town. By 1884 the area had really been bitten by the telephone bug — there were eighteen telephones in town.

*Courtesy of the Telephone Historical Collection, Bell Canada*

*These guys were proud of their high-wire act. Seventeen telephone company linemen were photographed on this Main Street pole in 1906, when the area was first wired for phones.*

Exchanges were installed in both Newmarket and Aurora and linked by wire in 1884. Later that year they were wired into a central exchange in Toronto. The eighteen Newmarket subscribers could then call all over the province. During those early years only insurance agent David Lloyd, who lived on Pearson Street and was the Bell Telephone Company's

Newmarket agent, and merchant W.W. Playter, who lived on Prospect Street, had phones in their homes. The rest were in business locations.

The first switchboard was in Lloyd's office at Main and Botsford Streets and operated from 8:00 a.m. to 8:00 p.m. weekdays, 2:00 to 4:00 p.m. Sundays, and 10:00 a.m. to noon and 2:00 to 4:00 p.m. holidays. Bell brought in twenty-four-hour service (except on Sundays) in 1903. The early telephones were single units that were held alternately to the mouth and ear for talking and listening. Once the Bell Telephone Company was incorporated in 1880, it immediately began taking over the small private lines. Ten years later the first transatlantic call from Newmarket was made when a John Kirstine is recorded as having called Dulwick, England, and talked for eleven minutes.

By May 1911 the town had two hundred phones, and a year later three hundred. Newmarket didn't hit the five hundred mark until 1920. In 1956, Bell built its new exchange on Millard Avenue, introduced dial service, and everybody had to get used to new and longer numbers. The old three-digit numbers gave way to an exchange (Twinning, TW for short) and a five-digit number. Eventually the TW became 89 and TW5-6581 became 895-6581.

## ❧ Newmarket Regatta: An Annual Event ❧

SAILING WAS A great hobby in colonial Upper Canada. If one didn't have a full-sized boat, one built a model. It was during the summer of 1863 that the first Newmarket Regatta was organized. Six model yachts and schooners raced against each other on the waters of Sutherland's Pond (Fairy Lake). The *Royal Albert*, *Seagull*, *Cushla Machree*, *Ariadne*, *Paddy Whack*, and *Maid of the Mist* were all after the big silver cup. Each vessel was exactly three feet in length and an accurate scale model.

It was a sunny afternoon and the shores of the lake were lined with spectators. A W.S. Murray, clad in the uniform of the Royal Canadian Yacht Club of Toronto (founded 1852), embarked in a handsome bark canoe and paddled across the water. At three o'clock the starting signal was given, the breeze stiffened to fill sails, and each craft headed for the opposite shore. Each vessel displayed its flag — Albion, Erin, France, two for Canada (2), and the United States — otherwise the ensign of

St. George, the Union Jack, the Harp and Shamrock, the Tri-colour, the Maple Leaf and the Stars and Stripes. The winner of the race, the *Ariadne*, crossed to the opposite side of the pond and returned followed by the *Sea Gull*, *Cushla Machree*, and the *Maid of the Mist*. According to the news report the others went astray and didn't finish. This first regatta was considered to have been successful and plans were made to have a race every Saturday afternoon, with prizes.

The model yachts continued to compete for a number of years and the Pond continued to grow in its significance as a recreational centre for the community. Today, it and the surrounding park are in continual use for festivals, exhibitions, an outdoor Shakespearean theatre, craft shows, boat races, canoeing, and many other events.

## Politicians Didn't Keep Their Promise

EVER NOTICE THAT the clocks are missing from the tower of the Christian Baptist Church at the top of Main Street hill in Newmarket? Those blank, round clock faces have been staring out over the town since 1875 because the municipal council failed to keep a promise. When the church was built in 1874 its construction was quite an occasion for the then village of Newmarket. As an earlier story related, the governor general of Canada, Lord Dufferin, laid the cornerstone on July 25, 1874. Triumphal evergreen arches were erected over a flag-draped Main Street at Water Street, Timothy Street, opposite the church, and at Ontario Street — and a special train that stopped at a decorated temporary platform at Water Street brought the vice-regal party from Toronto.

The village council of the day promised to furnish a four-faced clock for the tower if the church elders built it to accommodate one, but the councillors never approved the money for it. The deal was that the town would provide the clock in return for the church allowing the town free use of the bell in the bell tower. Also, that the weight of the proposed bell would be double that of the existing village bell. Town fathers figured that the striking of the clock would eliminate their expense of ringing the village bell several times a day, a service that cost them $40 a year. However, the proposal was put to the ratepayers and resulted in a tie vote. Council,

*Those blank spaces on the Christian Baptist Church steeple have been waiting for their promised clocks since 1875.*

faced with the decision, voted not to provide the money for the clock.

So that's why, all these years later, the tower of the church at the top of Main Street hill is still waiting for its four-faced clock.

## ✑ Glenville Once a Thriving Village ✑

MANY OF NEWMARKET's neighbouring villages of pioneer days have fallen into decline and stagnated. Some have disappeared altogether, leaving nothing but a crossroads sign and sometimes a millpond to mark their passing. Glenville, a once thriving little rural village set in the rolling hills of northern King Township, one-and-a quarter miles west of Newmarket's present boundary, is one of the latter.

A modern highway (Highway 9) has obliterated the old road track along which the village grew up during the nineteenth century, and the mills, distillery, stores, hotels, and other businesses have all disappeared without a trace. Only the ponds around which the village flourished as a milling site remain, but because the new highway has been graded through many feet higher than the old track, it is hard for newcomers today to visualize how the old gravel road clung to the side of the pond only a few feet above the water; or how it served as the jumping off place for small boys who bicycled out from Newmarket for a summer swim.

According to Elizabeth Gillham, whose book *Early Settlements of King Township* devotes a whole chapter to Glenville, a sawmill was built on the south pond in 1807 (there are two small ponds south of the highway separated by a marsh) by an emigrant from Pennsylvania, William Lloyd. He used an up-and-down saw to rip through the large pine logs taken from the surrounding countryside. This mill burned down in 1898.

Newmarket businessman William Cawthra built a big frame flour mill on the north pond in 1836. This one burned in 1916. A third Glenville mill was operated by Fred Webster, a descendant of the Webster family, early settlers in the Glenville area who arrived during the first years of the nineteenth century. In 1934 Webster's mill was also a victim of fire.

When Newmarket merchant and fur trader William Roe ran for Parliament against Louis-Hippolyte Lafontaine in 1841, he was the owner of the Glenville Distillery, which at that time was selling whisky for 25 cents a gallon. Lafontaine had resigned his candidacy in his own Quebec riding of Terrebonne that year, charging unfair elector practices, and Reform Party leader Robert Baldwin parachuted him into the Fourth Riding of York. As discussed earlier, Lafontaine defeated Roe, despite the latter's access to whisky, a key election ingredient, and represented the riding from 1841 to 1844.

In addition to the mills and distillery, in its heyday Glenville boasted three blacksmiths, a blanket-and-carpet-making establishment, a store that became renowned locally for the felt hats made and sold there, and two hotels, the Sand Bank and the Central. The village also had a church, a school, and an active Temperance Society with its own hall.

Not big enough to have its own minister, the Glenville Methodist Church was on the Holland Landing circuit. The church was a white frame building without a basement but with a large shed for stabling horses. It stood on the north side of the road (old Highway 9). In 1902, it became part of a circuit with Kettleby, Pottageville, and Snowball. In 1925, it joined the United Church of Canada, but by 1952 the congregation had dwindled to the point where it was difficult to find a minister to serve the four churches, and services were discontinued. The church was sold in 1959.

West of the church, on the south side of the road, stood Temperance Hall. It was taken down in 1932. The first Glenville school was built in 1839, and in 1885 a new brick school was built on the crest of a hill, west of the milling centre. It continued to serve the community until 1953, when it was sold, and is now a private home.

In 1900 Glenville was granted its own post office. Until then its residents had to go to Newmarket for mail. The post office was in the gristmill, and remained there until rural mail delivery was inaugurated in the area in 1914.

Not much is left of the old milling centre of Glenville today. Highway 9, the westerly extension of Davis Drive, has been repeatedly rebuilt over the years, and each time the level of the road has been raised. Now speeding cars and trucks pass through the glen on a four-lane thoroughfare and the only clue for drivers that there was once a valley there is the pond on the south side, well below the highway. All traces of the mills, hotels, stores, and other businesses have disappeared.


## ॐ Merchant Found Shot Through the Heart ॐ


THE STORY OF one of Newmarket's earliest merchant families came to a bloody end in a cold basement room on the night of February 26, 1890. The story begins with Robert Hall Smith, a young man who early in 1838, with his cousin Michael P. Empy, opened a Main Street dry-goods store immediately north of the North American Hotel.

It is the story of family intrigue, wealth, and success; a difficult and controlling widow, a wild son who spent years as a rootless sailor on the Great Lakes, and a second son who took over the failing family business after his father's death and brother's departure, and made it a success. Even Robert Simpson, the Toronto department store tycoon, figures in the Smith family story.

After a short time in partnership, Smith and Empy split, with Empy opening a Bogarttown store about one mile southeast of Newmarket. A few years later Smith built a new store on the northwest corner of Main and Timothy Streets. In 1857, he sold his dry-goods business but bought it back two years later. He continued for thirteen years until a fire forced him out of business. His eldest son, John, purchased what was left of the stock, but did not succeed in business. John Marshall Smith was the dissolute son who failed at business and disappeared for twelve years. It is not recorded why he abruptly left, or what tensions were tearing at the Smith family when he returned. However, feelings ran so high that younger brother Robert Arthur Smith banned John from his store after he picked up the pieces of the business, and directed his staff not to allow John behind the counter if he showed up.

On the Wednesday night of February 26, Mary (Mrs. R.H.) Smith; her daughter, Felicia; Robert's bride of six months, Ida; and some neighbours were going to a concert. Son John stayed at the family home, the Cedars, part of an estate stretching from Main Street to today's Lorne Avenue; the mansion had been built in 1857 by R.H. Smith. John said he didn't leave all evening, but many doubted it. Robert was tending his store, but promised his mother he would close early and come to the concert. They saved him a seat, but he didn't show up.

After the concert, Robert's young wife returned to her home above the store, but couldn't get in. She went to the Cedars, but her husband wasn't there either. The two women, Ida and her mother-in-law, Mary, went back to the store, where a neighbour, C.M. Hughes, helped them force a window.

They searched home and store, and were horrified to find Robert Smith's body, cold and lifeless, on the floor of the furnace room. The call went out for help. Soon Constables Savage and Bogart, the coroner Dr. Stuart Scott, Mayor Erastus Jackson, and a coterie of family friends were

Photo by author

*This Georgian style mansion, photographed in 2010, was erected around 1856 by Robert H. Smith, one of Main Street's early merchants. It sat amid his sixteen-acre estate that ran west from Main Street to the present Lorne Avenue, between Millard's Lane (now Millard Avenue) and Botsford Street. Smith called his home The Cedars. He and his wife, Mary Bogart, had six children. Over the years, most of the estate has been subdivided.*

on the scene. A seven-chamber revolver with one chamber discharged was found near the body. R.A. Smith had a bullet through the heart.

An inquest was convened the next week. On the jury: T.H. Brunton, foreman, H. Richardson, R.J. Davison, J. Stallard, A.E. Roe, Wm. Brown, James Allan, B.H. Millard, Morrice Foster, J.E. Souch, James Sutherland, and Joseph Belfry. The coroner summoned twenty-one witnesses who provided the packed hall of over four hundred spectators with details of Mrs. R.H. Smith's meanness and controlling ways in dealing with the family money and properties, including her opposition to Robert's choice of a bride even though he was thirty-nine years old. The long-standing tension between the two brothers and the intrigues over property were aired publicly.

Testimony from a number of witnesses verified that Robert seemed perfectly happy that night when the family left for the concert, and was well-contented with his new bride and thriving business. In the end the jury balked at pointing a finger. It found "said Robert Arthur Smith came to his death from a pistol shot wound, but whether the said shot was fired by his own hand or by the hand of some unknown person we are unable to say."[2]

The founder of the business, R.H. Smith, had been born in Penetanguishene in 1817, but the family moved to York when he was two. His father died shortly afterwards and his mother subsequently remarried James Marshall of Aurora. Smith worked in Mosley's general store in Aurora from 1833 to 1835, then took over his step-father's business in Aurora. During the 1837 Rebellion, Marshall, Smith, and Empy, who also worked for Marshall, were all named as rebels. Smith and Empy were imprisoned, and James Marshall fled to the United States. When Smith and Empy were released they found their store wrecked and looted. They decided to start over in Newmarket as Smith & Empy.

R.H. Smith was not a man of robust health. He suffered from "a nervous heart." Today it probably would be called angina. In 1858 he sold his business, but not the building, to Moses Bogart, his brother-in-law, and went into the bank brokerage business. In 1862, Bogart took on a partnership with a young Robert Simpson, and Simpson & Bogart operated in the Smith family store at Main and Timothy Streets. After three years in business they moved across the street to larger premises in the Caldwell Block. On October 29, 1870, the store burned, and although it reopened as The Robert Simpson Co., Simpson moved to Toronto in June 1871 and founded a department store chain.

R.H. Smith's heart gave out in 1883, and his widow lived on alone at the Cedars, which can still be found on Victoria Street in Newmarket's Heritage District. Strangely, another Smith (R.A.) of no family connection opened a store in the same building selling groceries and high-class china. He called his store "China Hall." William L. Bosworth, his adopted son, succeeded Mr. Smith and the entire stock was transferred across the street to the building on the northeast corner of Main and Timothy.

R.H. Smith's wayward eldest son, John, disappeared after his brother's murder, never to be seen again. No charges were laid. The jury found evidence was inconclusive as to whether it was murder, an accident, or a suicide. No record could be found of Robert's widow, Ida, following the murder.

## ❧ Department Store King Started on Main Street ❧

ROBERT SIMPSON STARTED his business life as a twenty-two-year-old shop

Author's collection

*This photo was taken very early in the twentieth century. The building labelled China Hall, located on the northwest corner of Main and Timothy Streets, was where Robert Simpson and his first partner, William Trent, went into business. Although the painted signs on the Timothy Street wall are gone, and the storefronts have changed over the years, the building still serves as commercial space on Main Street.*

boy in a Main Street general store in Newmarket, and finished it as founder and owner of one of Canada's greatest mercantile empires.[3] As a boy, Robert worked in his father's general store in Inverness, Scotland, and when he immigrated to Canada he chose Newmarket as his home because a cousin, Mrs. James Sutherland, already lived here. Robert went to work in the Sutherland family store, D. Sutherland & Sons.

After two years, Simpson and his friend William Trent founded Simpson & Trent Groceries, Boots, Shoes and Dry Goods. In 1858, they opened up for business on the northwest corner of Main and Timothy Streets. In 1862 Trent went his own way, and that was when Moses Bogart became Simpson's partner. A shrewd businessman, Simpson became noted among farmers for borrowing from them in the fall, giving notes for the loans against which the farmers bought merchandise from his store during the lean winter and spring months. To sweeten the pot, he paid 10 to 15 percent interest against the prevailing 6 percent bank rate. He still came out ahead because the farmers invariably overspent the notes and wound up indebted to the store.

The firm moved to larger premises across the street, but fire destroyed that store in October 1870. Less than two months later Simpson dissolved the partnership, rebuilt, and reopened as the Robert Simpson Company. The following June he moved again, this time to downtown Toronto. From that beginning, the Robert Simpson Company grew into a national department store chain and made Robert one of the wealthiest merchants in Canada.

In 1894, Simpson built a six-storey depart-ment store at Queen and Yonge Streets, but had to rebuild a year later after a disastrous fire in the area. The new store opened in 1896 with over five hundred employees and thirty-five departments. Robert did not live to savour his success. He died in 1897. His widow, the former Mary Anne Botsford of Newmarket, sold the business to a syndicate of Toronto businessmen the next year, 1898.

In 1978, the Hudson's Bay Company bought what was by then a chain of department stores in Toronto, Montreal, Halifax, Regina, and London, Ontario. By 1991 all the Simpson department stores had been merged into Bay stores and the Simpson name disappeared from Canada's business landscape. A separate mail-order firm had been formed in 1952, in partnership with the Chicago-based Sears, Roebuck and Company, called Simpson-Sears Limited. It eventually opened department stores across Canada as well, and today those stores operate under the name Sears.

There is an Ontario government plaque dedicated to Robert Simpson near his birthplace in Inverness, Scotland, a plaque on the Queen and Yonge Streets building that was formerly his flagship store, and several others on various Simpson buildings around the city. Newmarket has one monument embedded in the Main Street sidewalk in front of one of his former stores.

## ✑ "Old" Town Hall Is Really Our Third ✑

MANY PEOPLE THINK the "Old" Town Hall on Market Square is Newmarket's first town hall, but in fact, it is the third. This old lady of Market Square, restored one hundred years after it was first built as a town hall and farmers market building, now serves the community as a theatre and meeting hall.

The first town hall was a small frame building on Timothy Street with an entrance door in the centre of its west side. The date of its construction is not known, but since it became outdated and was replaced by a new

Author's collection

*The ornate bell tower that crowned the 1883 town hall and market had been removed mid-century and was replaced with an exact replica in 1983. Above, the new tower is put into place.*

town hall in 1861, it was probably the community's first public building. It also served as the courthouse. The building stood to the west of the hotel parking lot (then the Forsyth House, later the King George Hotel) on the south side of Timothy Street. Apparently the old building was still standing in November 1897, for records at the Registry Office indicate at that time James Pipher, then operator of the hotel property, leased it to the town for twenty-five years for the nominal sum of one cent per year.

Records indicate the building was torn down to make way for the brick home on the westerly portion of the hotel property that Mrs. Nellie Forsyth built for herself sometime after getting out of the hotel business. She sold the hotel property in 1904, but kept the westerly 117 feet for herself. It seems likely it was around that time that the first town hall and courthouse disappeared.

In 1852, the population of Newmarket was at only five hundred, but the community was growing, and by the end of that decade many people felt a new town hall was needed. In August 1858 the first public meeting was called to discuss building one with money from the Clergy Reserve Fund.[4] The first of many such meetings, it sparked a heated debate in the community.

Some wanted the Clergy Reserve money spent only for schools, others didn't want a town hall at all, others wanted to debenture its cost, and others opposed debenturing. A group of businessmen from the south end of Main Street, led by William McMaster, a successful Main Street merchant with a store at the south end of the street, fought council's plan to build the town hall on Grammar School Lane (now Millard Avenue) just west of Main Street. They felt the location was too far north and wanted it built on the present site of St. Andrew's Church at Main and Water Streets.

When council passed bylaws allowing it to buy the north site and build the hall, McMaster sued on the grounds that the expense was excessive when the money was not in hand, and succeeded in delaying the project. But he couldn't stop it and the second town hall was built. A forty-foot by eighty-foot brick building, it contained a basement, an engine room, a lock up, a council chamber, and two additional rooms. Besides functioning as a council chamber, it housed the Mechanic's Institute with its library, lectures, and exhibitions. It remained in use until the building on Market Square was completed in 1883. The

Grammar School Lane building still stands but was long ago converted to very small living quarters.

Newmarket had always been the natural economic centre for the area. Farmers' markets such as the Butcher's Fair grew up during the community's early years. The Butcher's Fair operated until 1867, and its success made it obvious there was a need for a full farmers' market. In May 1867 a meeting was called and a committee appointed. Two years later, in April 1869, the committee bought a parcel of vacant land between Timothy and Botsford Streets (the present Market Square) and erected a shed on the west side of it.

The first market was held June 1, 1871, in a small shed with a sawdust floor, which stood on the west side of the square. It grew in popularity among residents who shopped for fresh produce, shopkeepers who came to buy in bulk, and farmers who brought in their produce to sell and then spent their money on the Main Street. The market was so successful that within a few years Newmarket's business community was again concerned about maintaining the edge it had established, and many foresaw the need for a substantial new market building with improved facilities.

It took one of the community's founders, former fur-trader William Roe, to get the wheels turning for construction of a proper market building and a new town hall. In 1876 he brought a petition bearing seventy-three names to village council asking that money be granted for construction of a town hall and market building. The idea touched off a community-wide debate that raged until March 1882, when council decided to hold a plebiscite asking ratepayers to approve borrowing $6,000 for the new town hall and market building. The debate did not centre on whether to build it or not, but on whether to include a second-floor auditorium with stage and a bell tower on the roof. Mayor William Cane, one of the town's leading industrialists, favoured the larger building, arguing, "We must grow and invest to prosper."[5]

On May 22 the referendum was held on whether to spend $6,000 on a new two-storey town hall and market building. It squeaked through by a sixty-five-vote margin. On Dominion Day in 1883 the third town hall, with space incorporated for a new market, was officially opened on Market Square.

During more than a century of service, the old lady of Market Square has been witness to many of Newmarket's most memorable events. It has also been a courthouse, a police station, theatre, reception hall, and many other things. Its rafters have echoed to the speeches of leaders such as Sir Wilfrid Laurier, Sir William Mulock, and William Lyon Mackenzie King. And it was there that plans were laid for the Newmarket barge canal and the radial railway. Nominations, elections, trials, council meetings, plays, operas, balls, and minstrel shows have all marched through its auditorium. In its halls soldiers have been recruited for far-off wars and feted on their victorious return. But most important of all to the citizens of the little town who voted $6,000 to build it, the building made Newmarket the major market centre in the north half of the county.

Reports carried in *The Newmarket Era* of the official opening indicate the first storey, designed exclusively for a market, had butcher's stalls, and a spacious market floor. The basement was for storage. Newmarket's market continued to flourish and bring business to the town. It spilled out onto the square in good weather and in its heyday attracted special trains of shoppers from Richmond Hill and Toronto.

But by the 1940s many factors combined to the decline of farmers' markets. Better roads and better cars and trucks made it easier for consumers to shop and farmers to ship, the advent of the grocery-market chains drew business away and the restrictions of an economy at war finally brought an end to the old market.

## ❧ Boer War Victory Celebration Ended With a Bang ❧

NEWMARKET GREETED THE end of the Boer War with a bang — a much bigger bang than anyone had anticipated.

The Newmarket-Aurora district led the nation in enthusiastic support for queen, Empire, and the British government in the disagreement with the Boer republics. In fact, when war finally broke out in 1899, Colonel Thomas H. Lloyd of Newmarket, commanding officer of the 12th York Rangers (the local militia unit), wrote Ottawa offering the whole unit for service overseas. When Ottawa replied suggesting the colonel was a mite over-enthusiastic and just maybe the whole unit hadn't volunteered, Colonel Lloyd fired back a letter listing the names of all twenty-eight officers and 336 NCOs and men who were ready to sail. All this was

Author's collection

*This late nineteenth-century dam on Fairy Lake also served as a platform for the town band performances on special occasions.*

before Prime Minister Wilfrid Laurier had even decided whether Canada should be part of Britain's little war.

Eventually Canada did join the war and feelings were running so high that every time a victory was announced, the bunting and band came out in Newmarket and the whole town celebrated. So, when Pretoria — the capital of the Transvaal state — fell, a really big celebration was felt to be in order. A holiday was declared, the Citizens Band mustered, and a party was planned at Fairy Lake. Mayor H.S. Cane was in Toronto when word of the victory arrived and council phoned him to buy fireworks. He purchased plenty and brought them home on the Radial Railway. In those days the Fairy Lake dam had a platform extending over the water with a railing. The rockets were to be set off from there.

The entire town and countryside assembled, the band played martial music, and the oratory was flowing when the first rocket was set off. Unfortunately, it took off backwards, landed in the box of remaining rockets, and exploded, setting off the whole box in a symphony of smoke, flame, and exploding fireworks. What followed must have looked like a

Laurel and Hardy movie. Everybody ran. Members of the band jumped into the water and came up floundering with their instruments. One rocket shot clear through the big base drum, ripping the heel off drummer W.H. Helmer's shoe. Aside from dampened spirits, doused bandsmen, and fire damage to the dam, there were no casualties.

The same can't be said for Newmarket's military contingent overseas. Although Colonel Lloyd's offer wasn't accepted, a number of local men did see action in the war. One didn't return. Walsley Haines, a private in the Royal Regiment of Canada, died of enteric fever and was buried in South Africa. In September 1900 a public meeting decided to raise money for a memorial to the young soldier, and a bust by sculptor Walter Allward of Toronto was commissioned.

It is a fine early example of the work of a man who went on to become one of Canada's most distinguished sculptors and who, after the First World War, was commissioned to do the massive monument at Vimy Ridge. The Haines monument was erected on the waterworks lawn at the foot of Main Street, which at one time had been the property of the Haines family. Town council moved it from its historic location in the 1970s, placing it with the First World War peace monument in the little park on the southeast corner of Church and D'Arcy Streets, where it can be found today.

## ❦ Minnie Murdered Susie ❦

POOR SUSIE SAXTON. Shot in the back, then three times in the front, on a Monday morning while she was doing the wash.

Susan, thirty-seven years of age and about to be married to wealthy North Gwillimbury farmer Dan McMillan, lived with her sister Minnie Saxton, thirty-four. They were the daughters of prosperous Main Street jeweller Fred Saxton. The murder took place about 7:00 a.m. Monday, August 22, 1896, in the kitchen of the large, rough-cast home, on Water Street near Main, that the two women shared after the death of their widowed father two years earlier. The weapon was an old British Bulldog .38-calibre revolver that Fred had kept around the house because he often brought valuables home from the store. The murderer was Minnie Saxton.

184

Next door neighbour W.C. Widdifield, the women's lawyer and friend, was awakened that Monday morning by his servant who reported that a hysterical Minnie Saxton had arrived at the door demanding to see the lawyer. "Susie is dead," she told the servant. "I have shot Susie and she's dead." Hurriedly getting dressed, Widdifield went downstairs and was immediately confronted with the same confession. "I have shot her — she's dead."[6] Hurrying next door, he found Susie, stretched on the floor, with four bullet wounds. He immediately called the police chief P.J. Anderson who in turn called the coroner Dr. Stuart Scott, and the undertaker John Millard.

Minnie, it seemed, had always been considered "weak-minded" by the neighbours. She was prone to bouts of hysteria and often did odd things. Susan had given up an independent life to live with Minnie, and Minnie had become very possessive of her older sister, particularly since their father died. Susan occasionally had gentlemen callers, and on such occasions Minnie's hysteria would manifest itself. "She was never violent, however, except when the devotion of her sister to her seemed to be shared by someone else," Susan's inquest was told.[7] Minnie would brood for days. At one point in 1893, Minnie had been committed to the Toronto Asylum at her own request. She stayed there for a year, and when her father brought her home, she was pronounced "cured" by her doctors.

That summer of 1896 Susie had been seeing a Mr. McMillan without telling Minnie. The August Saturday before the murder, she broke the news to her sister that she was to be married early in September. Susan had taken the precaution of hiding the old pistol, but Minnie found it. She had brooded all weekend, Minnie later told lawyer Widdifield, and was irresistibly carried on to do the murder. She said she fought against it, but the hysteria of her mind overcame her.

Community business moved quickly in nineteenth-century Newmarket. After the coroner had examined the body, undertaker Millard laid it out in the parlour in preparation for the funeral to be held Tuesday afternoon. Dr. Stuart Scott called the inquest for Tuesday morning at the town hall. The thirteen-man jury visited the Saxton house to view the body, then returned to the town hall to be sworn in. Some of today's legal niceties were absent. Coroner Scott conducted proceedings, but also testified, as Dr. Scott, the Saxton family's physician. Mr. Widdifield testified as a key witness to the previous mornings' proceedings, but also represented Minnie as her lawyer.

Other witnesses included Constable John Savage who gave details of the position of the body and the state of the house; Rebecca Greensides, Widdifield's servant; Dr. Campbell who conducted the postmortem; and George Partridge, the milkman who had heard what sounded like a quarrel early in the morning, then at about 7:00 a.m. had heard the four shots followed by laughter, so he concluded all was well.

The jury retired for ten minutes, returning with this verdict: "We find that the said Susan Saxton came to her death upon the 22nd August instant through wounds received by her from a revolver in the hands of Minnie Saxton."[8] A Magistrate's Court was convened immediately with justices of the peace H.S. Cane and J.J. Pearson on the bench. The prisoner pleaded not guilty to a charge of murder, the dispositions from the inquest were taken as evidence, and Minnie was committed for trial and whisked off by train to jail in Toronto.

The trial was held early in November, and, after hearing the evidence, the trial judge, Chief Justice William G. Falconbridge, decided no defence evidence was necessary. He instructed the jury to find Minnie not guilty of murder by reason of insanity, and the jury so found without leaving their seats. Minnie was committed to the Asylum for the Insane. She is buried in Newmarket Cemetery.

*Chapter Ten*

# A NEW CENTURY

## ❧ The 1899 Electric Train: To Toronto in an Hour ❧

IT'S BEEN WELL over a century since the tracks of one of the finest rail commuter services of its time reached Newmarket. At the turn of the twentieth century, when Newmarket's population hovered around the 2,000 mark, it was linked to downtown Toronto by an electrical railway system that whisked passengers into the city faster than we can drive there today. The Toronto and York Radial Railway reached Newmarket in August 1899, and, according to its schedule, made five trips a day between its northern terminus in front of the King George Hotel and downtown Toronto. It carried freight and passengers, and eventually its tracks reached as far north as the then-booming Lake Simcoe resort areas of Sutton and Jackson's Point.

The old radial, which would be so welcome an addition to today's commuting picture, finally faded from the scene in 1948. The last remaining portion, the TTC streetcar line to Richmond Hill, was discontinued that year. It ceased to run north of Richmond Hill in 1930. Traces of the system are still visible on our landscape. Parts of its roadbed can be seen running through farm fields in the area, and there is a huge concrete arch near the Queen Street Bridge that once supported a trestle taking the tracks down to the river flats. Long-time Newmarket residents will

*The Toronto & York Radial Railway Company's tracks up Yonge Street reached Newmarket in 1899. New owners who took over in 1904 built a high-speed track to Jackson's Point (1907) and Sutton (1909). Above is the first car leaving Newmarket on those tracks in 1907.*

remember the radial station that stood on Botsford Street across from the Old Town Hall. A length of radial track was found during reconstruction in the Market Square area between Botsford Street and Park Avenue, and was left exposed when the area was paved.

The radial tracks came north on Yonge Street to Armitage (corner of Yonge and Mulock Drive), then cut northeast into town. They emerged from the fields at William Street, followed it over to Eagle, then around to Main Street, and north on Main. The King George Hotel served as the Newmarket terminal in those first years.

Horse-drawn vehicles and clanking radial cars proved to be an unfortunate combination on the narrow Main Street. The cars scared the horses, so shoppers stayed away, merchants said. As a result the tracks were moved west of Main Street, passing through Market Square west of the town hall to a station on Botsford Street, then over to Raglan Street, north to Queen Street, and east to the bridge and down the trestle. But the late nineteenth-century dream of a system of electric railways radiating out from Toronto was dead. In fact, despite the fact that in their heyday the electric railway companies operated over 130 miles of track, they never did become a rationally organized system of transportation. Some of the lines were little more than suburban extensions of city streetcar lines; others were proper inter-urban lines joining Toronto to its hinterland. The major problem of the radials was that there was no central, downtown terminus from which all the lines radiated. There was an attempt later to remedy this problem by constructing a belt line around the perimeter of the city, which would have joined the various radials. This proved unsuccessful and after a couple of years of operation in the mid-1890s the project was abandoned.

The largest of the Toronto radials was the Toronto and York Radial Railway, which grew from the Metropolitan Street Railway Company (1877). This line was slowly extended up Yonge Street, was electrified in 1890, reached Richmond Hill in 1896, and, by 1899 had a service all the way to Newmarket. In 1904 the road became part of the Toronto and York Radial Railway Company (chartered in 1898), owned by the Sir William Mackenzie interests, which also owned the system within the city. Under this new direction, a high-speed right-of-way was extended to Jackson's Point (1907) and Sutton (1909). A fourteen-mile railway spur line, which ran from Bond Lake south of Aurora to Schomberg, was acquired in 1904, and the steam trains were replaced by electric cars in 1916. The Toronto terminus of the Toronto and York Radial originally was on Yonge Street at the Canadian Pacific crossing north of Bloor Street. In 1915, the city forced the line to end at Farnham Avenue.

Growth of the lines was most impressive. From 350,000 riders in 1900, it grew to 2,240,000 in 1905, and hit a peak of 11,689,000 in 1921. During the previous year, the City of Toronto had acquired the York line from Mackenzie. The Toronto and York Radial had two other lines. One ran from Sunnyside west, and, after being acquired by the Toronto and York Radial in 1904, it was extended all the way to Port Credit. In the east end a line ran from Kingston Road and Queen Street eastward to Halfway House, a hotel and tavern on Kingston Road in east Scarborough (it is now part of Black Creek Pioneer Village). In 1904 this line became part of the Toronto and York Radial, and the next year track was laid to West Hill.

Following acquisition by the City of Toronto, some of the sections of these lines became regular streetcar lines and the others were turned over to Ontario Hydro, which, under Sir Adam Beck, was planning a high-speed system of electric, inter-urban railway lines. Although this scheme never materialized, Hydro did operate some of the lines until 1927.

The lines were re-acquired by Toronto in that year. The Scarborough and Mimico lines were incorporated into the Toronto Transit Commission (TTC) service, the Schomberg branch was closed, and the service to Sutton operated as a separate entity with the TTC as agent. After 1930 the line was operated only to Richmond Hill, and, in 1948, service north of the city limits was abandoned. The Yonge Street line ended on the south side of Hogg's Hollow.

The Toronto Suburban Street Railway was incorporated in 1894 and built from Keele and Dundas Streets to Lambton Mills and Weston. A streetcar line also ran from Bathurst and Davenport to Keele. In 1911, Mackenzie bought the Toronto Suburban Street Railway and the line was extended to Guelph via Georgetown. The work was slowed down by the war and cars did not commence service until 1917. The line had already been extended to Woodbridge. The company's parent, the Canadian Northern, was acquired by the new Canadian National Railway (CN). Portions of the line were incorporated into the TTC in 1923: the old Lambton line was acquired by the Township of York and abandoned in 1928 and the Weston section was sold to Weston and York Township in 1925 and operated by the TTC until it was abandoned in 1948. CN continued to run trains to Guelph until 1931 when service, always unprofitable, was discontinued.

The lack of co-ordination, the competition from inter-urban bus service from the mid-1920s on, the growth of the private use of the automobile, and the Depression were the chief contributors to the failure of these electric railways. It is ironic that today government agencies and individuals who are looking for cheap systems of rapid transit regret the short-sightedness of those who allowed the radial railways to decline and fail.

## ❧ Amusement Park at Bond Lake ❧

BOND LAKE, THE little kettle lake set in rolling hills on the Oak Ridges Moraine, a few miles south of Newmarket, was once York County's biggest playground. One factor encouraging this development during the last years of the nineteenth century was the efficient electric railway service down Yonge Street linking Newmarket to Toronto.

The Metropolitan Street Railway Company, operators of the line, acquired Bond Lake and the land around it. Around 1891 they built a steam-powered electricity generating plant there to supply power to their railway line and created a two-hundred-acre amusement park on the shores of the lake, hoping to develop a destination that would keep their cars full on weekends, holidays, and during the summer slow periods. It became a famous destination for Sunday school picnics and other outings during the first two decades of the twentieth century.

The park had a fleet of company-operated boats so patrons could row around the thirty-three-acre lake. A merry-go-round, refreshment stands, and a bandstand offered entertainment. It operated for over twenty years and in its heyday drew large crowds to what was then a very rural destination for many Torontonians. It was used by Newmarket and Aurora folks as well. One account in *The Newmarket Era* tells of the railway company providing three special cars on a summer Sunday afternoon in 1900 for a moonlight excursion from Newmarket to Bond Lake. When the travellers arrived at the park they mingled with 2,000 others on the grounds, and the British-Canadian Band provided musical entertainment.

Local legend, still in circulation when I was a boy in the 1940s, was that Bond Lake was bottomless because it was fed by an underground river that flowed to Lake Ontario. It didn't deter young swimmers coming to the park from plunging in, however. Actually, a York Region engineer told me years later the lake isn't even in a water table linked to Lake Ontario, but fluctuates in direct relation to Lake Huron. Said to be 110 feet deep, the lake is one of a string of kettle lakes across the Oak Ridges Moraine that were scooped out by a retreating glacier during the last Ice Age.

## ❧ Area Families Colonized the West ❧

MANY NEWMARKET-DISTRICT families were looking for greener pastures by the 1880s, and Canada's great northwest offered them. Families emigrated singly and in groups. One large group departed from the Newmarket railway station in May 1883, complete with a nine-man brass band, and were seen off by a crowd of over two hundred well-wishers. They travelled in a special Grand Trunk car that took them directly to their destination in the new colony without the necessity of making changes along the way. The railway car was stocked with "a bounteous supply of edibles."[1]

A week earlier, William Mackie, Thomas Blizzard, and Charles Traviss, all of Queensville, had left for Regina with the stock cars carrying their cattle and horses. A week after the main party's arrival, the Regina *Leader* carried this report:

> The Sharon Colony comes from near Newmarket, headed by a brass band numbering nine. They brought up everything, wagons, ploughs, etc. and are ready to commence farming right away. They have rented their farms in York County and intend to bring up their wives and family next season. They expect them to take an excursion west this fall. They are all of English descent. They have wandered about Regina and can hardly express how much they are taken up with the country. They are all highly delighted. Mr. Doan took up some land and broke it in his hand and examined it where it had been broken up in the fall and you could take the harrow, and, instead of backsetting you could make it fit for seeding by the harrow. Further, that he went down deep below that and found it of the first quality. They bring with them one yoke of cattle, black and white, owned by Jesse Doan. They were in such a condition notwithstanding their long journey, that a butcher said, "They are beef," offering 10 cents a pound live weight. They are acknowledged to be the finest cattle which have overcome to the North-West and Mr. Doan

has been offered $425 for them. Two fine yoke owned by G.M. Doan, a brother, came through in very find condition. Another yoke, owned by Thos. Blizzard, came through in fine shape. Ten yoke were brought in altogether, and Mr. Traviss had with him two pair of very nice, well-bred horses for which he was offered $575. Some of the party were considerably surprised at the bill of fare they got at the Commercial, and they sent it down to their friends to show them the style of hotels in Regina. Amongst other things the Doans were told that there were no ladies in Regina. But the Sharon Colony saw on Sunday the ladies promenading Broad street, and thought them very nice. On the morning of their arrival they serenaded their old neighbour, Mr. Brest, the proprietor of the Commercial, who stood like a General of a Division in front of his men.[2]

There were many family names still familiar in this district today among the men on the train: George M. Doan, John Doan, G.R. Doan, Jesse Doan, Marshall Kitely, Henry Kitely, Robt. Briggs, G.P. Smith Jr., and A.P. Smith of Sharon; C.F. Lundy, Robert Lundy, and William Roadhouse, of Newmarket; Thomas Traviss, Stephen Traviss, William Mackie Jr., R. McFarland, and Silas C. Soules of Queensville; and James Taylor and John Chapman of Holland Landing — all heading for Regina. John Soules of Queensville went to Brandon; Dr. Thomas Bentley, Edwin Hill, James Druery, Thomas Druery, and Mort Terry, all of Newmarket, settled in Winnipeg.

## ❧ Sir William Mulock: Father of Penny Post ❧

MULOCK IS A name that has been associated with Newmarket over much of the town's two-hundred-year-plus history, but many of our newer residents have no idea of the nature of that association.[3] Small wonder, for the once-prominent political family disappeared from the public eye many years ago. However, the Mulocks made a brief reappearance in 1999 when the family donated eighteen acres of parkland to the town from the remnants of its Yonge Street estate. The park is named for William Thomas

Mulock, a great-grandson of Sir William Mulock and an artist, who died in 1998. He was the son of Mr. and Mrs. Thomas Mulock.

Sir William, founder of the family fortune, grew up in Newmarket in the mid-nineteenth century. His mother's family, the Cawthras, were among the town's early settlers. Young William's father, Dr. Thomas H. Mulock, was a doctor in Bond Head, about four miles west of Bradford, who died when the boy was very young. Mrs. Mulock (Mary Cawthra) moved back to a house on Pearson Street in Newmarket where she would have the support of her family. William, born in 1844, attended Newmarket Grammar School on Millard Avenue, and graduated in law from University of Toronto. He returned home to complete his training, articling with Newmarket lawyer Alfred Boultbee.

Practising in Toronto, the young lawyer quickly won prominence, became a leader of the Ontario bar, and, in those pre-income tax days, became very wealthy. A switch to politics in 1882 brought him home again, and he was elected to the House of Commons in the Newmarket-

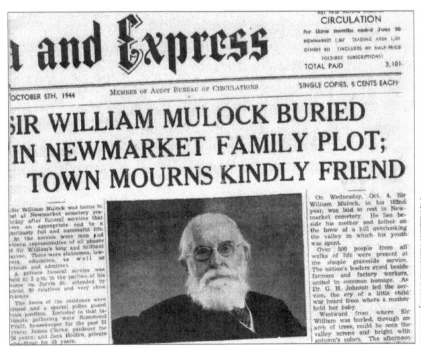

*Newmarket native Sir William Mulock was knighted for spearheading the creation of the penny post in 1898.*

area riding of North York, a seat he held for twenty-three years, from 1882 to 1905. He entered Sir Wilfrid Laurier's cabinet as postmaster general in 1896, and, two years later, was responsible for the introduction of the "imperial penny postage" within the British Empire, an accomplishment that earned him a knighthood. As the first federal minister of labour he brought a brilliant young man named King into government as his deputy minister. That young man later became Canada's longest-serving prime minister, William Lyon Mackenzie King.

Although Sir William maintained his main residence in Toronto, he built a country estate on Yonge Street at Armitage, today the corner of Mulock Drive and Yonge Street, where he spent the summers. In 1905 he left politics upon his appointment as chief justice of the Exchequer Division of the Supreme Court of Canada. In 1923 he became Chief Justice of Ontario. He retired from the bench in 1936. In his final years, Sir William Mulock was known as Canada's "grand old man." He died in 1944 at the age of one hundred.

The Ontario government historical plaque to Sir William is at Bond Head, the village where he was born. Descendants have sold off all but ten acres and the mansion of his summer estate in Newmarket. A member of the family still lives there.


## ❧ Canal Almost Finished Then Abandoned ❧

NEWMARKET AND AURORA came close to being part of the Trent-Severn Waterway in the opening years of the twentieth century. Imagine what that would mean today! Instead of ball diamonds and tennis courts in Newmarket's north end, the town council might be administering a marina. The chamber of commerce wouldn't be worrying about how to bring tourists into the area — we'd be on the canal. Newmarket and Aurora would be the marine gateway to Lake Simcoe and the delights of Ontario's vast waterways.

Construction of canals along the waterways from the Bay of Quinte to Lake Simcoe was originally to provide communications for the new settlements founded around Peterborough by one-time Newmarket resident Peter Robinson. After 1880 pressure increased on the federal government to complete the waterway all the way to Georgian Bay, and the final stage of construction began in 1895. Ontario was caught up in canal fever.

The idea to connect Newmarket and Aurora to this water network came from Sir William Mulock, then the area's member of Parliament. At a meeting in Newmarket town hall in September 1904, Mulock called to discuss the effect of freight rate increases, ranging from 33 to 50 percent, being levied by the Grand Trunk Railway, and he predicted that the deepening of the Holland River would make the two towns thriving centres. Farmers were attracted to the idea of cheap water transport to places like Peterborough, where the Quaker Oats Company used 20,000 bushels of oats a day. William Cane & Sons, the Newmarket wood-products firm that brought logs in from forests that were being pushed farther and farther north, also liked the idea.

Planners predicted the canal would be extended to Aurora, to Schomberg by the west branch of the Holland, and to Sutton by the Black River. Plans for a small canal from Newmarket to Lake Simcoe were prepared. The plans entailed dredging the Holland River, building four locks at three locations, a swing bridge, three dams, retaining walls, and a dock. Total cost was $360,220.

Later plans to extend the canal to Aurora brought the cost to $822,498. The plans did not include the cost of acquiring land nor were calculations on water supply very accurate. They were designed more to keep Minister Mulock and his North York riding constituents happy. Mulock, in turn, had proposed the canal to increase his chances in the 1904 election. However, government engineers were railway men and opposed new canal construction. They increased the canal's specifications with the intent of making it so expensive it would be dropped. But no one wanted to take on Mulock. First tenders on the canal were called in October 1906, and work started in May 1908.

Debate continued to rage over the project, but by January 1912 three locks had been almost completed, 80 percent of the excavation to Holland Landing finished, three swing bridges installed, and a turning basin built just north of Davis Drive (then Huron Street), but almost nothing had been done from Holland Landing to Lake Simcoe. The turning basin has since been filled in and is a parking lot today, but bollards, the large iron fixtures used for tying up barges, and other remnants of the canal can still be found along the river there. A park trail now runs along the east side of the canal/river from Davis Drive north to the Newmarket boundary.

*A dredge works on the canal north of Newmarket. The basins and turning circles created for barges have all been filled in, and today only an outline of the canal is visible cutting through the countryside, although remnants of three liftlocks and some bridges remain.*

*The first phase of the canal was to terminate at the turning basin next to the Davis Leather tannery. Although this part of canal and basin were completed, no barges ever used it.*

There has always been a question of whether the canal would have had enough water to serve its purpose. Its designers proposed a chain of reservoirs on the high land south of Newmarket, and dams on Musselman, Bond, and Wilcox Lakes to supplement the natural flow in the river. None of these ideas ever reached development stage and had the Liberals been able to complete the project, they may well have found that the canal did not live up to expectations.

Mulock won re-election but retired from politics in 1905. Allen B. Aylesworth succeeded him in the riding and inherited the controversial canal project. It eventually became nicknamed Aylesworth's Ditch. Aylesworth did not run in the 1911 election, and Lloydtown farmer R.C. Robinette won, campaigning for the Conservatives and against the canal. The new Conservative government under Prime Minister Robert Borden immediately was told by chief engineer W.A. Bowden that the locks (excluding the gates) had been finished, as had 80 percent of the excavation, three swing bridges, and the turning basin in Newmarket, with most of its stone protection lining. Total cost to that point was $818,642. Bowden estimated the government could save $393,000 by abandoning the works. Two days after receiving the report, the minister of Railways and Canals, Frank Cochrane, cancelled the contract. By August 1912 all work had stopped. It never resumed.

Parts of the canal north of Newmarket are still identifiable by their straight banks, and the three locks are still there. The mechanism of one swing bridge remains intact at Green Lane, although it's now bypassed by the road.

The canal fiasco created a difficult time for the citizens of Newmarket and surrounding area, comments James T. Angus, author of *A Work Unfinished*. The business community, once solidly behind the project, divided, principally along political lines. The town became the laughing stock of the province, if not of the country. Everyone was embarrassed, not the least the government engineers responsible for the greatest engineering failure on the waterway since the 1830s.

## First Toronto Santa Claus Parade Started in Newmarket

TORONTO'S FAMOUS SANTA Claus Parade, which has been going for over one hundred years and for many years was sponsored by the T. Eaton

Company, had its beginnings in Newmarket. The first Santa Claus Parade took place on Saturday, December 2, 1905, as a publicity stunt to herald Santa's arrival at the Eaton's Store in downtown Toronto. Mr. and Mrs. Timothy Eaton met Santa at the Union Station and walked him to the Eaton's store as a few hundred people watched from the street.

The Cane Company, a Newmarket woodenware manufacturing company that operated from 1874 to the 1930s, built a log-house float for the T. Eaton Company for that first parade. The small parade formed here in town and headed for Toronto by train, with Santa seated on the chimney of the house.

In subsequent years, Santa's arrival in Toronto became more extravagant, with a horse-drawn carriage, footmen, and trumpeters heralding his journey from the North in 1906. By 1910 his arrival was switched to Toronto's North Station and his coach was pulled by eight reindeer imported from Labrador. In the very early years Santa's Court was held in Massey Hall, where over 9,000 children saw him during three daily receptions. The use of Massey Hall ended in 1915 when Santa rode through the city streets and then went to the Eaton's store.

Up until 1912 the parade originated in Newmarket and Santa took his time heading south, visiting children and handing out goodies at stops along the way, and staying overnight in York Mills. Today, the parade is billed on its official website[4] as the longest-running children's parade in the world. Eaton's dropped out as a sponsor in 1982, and the parade has been run by a not-for-profit organization since.

When Santa left Newmarket in 1905, he was a one-man parade. Today, more than twenty-five floats, one hundred celebrity clowns, 1,500 costumed participants, and many bands accompany him on his route through downtown Toronto.

## Salvation Army Soldiers Took Newmarket by Storm

THE SALVATION ARMY took Newmarket and district by storm when it arrived in January 1883.

The Newmarket Corps is one of the oldest in Canada. It was established only six months after the Salvationists officially arrived in

Artist, Thomas Mower-Martin R.A.C., with permission of the Salvation Army Archives, Canada and Bermuda Territory

*The Salvation Army meetings were often a focal point of interest on street corners in many Ontario towns at the beginning of the twentieth century. Above, a painting of an open air meeting on a Toronto street corner in 1895, illustrates the intensity of the gatherings.*

Canada and launched their crusade with meetings in Toronto, London, Hamilton, and Chatham. These unusual evangelists descended on mid-Victorian Newmarket with drum and cymbal, parades and singing, hellfire and brimstone, and turned life in the quiet backwater on its ear. People watched the parades, all-night meetings, and other boisterous activities with fascination.

At first, many joined in the activities. Wagonloads of country people came into town for the meetings, and that must have been good for business. But within six months the novelty wore off, the disruptions to the life of the little community became annoying, and finally people began calling for controls. There were angry letters to the editor, hostile editorials, merchants complaining about business being scared away, street fights breaking out, and rotten eggs being hurled at Salvationists. On some occasions Army supporters wound up in jail.

Captain Tom Mitchell, probably one of the first English officers ordered to the Canada by founder William Booth, came to Newmarket "to open fire on this town against sin and the devil on Sunday next in the

Mechanic's Hall" as the local newspaper reported.[5] "Salvation for nothing and heaven for everybody' is their motto," wrote *The Era*'s editor.[6]

An Army record of Mitchell's arrival says, "On Dec. 30, 1883, the citizens of Newmarket were amazed to see a young man wearing a hat similar to those worn by railway employees, but wearing a red band, with words in yellow, saying THE SALVATION ARMY."[7] Things got off to a lively start on that first weekend of January 1884 when a detachment of eighteen arrived at the railway station to help Mitchell "open fire." They marched to the Mechanics' Hall on Lot Street (Millard Avenue) lead by drum and cymbal and singing all the way.

*The Newmarket Era* reported, "On Sunday morning, they proceeded from the 'barracks' by way of Main St., and the unusual beating of drum and cymbals with shouting of song in the streets created no little excitement. The barracks was crowded three times on Sunday and good feeling was manifested in their meetings. They drew a crowd every night and their peculiar songs are no small attraction."[8] Crowds continued to attend the services throughout the month.

"The whole surrounding country appears to be interested and people come in by the sleigh load," said an early February report.[9] On February 8, Richard Wells of the Queen's Hotel in Aurora offered the Army a free hall if it would come, and by the end of February meetings were going on there too. By late March some less-than-glowing reports were beginning to appear in the local press: "The juveniles who attend the Salvation Army took a tramp around town last Saturday afternoon to the beat of the drum and the cymbals," sniped *The Era*, on March 8th. Some of the Army's new recruits seem to have become pretty colourful Salvationists. "Little Johnny and Happy Tom" kept Mount Albert under constant bombardment. In April they were reported to have captured a number of "prisoners." By April 11, *The Newmarket Era* was saying, "It is their intention to keep steady on sin and the devil until the whole village is captured," perhaps a little tongue-in-cheek. In May fights broke out when the Army held Saturday night meetings in front of Newmarket's north-end liquor store.

"There is some talk of warrants being issued" (against the ruffians who roughed up the Salvationists), reported the *Newmarket Era*, "but as a rule people are getting tired of stepping into the ditch or being jostled off the sidewalk while monopolized by the Army."[10]

The novelty of this new phenomenon was definitely wearing thin, but the box score was impressive. In its first six months, the Army signed up eighty-two members in Newmarket and eighty in the outposts of Aurora and Bradford.

The meeting held Sunday, June 8, to mark a change of command — Mitchell and his wife and the post's other officers were off to new assignments — gives a pretty good idea just where it was wearing thin. Sunday evening after the officers gave their farewell addresses to a crowded barracks, a prayer meeting went on until 5:00 a.m. "when the big drum was pounded through the streets, announcing the opening of their big day."[11] Twice during the day processions marched to the railway station:

> ... flags and banners flying, to the number of probably 300, with three big drums, triangles, tambourines and other musical instruments too numerous to mention, and marched to the other end of Main St. amid the din, disorder and confusion of so many people singing and shouting, apparently without any regard for time and harmony.
>
> They then returned to the barracks in a body after which, during the remainder of the afternoon, squads of different numbers kept up a continual noise between the barracks and the town hall.[12]

Major Albert Coombs, commander of the Salvation Army in British North America, spoke to a banquet in the town hall that Monday, June 8th. The banquet meeting "resolved into a prayer meeting about 12:00 o'clock [midnight], and the beating of the big drum on the street about 4:00 o'clock next morning announced its dismissal to our slumbering and very frequently disturbed citizens residing in the vicinity of Main St."[13] That weekend's activities finally spurred *The Newmarket Era*'s editorialist into action.

On June 13th, under the heading, "Intolerable Nuisances" the paper flayed away at "the abominable nuisance of singing and howling, indulged in almost nightly, after orderly people have retired." It termed the drum and cymbal playing and the singing on the streets on Sundays during church services, the greatest nuisance of all. Apparently the noise outside the Methodist church that Sunday had become so loud that the minister,

Reverend J.H. Starr, could not be heard. He had to stop preaching and call upon the choir to sing. "The time has come that this nuisance must be stopped," thundered *The Newmarket Era*.

Things quieted down a bit after that. Sunday evening parades were stopped. "It was the first calm and quiet Sunday evening we have had since the opening of the present year and was highly appreciated," commented *The Newmarket Era*'s next edition on June 20, 1884.

As Newmarket's Salvationists settled into their work of reclaiming fallen humanity, the noisier action must have shifted to outlying districts. From August 22, 1884, comes this report: "The Salvation Army [of Mount Albert] made a raid on Blake's Station and Knight's Sawmill last Tuesday evening, bombarding the whole settlement nearly all night. Nobody was hurt but a good quantity of mosquitoes and black flies suffered."[14]

Over the years, the Salvation Army has occupied a number of buildings in Newmarket. For the first five or six years their barracks was at the Mechanic's Hall on Millard Avenue, then it moved to a building on the east side of Main Street, opposite Botsford Street. From there, the Army took over the Old Kirk, a former Presbyterian church on Timothy Street near the trading tree, then moved to a hall on the post office site, and, in 1896, purchased the brick building (a former church) on Queen Street.

A new citadel was built in 1991 off Mulock Drive near Bogarttown, but it has already been outgrown. The congregation decided in 2006 it must relocate, and a five-acre site near Leslie and Wellington Streets in Aurora was purchased. Construction of the new citadel was scheduled for 2011. Now called Northridge Community Church of the Salvation Army, it strives to meet needs throughout central York Region. Among Northridge Church's many activities: help for people through food banks, clothing and furniture assistance, counselling, help to seniors, help for people seeking shelter, a summer youth camp, and emergency disaster relief.

## Gas and Oil Beneath Newmarket

NEWMARKET SITS ATOP a natural gas and oil deposit, according to dusty old records that have been unread and neglected for many years. The tales of gas and oil lying beneath the fields south of Gorham Street are well documented, although there remains some question about how much of the "black gold" is there.

Gas bubbled up through a natural spring on the Gorham farm from the earliest days of settlement, but it wasn't until the mid-1870s that teacher Alexander Muir stirred up interest in the phenomenon with a March 1875 letter to the editor of the *Newmarket Era*. He pointed out natural gas had been rushing up through a spring on the Gorham farm for more than half a century, so was not from surface decomposition of organic matter.

"The gas escaping from the Gorham spring is of great value and could be used for illuminating, heating and cooking — sufficient was escaping to light the (Gorham) woollen factory at night and a certainty there is sufficient to light Newmarket," he wrote.[15] Muir said on a visit to the spring he found a continuous commotion on the surface of the water, which was on a level with the surface of the ground: "The spring was curbed by a box about two feet square and four feet deep. The spring itself was approximately five feet deep. It had a clear, sandy bottom, the water never freezes during the winter and gas escapes winter and summer."[16]

*Courtesy of Newmarket Historical Society Archives*

*Alexander Muir only lived and worked in Newmarket for a short time, but left an enduring imprint on the community. He was principal of the Common School from December 1872 to December 1874, village clerk for about nine months, then left to resume teaching in Beaverton. Muir was already famous when he arrived in Newmarket as the composer of the popular anthem, "The Maple Leaf Forever," in 1867.*

The high school principal, Dr. John Morrison, got into the act with a letter pinpointing the gas as carburetted hydrogen, the same gas then being commercially exploited for lighting in Pennsylvania and New York. In August, oil experts from the booming American oil fields in Pennsylvania were brought in, leased an acre of the Williams farm (later the Pickering College farm), and promised to return to sink a test well. They evidently didn't come back, but others did arrive. By November, another group of United States oil men was negotiating with Nelson Gorham for rights to sink a test well near the spring, and a Canadian mining company was talking of building a smelter in town, fuelled by the gas, which would handle "five or 10 tons of ore a day."[17] None of this came about, and things settled down again until July 1884, when an attempt was made to organize a gas company in town to furnish light for stores, factories, homes, and streets. Imagine — no more candles and coal oil lamps! (The first electricity wasn't available in Newmarket until 1886.)

A public meeting was called, and a "man of practical experience" from Listowel invited to speak. Enthusiasm ran high and a study group was established, but again nothing was done. In June 1899, two Ohio oil men, the Cox brothers from the Brantford Gas and Oil Syndicate, came to town. After examining the gas sites, they said there was a natural gas bed about three hundred feet wide, running southeast and northeast, on the east side of town. The Cox Report, submitted later, said, "I have found traces of oil and very strong deposits of gas in the shallow formation, 400 to 500 feet below the surface, and also in the Trenton limestone above the granite, about 1,200 feet from the surface, in which you ought to get very large gas wells. Discovery of oil and gas would boom your town if it was developed," predicted Cox.[18] But by then the old lamplighter had been retired, and electricity had come into its own. The town had its own generating plant and it was making money. People weren't too interested in gas lighting any more.

One final attempt was made to exploit Newmarket's natural gas reserves. In May 1900 Newmarket businessman W.C. Widdifield asked town council to grant him an exclusive franchise on the streets of town in case he organized a gas company to exploit the well on the Williams farm. By 1904, Mr. Widdifield and his Newmarket Development Company were back asking council for permission to lay mains along town streets to supply natural gas for heating purposes. But it wasn't to be. The development company didn't get going, the gas reserves were never tapped, and in the ensuing years of cheap energy it was all but forgotten that Newmarket once dreamed of an oil and gas boom. The area is now totally covered by residential development.

## ॐ Steam Whistles Sounded Daily ॐ

STEAM WHISTLES WERE a major means of communication in Newmarket during the first half of the twentieth century. There was a town whistle that blew daily at 6:00 a.m. and 6:00 p.m., and it doubled as a fire whistle, signalling with a combination of long and short blasts to identify the intersection where the fire report had originated. Fire-alarm boxes with crank handles from which citizens could send in a fire alarm were installed on telephone poles all over town in 1887. They remained in use until 1954. The three major employers in town, the Office Specialty, Davis Leather, and William Cane & Sons (later Dixon Pencil) all had whistles to signal work hours.

In the first years of the new century, Newmarket generated its own electricity at the south end of Main Street using coal-fired boilers to operate a large steam engine, which in turn drove a direct current dynamo. The high-pressure steam also was used to blow the town whistle. This whistle had a deep-throated sonorous tone that could easily be differentiated from the other whistles in town, according to the former Newmarket Historical Society president, Elman Campbell. When it was decided to end the use of a town whistle in the late 1920s, the Office Specialty factory whistle on Timothy Street was used to turn out the volunteer firemen and tell them what part of town required their assistance.

At the time, Newmarket was only a town of a few thousand and everyone knew the fire signals by heart. The sound of the fire whistle was enough to send a crowd to the corner concerned on very short notice. Small boys on bicycles often got there well ahead of the firefighting volunteers.

The Office Specialty whistle was actually two whistles joined together so they blew simultaneously. The smaller shriller one blended with the deeper sound of the larger one to make a distinct mellow tone with great

Author's collection

*William Cane & Sons, Newmarket's largest nineteenth-century employer, turned out all kinds of woodenware, as well as lard, candy and spice packages, jugs, pails, tubs clothes pins, and snow shovels. Workers here pose for a photographer in the summer sun.*

carrying power. The Cane factory whistle was a single whistle that gave a more musical tone. The factory ceased to use it in the mid-1920s. The Davis Leather whistle was the most distinctive of all. It consisted of two whistles controlled by a valve. When the valve was first opened, the high-pressure steam made a shrill sound in the smaller unit, and then as the valve was opened farther the small unit was shut down and the full force of the steam entered the larger unit. The process was reversed when it was shut down. The effect was a high-pitched siren wail. The tannery stopped using its whistle in the late 1940s.

There were other whistles around town a hundred years ago. The Grand Trunk Railway's steam locomotives blew two long, wailing blasts coming into town, and two short blasts at the three crossings (Huron, Timothy, and Water Streets), and the electric radial cars, which went directly through the heart of town, had shrill compressed air whistles that they used at the many street crossings as they moved through town.

No factories blow whistles in Newmarket today. The only whistles heard now are those of the GO Transit commuter trains; five run south from Barrie and Bradford in the morning, and five return later in the day. They whistle at the Mulock Drive, Timothy Street, and Davis Drive level crossings.

## First Subdivision a Flop

SINCE THE END of the Second World War there have been few years in Newmarket when at least one subdivision was not underway, but before 1945, only one was tried. It was not a success!

Newmarket saw a growth spurt between 1900 and 1914, and many of the new arrivals were from the British Isles. Town council decided more building lots were needed, and in 1912 it purchased a thirty-five-acre farm on the north side of Srigley Street, opposite William Denne. The land ran north to Queen Street and bordered the Stickwood Brickyard.

*In 1914, this smiling group attended the turning of the first sod for Connaught Gardens, Newmarket's first subdivision located off Srigley Street, a block east of Prospect Street.*

It was laid out in fifty-foot lots with streets, mostly named for town councillors of the day, all bearing cement sidewalks on both sides. Today, only Pleasantview Street, at the west end, and Wesley Street, named for Dr. J.E. Wesley, remain. The town did not grade the subdivision, so the streets ran up and down hills. There were no culverts either, and no provision for runoff from higher land. The lots were not serviced with water, sewers, lights, or telephone.

The development was named Connaught Gardens in honour of the governor-general of the day, the Duke of Connaught. In July 1914 there was a grand opening and lots were offered for sale. A large platform was erected with a big sign showing the plan of the area with all the lots numbered. Huge platters of sandwiches, cakes, and cookies were put out, to be washed down by lemonade and orangeade. There were plenty of sales at $50 per lot, but timing was bad. Only a month later the First World War broke out, and it was followed by years of high prices, the Depression of 1929–39, and then another war. Most of the lots, except for a few on Pleasantview, Srigley, and Wesley Streets, were taken back by the town for unpaid taxes.

## First Hospital on Main Street

THE MAIN STREET once-elegant Victorian mansion where York County Hospital (now Southlake Regional Health Centre) was first located is now hidden behind an ugly one-storey office addition. The large brick house was built at the top of Main Street hill in 1896 by Dr. Walter G. Hutt. Newmarket at that time had a population of 4,000 and was a stop on both the Grand Trunk Railway and the radial railway. Dr. J.H. Wesley, Dr. Lowell Dales, and Beatrice Dales purchased the building from Hutt's estate in 1920. The hospital was started there as a tiny private corporation that opened in June 1922 with six beds and two nurses on duty. By the end of that year twelve beds were in use.

The house served until the opening of a new building at Prospect Street and Davis Drive in 1927. In the late 1950s, lawyer Joe Dales, the son of Dr. Lowell and Beatrice, added a one-storey office building to the front of the old house and moved his law office into it.

*Newmarket's first hospital began in 1920 in this Main Street residence belonging to Dr. Lowell Dales and two partners.*

By 2008, Southlake Regional was recognized as one of the fastest-growing hospitals in Ontario. It then reported a staff of 2,651 and 387 doctors. As of 2010, the hospital has 2,400 employees, 380 physicians, and five hundred volunteers, with a state-of-the-art cardiac centre, a nationally renowned reputation for delivering excellence in arthritis care, child and adolescent eating disorders, and shoulder surgery, a world-class cancer centre, a Level 2 Paediatric and Prenatal Care Centre, and an Eye Institute with the capacity to perform 9,000 surgical cases per year. Southlake has undergone a stunning transformation from a local community hospital to a foremost regional health-care centre. According to the hospital's website its state-of-the-art buildings house leading-edge technology and facilities comparable to, and in some cases exceeding, what is offered anywhere else in the Province of Ontario.

*Chapter Eleven*

# WAR AND DEPRESSION

## ◌ᵔ The 127th Was Newmarket's Battalion ᵔ◌

THE FIRST WORLD War, the "war to end all wars," seems to be ancient history today, but in the late spring of 1916 it was a very personal matter for Newmarket-area families, many of whom had men fighting overseas. But more men were needed. Two years into the conflict the call went out for volunteers for a new York County unit, the 127th Battalion.

"Newmarket is inseparably associated with the 127th Battalion," wrote its official historian, Major J. C. Boylen.[1]

The first recruiting depot of the unit was in Newmarket, and the 127th Battalion was formed there as a unit. From that mobilization on the 9th of April 1916, until the Armistice, the battalion maintained its existence as a distinct unit. After arriving in England, it was not broken up as were nearly all other units arriving at that time and afterwards. It became the 2nd Battalion of the Canadian Railway Troops and therefore a foundation unit of that special Canadian engineering service created for the British Armies in France. Not only did the Battalion go to France as a unit, but it did so under the commander who started with it from Newmarket, Colonel F. F. Clarke. At the Armistice his adjutant was Captain J. Murray Muir, its first Newmarket recruiting officer.

The people of York County took a particular interest in "their" battalion.

Newmarket's Davis Leather Company donated a set of band instruments, tents, and marquees. Ladies auxiliaries, Red Cross branches, and chapters of the Independent Order of the Daughters of the Empire (IODE) rallied around, providing extra clothing, field kitchens, and recreation facilities. York County Council voted $4,000 for recruiting expenses. When Colonel Clarke marched his new battalion down Yonge Street to barracks in the Kodak plant in Mount Dennis (now part of Toronto), so many people along the route called out a reminder that 104 years earlier the York Militia had followed the same route in response to General Brock's summons that each reminder was greeted with a resounding cheer from the troops.

By January 1917 the unit was serving in France. It saw action along the whole front from the channel to the Oise River in northern France, building and maintaining railways in the battle zones. In those days of poor roads and scanty motor transportation, railways were a necessity for getting men and supplies to the front, and the wounded back from front line aid stations to hospitals in France and Great Britain.

"Many times the crews would go to enormous trouble to clear away the debris of an already damaged track, lay a new section under constant harassment by enemy artillery, finally get a supply train moving with goods to the front, only to have the whole thing smashed up by more shelling. Occasionally the 127th men were bombed from the air. Gas shelling was particularly hard to cope with," wrote Canadian military historian Major Stewart Bull.[2]

Inevitably there were casualties. Thirty were killed out of the 1,157 (all ranks) recorded when the battalion was filled out at the camp at Mount Dennis, and scores wounded. A report compiled after the November 11, 1918, end of fighting showed that in two years of operations, the 127th (2nd Railway Battalion) had built 286 miles of railway line, and had maintained and ballasted as many more — a tremendous achievement by these hardy York County soldiers.

## Little Town Lost Eighty-Three on Europe's Battlefields

"LEST WE FORGET." That is what we always say on November 11th and other such occasions. And indeed in general we have not forgotten. Tribute is paid each year to those who laid down their lives for their country in our wars.

But a list of those from Newmarket lost in the First World War, "the war to end all wars," is a different matter. A list did exist of forty-seven names evidently gathered some time after the end of the war, but it isn't on any memorial and no one is sure where it came from. Forty-seven men, for there are no women in the list, seemed an enormous sacrifice for one small community of about 3,800 residents.

A little research soon revealed three things: there were names on the list of men not linked to Newmarket, there were mix-ups and spelling errors, and there were many soldiers with solid links to Newmarket who died in service and were not on the list at all. Newmarket's contribution in lives was much higher than that preliminary list indicated. I found the names of eighty-three Newmarket men who gave their lives in the services between 1914 and 1919, when the last wounded Newmarket soldier died in hospital. The vast majority of these lost soldiers, airmen, and sailors were young — mostly in their late teens and twenties, although the oldest is fifty-four, a veteran of the Boer War who had re-enlisted. There is also a father and son, two sons of a Newmarket bank manager, and two cousins. Most were in the army, but the community also lost some fliers and one sailor.

Consider a town of 3,800 residents with an average of four to a family home — roughly 875 families in the town. A loss of eighty-three men. Everybody in Newmarket was touched by tragedy and Newmarket's numbers are paralleled by Canada's as a whole. A nation of barely seven million people, we sent 600,000 men and women to war, and 60,000 lives were lost.

Newmarket's honour roll contains men decorated for valour:

Pvt. Herbert Blackhall: Military Medal
Pvt. Sherman Brock: Croix de Guerre (France)
Lieut. Reginald Ruston Brunton: Military Cross
Capt. Robert Dunlop: Military Cross
Sgt. William Eldridge: Distinguished Conduct Medal
Cpl. William Elvidge: Military Medal
Sgt. Douglas Gordon Mitchell: Military Medal
Pvt. Irvine Dudley Ross: Military Medal
L/Sgt. Clifford Dare Windsor: Military Medal

Canada entered the war against Germany when Britain declared war on August 4, 1914. Militia minister Colonel Sam Hughes issued an immediate "call to arms" and directed that 30,000 men be recruited and concentrated at a camp to be constructed at Valcartier, near Quebec City. Volunteers from the York and Peel militia regiments answered the call, including a number of Newmarket men then serving as reservists in the 12th York Rangers. The York men were absorbed into new units, with most becoming members of the 4th Battalion of the First Division. The Canadians arrived in England on October 14, 1914, for four months training on Salisbury Plain. In February 1915 the First Division arrived in France to take over a section of the front line around Armentières. The York men fought in the second battle of Ypres in April 1915, where the Germans introduced gas attacks, and were part of the British Army at Festubert and Givenchy.

Recruiting continued on the home front, and in the spring of 1916, as previously noted, the 127th Battalion, York Rangers, was mobilized at Newmarket. Many of its members were Newmarket men. The 127th was kept together as a unit and served until Armistice on November 11, 1918. No sooner was this first contingent organized than the call went out to raise more battalions. The first of these involving the York Rangers, our local militia regiment, was the 20th Battalion, which was commanded by Lieutenant Colonel J.A.W. Allan of Newmarket. After the Battles of Ypres Salient in April 1915, it was ordered overseas. The unit reached England on May 24, and went into camp in Kent. This second division, of which the 20th was a part, landed in France on September 15, and eleven days later was in the line. The 20th fought in most of the major engagements until the end of the war, suffering heavy casualties. In 1918 it was designated an occupying force and stayed in Germany for some time as part of the Allied Occupation Force that took over a conquered Germany.[3]

Many Newmarket men enlisted in other units. Alexander Brodie, whose father George was an importer of purebred heavy draught horses and farmed the former Millard farm on the west side of town, had gone west with Levi Hoover of Whitchurch Township in 1912. The boys joined the Alberta Regiment, 49th Battalion. In his last letter to his mother, dated May 22, 1917, Alexander tells of the death of Levi a week earlier. "Levi's end was very painful but short. The rest of his mother's life, if I judge rightly, will be almost unendurable." He went on to reassure his mother, "There have been many 'Blighties,' many 'nah poohs' [artillery shells]. Either may come to me any time, but I have a feeling that I shall get through without a scratch. I have always had a great measure of luck, and I hope to be lucky until the end of this war, at least." Later in the letter, he added, "I had two letters written and ready to send a few days ago when a 5.9 came along and buried them. I was much relieved when I discovered the fact that I had not been with them. A 5.9 is no respecter of persons. It is a shell about the size of a three weeks old pig, and when it hits the ground it creates a vast disturbance."[4] Alexander Brodie was killed June 9, 1917, at the age of twenty-two.

Sergeant W.G. Eldridge wrote home in June 1917, explaining he won the Distinguished Conduct Medal "for leading his platoon 14 times to the front line with bombs [falling], after my officer was wounded, and for saving our position in desperate counter-attacks." He went on, "It was worse than any trip in the Somme, for there are so many houses. Fritzy down in the cellar and you upstairs. This street fighting is not very good."[5] The sergeant was killed November 7, 1917.

Eighty-three men, many born, raised, and educated in Newmarket, and others who had moved here to work often bringing families — lost on the battlefields of Europe. That's a tremendous contribution. And there may be others the records have not yet revealed, for only in recent years have the records of that war been commonly available.

## ❧ Riding Refused to Re-Elect Prime Minister ❧

A PRIME MINISTER of Canada once represented this area in the House of Commons — the old federal riding of North York, which included most of York County. And the riding's voters refused to re-elect him.

Mackenzie King became the leader of the Liberal Party, and leader of the Opposition, while he was out of office after an election defeat in North York in 1917, but after he had been nominated by the riding's Liberals for another run. King had stepped down as one of the bright young men of the Sir Wilfrid Laurier administration's civil service, where he served as deputy minister of labour, and had won election in his home riding of Waterloo North in 1908. But in 1911 the Laurier government was defeated on the reciprocity issue (a version of free trade with the United States) and on the Newmarket Canal issue. King lost Waterloo North by 315 votes. Determined to remain in politics he turned to North York, the seat once held by his grandfather, William Lyon Mackenzie. Traditionally a Liberal seat, it had gone Conservative in the 1911 sweep by a narrow margin, and King felt he was the man to win it back in the December 1917 election.

But it was not to be. The First World War was raging, and the conscription issue was splitting the nation. North York had made a heavy contribution of young men to the fighting units at the front, and King opposed conscription. The campaign both here and across the nation developed into a bitter one, as this extract taken from the Newmarket newspaper, *The Express-Herald,* shows: "A vote for Armstrong is a vote for reinforcement for our boys on the firing line. A vote for King is a vote of betrayal to these same lads who bank on our immediate support."[6]

King biographer MacGregor Dawson noted:

*William Lyon Mackenzie King stands with supporters in front of the radial railway station on Botsford Street near the Old Town Hall. The occasion was an election campaign, but it is not known if the photo was taken during King's 1917, 1921, or 1925 campaign.*

In a country in its fourth year of war, and in a constituency which had contributed heavily to the troops at the front, there could be only one result. King was defeated in North York by 1,078 votes — a remarkably good showing, however, when it is remembered that the Unionist majorities in six neighbouring Toronto constituencies ran from 5,104 to 18,237.[7]

But King's mystic bond with the successors to his grandfather's loyal constituents was not so easily broken. "It really looks as though Destiny had intended me to carry on the fight which Grandfather commenced so bravely on behalf of the common people in their struggle against autocratic power. His battle was against the political autocracy; mine must be against the industrial autocracy," he wrote his brother in February 1919.[8]

By March 1919 Sir Wilfrid Laurier had died, and King was debating whether to seek his party's leadership. The convention, Canada's first of its kind, was called for August 1919, and King not only allowed his name to be entered, but he won on the third ballot. An opposition leader needed a Commons seat, so King immediately accepted the nomination in Prince riding (Prince Edward Island) for a by-election, and won. But that September he accepted renomination in North York, and in the general election of 1921 carried the seat in a three-way race with a majority of 1,005. His Liberals were called to form a government, and he became prime minister.

But fickle North York was not to remain as true to Mackenzie King as it had to his grandfather, William Lyon Mackenzie, eighty years before. Herb Lennox, an Aurora lawyer who had represented York North, the corresponding provincial riding, as a Conservative from 1905 to 1919, opposed King in North York in 1925, and had the pleasure of defeating the prime minister of Canada by 494 votes. *The Newmarket Era* reported:

Premier defeated in North York. Majority for Lennox 252 and eight polls to hear from. Wild night in Newmarket. There was a torch light procession through the streets of the Town. At the same time Colonel Lennox arrived with a procession of autos from Aurora and a great crowd thronged the street while he thanked the electors for redeeming North York.[9]

King found a seat elsewhere. Lennox was returned to the House of Commons by North York voters in 1926 and 1930, and the man who had defeated a prime minister died in 1934 while still in office.

## Holland Marsh Became Canada's Salad Bowl

TODAY IT'S CALLED Canada's salad bowl and, for at least part of every year, tables in much of this nation are graced with vegetables grown in the fertile muck soil of the Holland Marsh. But turning the vast swamp, which from time immemorial hampered travel westward from the trails that became Yonge Street, into the nation's largest vegetable garden was no easy job. First schemes to drain the marsh were proposed early in the nineteenth century when settlers from the old countries saw it as source of peat for fuel.

In 1852, a provincial land survey proposed to lower the Washago outlet of Lake Couchiching so that water levels in Lakes Simcoe and Couchiching and the Holland River would drop, thus draining the marsh. The settlements on Lake Simcoe screamed bloody murder and that idea went on the shelf. In 1910, a Bradford grocer, N. David Watson, convinced of the agricultural potential of the marsh, persuaded Professor William Day, a physics lecturer at the Ontario Agricultural College in Guelph, to investigate its possibility. Day tested the marsh's compost-like muck, which ranges in depth from two to forty feet, and found it ideally suited to growing vegetables. The professor formed a development syndicate that bought about 4,000 acres in 1912 and started promoting a drainage scheme. But things didn't happen quickly.

By 1914 Canada was embroiled in the First World War, and the Depression after the war left little capital around for such "iffy" ideas as a 7,000-acre drainage scheme. It wasn't until 1925 that Day got the various governments on side and saw the Holland Marsh Drainage Commission formed. Under the supervision of engineer and surveyor Alexander Baird drainage operations were carried out between 1925 and 1930. Day soon discovered that the Canadian farmers he moved onto the new land didn't know enough about muck farming to make a living and many soon gave up and let their land go for tax arrears.

The solution to that problem came in the person of John J. Snor, Canadian representative of the Netherlands Emigration Foundation. Snor saw the answer to his own problem and Day's too. He had poor immigrant families in Canada who were familiar with the intensive farming techniques required for small muck plots, which are traditionally practised in the Netherlands. He quickly found fourteen families willing to farm undeveloped land and, in 1934, they were settled in the northern section of the marsh on the 3rd Concession line. They formed the nucleus of the present-day Ansnorveldt, the first organized community on the Holland Marsh. By 1960 nearly 40 percent of the Marsh's population was of Dutch origin.

The early years were the hardest. Small vegetable harvests in 1934 and 1935 were barely sufficient to sustain the Dutch community and in some instances the generosity of Bradford and Newmarket merchants was a deciding factor. The harvests of 1936 and 1937 were considerably larger and attracted new farmers as well as Toronto wholesale purchasers. Today, the Marsh is one of Canada's most important vegetable growing districts.

## Redmen Won 1933 National Title

NEWMARKET HAD LITTLE enough to cheer about in 1933 as the nation slid deeper and deeper into what became known as the Great Depression. But that April there was one very big bright spot. The town's favourite hockey team, the Redmen, battled its way all the way to a national championship. Here's the story from *The Newmarket Era* of Friday, April 14, 1933:

> The lone, gruelling, wearisome, championship trail that the gallant little band of Newmarket Redmen have been following ended in a blaze of triumph at Maple Leaf Gardens on Thursday night of last week when 7,522 fans saw them win their second straight game from Regina Pats, Western Canada titleholders, and capture the O.H.A. Memorial Cup, emblematic of the Canadian Junior hockey championship.

The Newmarket Era *gloried in the hometown team's national Junior C Hockey championship in 1933, as shown on the front page of the newspaper. Newmarket's first national hockey championship was big news for the local newspaper, but in the editor's judgment it didn't outweigh a story about local churches getting together for a Good Friday union service. The church story was given the top headline on the front page that week.*

It was one of those rough, hard-fought battles in which no quarter was asked or given and it was just a question of the breaks in the final reckoning. The Pats started out to wear the lighter Newmarket boys down with a hard-hitting campaign, but they failed to stop the gallant Reds, just as several other championship contenders failed, and the North Yorkers finished just as strong as their heavier opponents.

While the game was not a wide-open display of junior hockey, the teams waged a close, hard-checking campaign which had the fans in an uproar all night.

When the red light flashed for Wilson's winning goal, the fans burst in a mighty roar of approval. The Davis pets had finally managed to capture the highly-prized title for which they had withstood a terrific struggle through a long playoff schedule and they lost little time in showing their joy. Hats were tossed in the air and papers and program were thrown on the ice.[9]

The story carries on for two and a half more columns, bringing readers a play-by-play account. According to Stan Smith, the team manager writing in the mid-1950s, "No other town of our size, before or after, ever won a Dominion Junior Hockey Championship."[10] Smith outlined how Newmarket, population 4,000, managed to put such a powerhouse together. He gave credit to Andy Davis of the Davis Leather family, and Lyman Rose of Roadhouse & Rose Funeral Home. They began building during the 1928–29 season after the Newmarket junior team lost such stellar players as Bill Thoms, Dodger Collins, and Ellis Pringle, all of whom went on to NHL careers. For the first two seasons the Redmen were knocked out early. "In the winter of 1930–31 we added Sparkie Vail, Normie Mann and Red McArthur to such fellows as Herb Cain, Don Wilson, Larry Molyneaux, Bob McCabe and Bob Peters (again several went on to NHL careers). They made it to the Ontario semi-finals before losing to Owen Sound."[11]

A new coach, Bill Hancock, was imported next season. Davis and Rose were still footing the bills. Cain, Molyneaux, and Peters were off the team because of the age limitation, but a phalanx of new stars were imported, Pep Kelly, Howard Peterson, Frank Huggins, Silver Doran, and Ran Forder. Due to injuries, locals were added from the Town League for the final series, Aub Marshall and Mac Ogilvie.

"Boy, that was a hand-picked club if ever there was one," wrote Smith.[12]

On April 7, 1933, that club won the Dominion Championship. Members of winning team were: Ran Forder, goal; Jimmy Parry, sub-goal; Sparky Vail, Silver Doran, and Gar Preston, defence; Normie Mann, Don Wilson, Red McArthur, Frank Huggins, Pep Kelly, and Howard Peterson, forwards; Aub Marshall, Mac Ogilvie, later additions; Bill Hancock, coach; Stan Smith, manager.

Three-quarters of a century later, when old-timers tell hockey stories in Newmarket, the 1933 national championship and another won by Newmarket Jr. C. Smoke Rings in 1956 always come up. The town has changed enormously and grown in population from 4,000 to over

80,000. There have been many teams and many championships, but those two victories left indelible marks on the memories of long-time families.

## ✤ Remember the 1940s ✤

NEWMARKET WAS A town with a population of barely 4,000. It had three public schools (Alexander Muir, King George, and Stuart Scott) and one high school, two dairies (one with a malt shop on Main Street), and two bakeries. Fairy Lake still looked like a mill pond and the town dump was up Bayview Avenue where Richardson Park is today. With the first half of the decade being the war years, Newmarket was an army camp town.

It was resolutely dry — what town wouldn't be with thousands of young soldiers bivouacked within its boundaries? Dry that is, except for sixty-four bootleggers, some of whom ran quite sophisticated speakeasies. One lady on Main Street north of Davis Drive (or Huron Street as it was

*During the Second World War and after, Boy Scouts salvaged scrap paper. The Dixon Pencil Company, one of the town's largest employers, provided this storage shed for the Newmarket collections.*

then called) cleared her living room and dining room furniture out two nights a week, installed tables and chairs, opened a fold-out bar, and if she recognized you through the peephole in the door, you got in. Those two nights were the ones on which employees at the Davis Leather tannery, Dixon Pencil, and the Office Specialty were paid.

Here are some other things people remember when reminiscing about the 40s:

- Mrs. Germain's pop stand on her front lawn on the east side of Prospect Street south of Queen Street.
- The three cannons that graced the Waterworks front lawn at the bottom of Main Street — two War of 1812 mortars and a First World War German artillery piece.
- The mirror at the narrow corner of Church Street and Millard Avenue, which allowed traffic to see around the bend.
- The five places to buy gasoline in the downtown area — Keffer's station on Water Street, Freddy Thompson's City Service on Timothy Street, Nesbitt's on Main Street, Geer & Byers on Botsford, and the Shell on Eagle Street. The gas was raised manually from the underground tank to a glass tank on top of the pump by the attendant working a large handle on the side of the pump. It was easy to see how much you purchased — you could watch it drain from the glass tank with measurements painted on the side.
- The weigh scale that was big enough to handle trucks on Market Square near Timothy Street. The Square was gravel in those days.
- The big road scraper the town often parked on Market Square. It had two hand-turned wheels to regulate the blade and it could be pulled by either truck or horses.
- The Office Specialty whistle that sounded each day to tell employees it was time to come to work.
- Fire alarm boxes on poles around town. When calls were made from them, it resulted in the whistle being blown and the speedy arrival of the Bickle fire truck and as many volunteers as were available. The whistle was the Office Specialty whistle, and it blew a code (three long, two short, for instance) to tell volunteers where the alarm originated.

- Boy Scouts' collections to help the war effort — scrap paper, kitchen fat, aluminum foil, and milkweed pods to make kapok (the fluffy packing used to stuff life preservers and make them float — a wartime essential).
- Mosquito fighter bombers being test flown over the area. The sleek aircraft were built at the de Havilland plant in Downsview. They sometimes seemed to come down our valley at tree-top level.
- Hillsdale Dairy delivering milk with horse-drawn wagons, and proprietor Mo Hall's horse barn behind the post office on Main Street.
- The ice and coal storage warehouses at Geer & Byers on Botsford Street. They had once been a curling club.

Only folks who grew up in Newmarket during the 1940s and early 1950s will relate to most of these memories, and those people are becoming in pretty short supply. If that's your generation and you have similar recollections, jot them down.

##  Six Weeks to Become an Army Town

FOR SOME PEOPLE war is hardship and sacrifice. For some it is opportunity. For the citizens of Newmarket and district, the outbreak of the Second World War, in September 1939, was both.

Most families had fresh memories of the sacrifices Canadians made on the battlefields of Europe two decades earlier. Eighty-three Newmarket men gave their lives in that conflict. People saw little virtue in another round of trench warfare, poison gas, and bayonet charges into the mouths of cannons. They had also endured ten years of deep economic depression and now could only hope that if war did come it would stay in Europe, but create new demands for Canadian factories so the long lines of jobless might shrink and wind down the Great Depression.

They did not exactly see their wishes granted. War did indeed end the Depression, but the cost in lives of young Canadians was enormous. By its end long lists of names were being engraved on new war memorials in parks in every Canadian town.

Prime Minister Mackenzie King's government declared war within days of Britain and France declaring war on Germany. Canadian soldiers and airmen were soon heading for European battlefields, and Canadian Navy ships were fighting in the North Atlantic.

The factories finally came to life. And because so many young men and women were in uniform, there were lots of jobs on the home front. In fact, in Newmarket and many other communities even the local "gentlemen" who had managed never to hold an honest job in their lives found themselves on war-factory assembly lines, along with a number of women entering the workforce for the first time, and seniors brought out of retirement.

In the summer of 1940, Newmarket's town council sent a delegation to Ottawa in search of a war-effort payroll. Mayor Dr. S.J. Boyd, Reeve Fred Lundy, Deputy Reeve Joe Vale, and town solicitor Norm Mathews met with the minister of National Defence and offered him free use of the town's fairgrounds as the site for an army basic training camp. The offer was accepted. Wartime Ottawa proved it could move quickly when it wanted to. Six weeks later, in September 1940, the camp was completed and ready for service. Crews erected thirty-six buildings, including a large drill hall, barracks, cook houses, messes, guard rooms, recreation halls, washrooms, quartermaster's stores, and two canteens. An infirmary, churches and other buildings were added later.

In just six weeks Newmarket had become an army town. The camp processed 1,000 soldiers a month through basic training, and gave a huge

*Rows of wooden barracks were erected in 1940 as part of an army basic training camp, following the federal government's acceptance of the Newmarket town council's offer of use of the town's former fairgrounds for such purpose. The complete army camp was built and running in six weeks.*

shot in the arm to the local economy. Government money poured in to build the camp, pay the soldiers, and buy food, gasoline, and other supplies. And then there was the money the soldiers spent in the town. Although Newmarket and its market area have experienced their economic ups and downs in the half century since war's end, that growth spiral established by the war has never really ended.

Much of the old army camp is still there, disguised now as a late 1940s residential area. Drive east on Srigley Street to the top of the hill by Prince Charles Public School. That's where the gates to the camp and the sentry boxes used to sit. Turn south on Muriel Street and look at the neat rows of houses on Lowell and Arthur Streets. Those were the barracks. After the war, a local entrepreneur bought a big chunk of the camp, cut the oblong barracks buildings in half, moved the halves onto separate lots, and remodelled them into homes.

Down by Fairground Park there is a big building that now houses the curling club. That's the old army drill hall. The modern structure on Srigley Street, which serves as the home of Newmarket Branch 426 of the Royal Canadian Legion, started its life as the army officers' mess building.

## Fifth Column Scare Triggered Wartime Paranoia

THE FIFTH COLUMN — today most of us probably think of it as the place in the budget where we enter the HST. But in the summer of 1940 the words "Fifth Column" had a far different and darker meaning. The Fifth Column was thought to be a web of spies, saboteurs, and Nazi sympathizers hiding within our society, ready to strike crippling blows to our war effort.

An article on the Fifth Column scare in *The Beaver* (the former name of *Canada's History Magazine*) of January 1994, describes a "period of intense fear in May and June of 1940 when Canadians came face to face with Hitler's blitzkrieg. After eight months of 'phony war' Canadians realized with a shock that they were in a very deadly struggle. For those two months, in a moment of utter collective panic, Canadians suddenly doubted whether they were equal to the task. In their hysteria they turned upon an entirely imaginary internal enemy in a paroxysm of panic that has come to be called Canada's fifth column crisis."

It is important to remember what was going on in 1940. That April, Hitler's Wehrmacht invaded Denmark and Norway. The latter survived weeks, the former mere hours. Holland fell in five days, Belgium survived eighteen days. Five weeks after the first assault Nazi troops were marching through Paris. On June 12, 1940, Justice Minister Ernest Lapointe warned that Canada "could no longer rely upon the Allied armies and the British fleet for protection against invasion."[13] It appeared Britain would fall next and if it did, Canada — the only western hemisphere country to declare war in September 1939 — would face the entire force of the German armed might.

Small wonder thoughts turned to spies, sabotage, and fifth columns — sometimes in an almost hysterical manner. In May 1940, for instance, a rumour spread through the town that a man named C.C. Rachar, who was employed as Newmarket's light and water works superintendent, was a German spy, planted there to sabotage these vital utilities.

The poor man was defenceless. He published his family history in *The Newmarket Era & Express* to show that he had been born and raised in Arthur Township, Wellington County, where his family had lived since his great-grandfather had emigrated there from England. He pointed out he and his two brothers had fought overseas in the First World War. Town Councillor Arthur Evans issued an official denial that the man was a spy, and that too was published in *The Era & Express*. All to no avail. Before long, Mr. Rachar left his employment and moved his family out of town.

Mass meetings of ex-servicemen were being held in cities across the country, and they demanded government action against enemy aliens and the "fifth column." In Toronto, 50,000 attended such a June 9th meeting. Veterans organizations offered to mobilize on the home front. In Newmarket on June 6, Alf Smith, president of the Newmarket Veterans Association, asked town council to form a Home Guard unit. To spur council into action he reported a recent incident in which two men with a map had been spotted on the hill south of Bogarttown. They had been overheard saying the hill would be an ideal place for gun emplacements to shell Toronto. Smith said his organization's members were very concerned about sabotage and espionage and wanted to back up the police. The following week, the Newmarket Veterans Association passed a resolution asking the government to intern all enemy aliens.

On June 20, a Civic Guard was formed by town council. First World War veteran H.M. "Herb" Gladman was named its leader, and Alex Eves, another veteran, and Bert Morrison, owner of the Main Street clothing and gun store, were named his assistants. In Toronto a League of Patriotic Action was organized, and one of its first moves was to report to the Mounties a German-born resident of the city whom they suspected as a fifth columnist because he kept homing pigeons. The man was interned.

In June 1940 the tumult peaked. Decline began after the federal government banned Nazi and Communist organizations and began rounding up Communists and Fascists sympathetic to Italy. Britain held out after all, and the war took a different turn.

## Young Flyer First Lost in Action

A YOUNG MAN from Timothy Street was the first Newmarket serviceman killed in action in the Second World War. Bill Pipher was twenty-five, when the bomber he was piloting over Germany was shot down. His parents, Mr. and Mrs. Earl Pipher, received a cable on Friday, March 27, 1942, informing them their son was missing in action. His aircraft, they were told, had gone down over enemy territory on Wednesday, March 25, and the air force had no word on survivors. The Piphers had been waiting for a cable from Bill for a much happier reason. That Wednesday, the day he was shot down, was their daughter Lelia's wedding day to Fred Penrose of Newmarket. Bill had promised to cable his congratulations to his sister from his base in Britain.

Sergeant Pilot Bill Pipher enlisted in the RCAF in September, 1940 — the darkest days of the war — and had trained in western Canada. He won his pilot's wings in July 1941 and before long was posted overseas. He spent a short time in Iceland before joining a squadron in Britain. The young pilot had been making raids over Europe for five months when his aircraft went down. Bill had attended Newmarket High for five years and was described by Principal J.B. Bastedo as a good student, a talented pianist with the Glee Club, and an impressive athlete on the track and field team. Before joining the air force, Bill had worked in the fruit and vegetable department at the A&P store at Timothy and Main Streets.

The bad news about Bill was soon followed by reports of other local men killed, wounded, or captured as more and more of Newmarket's young men were called up and shipped out. Although Bill Pipher was the first of Newmarket's servicemen lost in action overseas, he was not the first casualty from the town. That grim distinction goes to another young flier, Leading Aircraftsman (LAC) Ross Cook, the son of Mr. and Mrs. Francis Cook of Newmarket. Ross was killed in a flying accident at Hagersville, Ontario, on December 4, 1941. His father was Newmarket's CNR agent.

# Chapter Twelve

# LATER IN THE CENTURY

## ☙ Davises Sparked Toronto's Theatre Life ☙

TORONTO'S VIBRANT AND multi-faceted theatre world owes a big vote of thanks to three modern-day pioneers from Newmarket. Brothers Donald and Murray Davis, and their sister Barbara Chilcott Davis, took a big chance back in 1954 in old Hogtown and opened the city's only full-time Canadian theatre in a converted movie house on Mount Pleasant Road. The Crest Theatre lasted twelve years, from January 1954 to June 1966, and it proved that actors could make a full-time living on the Toronto stage.

"In the 1940s there were no native producing theatres," said Donald. "There were places like the Royal Alex that brought productions in, but the working companies that were around were not fully professional."[1]

Davis, who became one of Canada's most distinguished actors, said even after renovations the theatre was a long way from ideal. But everything was done to establish a standard not seen before in Toronto. On the first opening night the curtain went up a half-hour late because no one would leave the party in the lobby. The opening of The Crest was a big event because "the idea of earning a living strictly from the theatre in Toronto was unheard of in those days, but we were able to show it could be done."[2]

The Davis family was one of Newmarket's wealthiest during the first half of the twentieth century. Their father, E.J. Davis, was one of three brothers who owned and operated the Davis Leather Company. During the 1940s the Davises made a success out of the Straw Hat Players, a summer stock company in Gravenhurst and Port Carling.

"We really didn't intend to stay there [The Crest] very long," said Donald. "We always had the unfulfilled dream to convince someone to build a theatre for us."[3]

Never quite a financial success, although it managed to present forty weeks a year of good theatre, The Crest finally closed in 1966, two years after losing a Canada Council grant in a political squabble that made entertainment headlines across the country. Murray stayed to the bitter end, but by 1966 Donald, the younger of the brothers, was a hit on Broadway. He left in 1959 for a year's sabbatical, which turned into twelve busy years of starring roles. Sister Barbara Chilcott, a mainstay of The Crest Company, remained familiar to Canadian theatre-goers and national TV audiences for many years. She married renowned Canadian composer Harry Somers in 1968. Murray eventually retired to raise beef cattle in the Collingwood area.

## Tall Tales About Past Pranks

IT MUST HAVE looked like a Newmarket old boys' reunion. A group of "young fellows" sitting around taking tea and talking about the good old days when they were kids with bicycles and Newmarket was but a town of 4,000. The reminiscing started when somebody asked whatever happened to Parachute Joe? No one knew, but that started the memories flowing.

Like the time two brothers who lived on the "east side," somewhere near Alexander Muir Public School, had nothing to do one hot summer day so they climbed to the roof of the old school and stuffed a wad of something down the chimney. The plug wasn't discovered until much later that year — in fact it was the nippy autumn day when the coal furnace was lit. The old two-storey school filled with smoke so fast that everybody got a day off school.

Glenville Pond was the town's favourite swimming hole in those days. It was about a fifteen-minute bicycle ride out of town on a lovely, quiet gravel road running west from the town boundary where Parkside Drive is now.

*"Parachute Joe," a local character around town in the 1940s, was so determined to enlist in the paratroopers during the Second World War that he decided to practise by jumping from a barn loft.*

Drawing by Creighton Henry

The old mill pond was deep, cold, and fast-moving, and located at the bottom of a winding hill. In the 1940s there were even a few vestiges of the once-thriving mill town remaining. It wasn't the paving of Highway 9 that killed the pond as a swimming hole. Before that happened, a new owner fenced it off, posted it, and stocked it with trout. That alone wouldn't have discouraged young swimmers, as one of the old boys pointed out, but the barbed wire and cedar branches strung about three feet under water below the bank sure did.

"What about the bag lady?" was likely asked by someone. Newmarket was probably ahead of its time in this respect, and because she was the only one we had, naturally for young lads there was something of an air of romance and mystery about this bedraggled creature who walked endlessly about town.

Was the story imagination or fact? We never knew. We did know she was often spotted around the train station, and that added substance to the story that she was still waiting for a handsome young soldier to return from the First World War battlefields.

Hallowe'en was a great source of tales or pranks, but the best one is the oldest — the story of the tipped over outhouse. It was probably the last outhouse in town and it was behind the old saltbox house on the southwest corner of Church and Botsford Streets. For years, no matter what its owner did, he was always outsmarted and found the outhouse tipped over on the morning of November 1st. But the year in question (sometime in the mid-1950s), he outsmarted the outsmarters. He simply moved the little structure back down the path about four feet and left it unguarded. Sure enough, the first kid down the path in the dark fell right in.

And what about Parachute Joe? He was determined to join the army and become a paratrooper, but the army wouldn't have him. To prove he was up to it, he made a parachute out of an umbrella, climbed to the roof of Dennis' barn, and jumped. The parachute didn't work, and Joe spent some time hobbling around on crutches.

## National Film Board Documentary Focused on Citizens Band

NEWMARKET ONCE HOSTED a world premiere of a movie. Granted it wasn't a Hollywood blockbuster, it was a National Film Board (NFB) documentary, but Newmarket was the star. In fact, not just Newmarket, but the Newmarket Citizens Band. The movie, *Goodbye Sousa*, was made in 1973 when the famous marching band was already 102 years old. It told the story of the survival of Newmarket's band when other small town bands all over the nation were fading.

The director was Tony Ianuzielo, and he won an Etrog for Best Theatrical Short at that year's Genie Awards for the seventeen-minute film. A Keswick native, Tony attended Newmarket High and Ryerson Institute of Technology (now Ryerson University) before spending his career as a cameraman, director, and producer at the NFB in Montreal. He had many old friends playing in the band.

In those days Newmarket's only movie theatre was on the Main Street, and when the local newspaper teamed up with the NFB to hold the world premiere, the Roxy Theatre agreed to supply the venue. It was a glittering affair with many local notables, as well as the band, invited to the showing and a reception afterwards at the home of yours truly, the editor of *The Era*.

## Hagen Taught Generations of Canadian Artists

FRED HAGEN LIVED and painted in Newmarket since moving there in 1941, earning a reputation as one of Canada's most respected artists and art teachers. Born in Toronto in 1918, he came to Newmarket as resident artist and master at Pickering College in 1941 after graduating from the Ontario College of Art. He married the former Isabelle Heald of Newmarket, and they had five children.

Hagen left Pickering in 1946 to study art in New York, and later that year joined the staff of the Ontario College of Art. In 1955 he became head of Printmaking, a position he held until his retirement in 1983. During his almost forty years there he shaped the talents of many generations of Canadian artists through his classes in drawing, painting, composition, and printmaking. He is a former president of — and, since 1965, an honourary member of — the Canadian Society of Graphic Art. He was also a member of the Canadian Society of Painter-Etchers and Engravers, the Ontario Society of Artists, and the Print and Drawing Council of Canada.

*Fred Hagen taught generations of Canadian artists. He began his career as a teacher at Pickering College in Newmarket, and lived in the town throughout his lifetime. Most of his career was on the staff of the Ontario College of Art. Today, a street in Newmarket is named Fred Hagen Crescent.*

His works hang in most major Canadian galleries as well as many corporate and private collections. It has been shown by, among others, the Ontario Society of Artists, the Royal Canadian Academy of Arts, the U.S. Library of Congress, and the Cincinnati Art Museum. In 1986, he was commissioned to design a set of four Canadian stamps honouring the discoverers of Canada: Henry Hudson, John Cabot, the Vikings, and the First Peoples. Newmarket named a street for him in the 1990s. Frederick Hagen died in 2000.

## ❧ Marsh Moonshine ❧

MOONSHINE, THAT ILLICIT, unlicenced, and untaxed distillation made in hidden stills, was once as much a part of the Holland Marsh as carrots are today. During the first half of the twentieth century, and earlier, a lot less of the marsh had been brought under cultivation and there were lonely and isolated places where only the most knowledgeable local inhabitants ventured — and they usually went by boat.

The illicit whisky trade on the Marsh never reached the proportions it did in the hills of Kentucky and West Virginia, where Prohibition era contests between government agents and still operators sometimes seemed like a civil war, but it nevertheless had its exciting moments. An edition of *The Newmarket Era,* published in December 1938, carried a court report of a raid on a Marsh still run by the legendary Holland Landing moonshiner Tom Foster. He was convicted and sentenced to six months in jail and fined $500 for operating a still. The fine was considerable in 1938 when a good annual wage for a man was $1,200.

Constables Vern Williams and Ron Watt of the York County Police Force were going through the woods between the old Holland Landing road and the river one day early in October when they found a milk can that smelled strongly of brew, an old fire with plates, and an old barrel sunk in the ground.

"We strongly suspected distilling had been going on in that place," Williams told the judge.[4]

From Tuesday to Friday the two policemen kept watch. When they arrived on Friday they saw smoke rising above the trees. Approaching quietly, Williams recognized Tom Foster and George Hollingshead, two Holland Landing men known to him, tending the fire and running a still over it. When Williams ran into the clearing, Hollingshead and Foster took off into the bush, with Williams in pursuit of Foster. After a 150-yard chase he caught up to him, but Foster turned on the officer with an axe and refused to be arrested.

"Rather than use too much force, I let Foster go on to his house and I said I would meet him there," Williams testified.[5] He then returned to the clearing and dismantled the still to use for evidence. But picking up Tom Foster wasn't so easy.

"We had Foster's house under observation after the still was found but we couldn't find Tom," said Watt.[6]

Finally, five days after seizing the still, the two constables spotted their man on a sideroad in East Gwillimbury between the 5th and 6th Concessions. He was driving a team of horses with a load of gravel on the wagon. But Foster spotted the police car about the same time the constables saw him. He jumped off the wagon, cleared a fence in one bound, and sprinted across a ploughed field. Three shots were fired, but they didn't slow down Foster who made it into the woods and escaped. The court reporter doesn't tell us when they finally caught up with the Holland Landing moonshiner, but it must have taken some weeks, for they didn't get him into court until December.

Another story was related to me by Arleigh Armstrong, the crown attorney in Newmarket for many years. He told of police laying a trap for a moonshiner at the Marsh landing on the Holland River where the man usually beached his boat. The suspect came ashore, hoisted two one-gallon jugs of amber liquid, one in each hand, and set off up the path. The police trap was sprung, the moonshiner put his jugs down, returned to his boat, and retrieved a rifle. A constable picked up the jugs. With deadly accuracy the moonshiner shot twice, knocking the bottom out of each jug.

"There ... you ain't got no evidence on me now," he crowed.[7]

He wound up in court anyway.

## Women's Christian Temperance Union Thought Water Best

ALMA AND ELMER Starr were among the last of the old-time Quakers in

Newmarket. They wore plain dress, and Alma wore a little black bonnet. The family had farmed at Bogarttown since early in the nineteenth century. One family member, Francis Starr, who was both farmer and teacher, was the first to be employed at the new red-brick Bogarttown school when it opened in 1856. Alma worked in many good causes but her favourite was the Women's Christian Temperance Union (WCTU), which at one time held powerful influence in Newmarket.

One of its many projects was to place an ornate iron fountain at the corner of Park Avenue and Main Street, a constant reminder that Newmarket at one time vanquished the demon rum. Erected in 1903, it was taken down to make way for the widening of Main Street in 1953, and never replaced. The fountain simply disappeared, taken away on the back of a town works-department truck, and in later years no one knew what happened to it.

The Newmarket WCTU had erected the fountain "for the quenching of thirst in man and beast free from the pocket and also free from the sorrow such as strong drink leaves in its wake,"[8] and was dedicated to the memory of a long-serving WCTU president, Mrs. Benjamin Cody. It was put up at a time when the WCTU was a political and social force to be reckoned with in the community, and at a time when its members were in the forefront of the battle for prohibition.

In pioneer Ontario, distilleries and breweries were as common as the mills they supplemented. They ensured millers and farmers a market for their surplus grain, and they turned out a commodity easy to transport and quick to sell. As a result, taverns dotted every highway and main street, and by mid-century whisky was selling in Newmarket for 25 cents a gallon. Innkeepers left a jug of the stuff on the bar overnight so late arrivals could help themselves. As the toll of intemperance weighed heavily on society, support for temperance grew stronger, and, in 1878, the federal government brought in the Canada Temperance Act, which permitted any federal constituency to hold a referendum and vote to abolish the liquor trade.

The WCTU, formed in Newmarket in 1885 to work for legal prohibition, became a loud and often strident voice. Early in 1910 a local temperance option was on the ballot, and it carried. On May 1, 1910, the village's bars and taverns had to close. The victory marked the zenith of the WCTU's power. The Union continued as a voice for morality in the community, gathering a two hundred-name petition in 1915 opposing "wet canteens for the men protecting our country," and in the twenties and thirties taking up the fight against such social evils as tobacco, gambling, lotteries, and "disgusting dress by girls."[9]

However, as the years passed interest in temperance waned, and after more than forty-five years, Newmarket voted (in 1957) overwhelmingly for the legal sale of beer and liquor at government outlets. The Newmarket WCTU continued to meet for many years after its heyday, although time diminished its numbers. The final meeting was held in York Manor Home for the Aged in the 1970s because, as Alma Starr told me in an interview at the time, "all the remaining six members are residents here."[10] By then even the green, iron WCTU fountain had been among the missing for many years.

*Alma and her husband, Elmer Starr, are shown reading the family Bible. Alma chaired the final meeting of the Newmarket WCTU when it was held at York Manor Home for the Aged, where the last six members were all residents.*

## ❧ Race to Build the First Mall ❧

ON THE CUSP of a growth spurt in the early 1970s, Newmarket was targeted by four major shopping-centre development companies, but Mayor Bob Forhan and his council decided only one would be allowed to build. Each firm promised a major shopping centre on land it owned, and so council made it a horse race, the firm ready to go first with the best proposal would win.

First off the mark was Schickedanz Developments Limited, which was just finishing its Quaker Hill subdivision. It proposed a strip plaza with offices for the Yonge Street frontage of its subdivision. Although the firm was not the winner, the plaza on the property today looks pretty much like the 1971 proposal. The other entrants all proposed to build the town's first enclosed shopping mall.

Corporate Properties Limited, an international shopping-centre builder that owned the farm on the southwest corner of Davis Drive and Yonge Street, said it would have a Hudson's Bay department store, supermarket, fifty-two-room Seaway Hotel, and retail stores. Over on the town's east side, Community Malls Inc. of Toronto proposed a mall with department store, supermarket, and three movie theatres. They were at Davis Drive and Sutton Road (now Leslie Street).

Regional Shopping Centres Limited was set up by department-store owner Simpson-Sears Limited and Cambridge Leaseholds Limited, one of Canada's largest builders of commercial retail space. It purchased the northwest corner of Yonge and Davis Drive and mounted a high-pressure campaign to convince councillors its plan was the best. It had detailed market surveys proving their mall would draw shoppers from as far away as Orangeville and Lindsay, slick brochures, and even chartered an aircraft to take councillors to see another of their malls in Windsor. Part of the campaign was a promise to start building in 1972. The proposal, of course, was for what became Upper Canada Mall, and it won the race, hands down.

And what of the unsuccessful sites? The Quaker Hill project eventually was built in a slightly reduced form. The other two firms simply decamped — sold their land and left.

# Epilogue

In the years since Upper Canada Mall was opened it has grown continuously, as has the town. By 2009, the mall had been through three expansions and now has 230 stores and 820,000 square feet of floor space. That same year Newmarket was packing 84,000 residents into its 14.2 square mile area, and is projected to reach a population of 98,000 by the year 2026.

Every square foot of that area is either built upon or about to be, so where will the town put all those new residents? It will have to grow upwards, said Mayor Tony Van Bynen, with high-rise apartment buildings and office towers along its major traffic arteries — Yonge Street and Davis Drive. Fortunately, the town is used to growth. Between 1991 and 2006 its population rose an astounding 63.4 percent, well over the Greater Toronto Area (GTA) average of 53.1 percent.

No longer considered a small town well north of Toronto, today's Newmarket is a thriving suburban community at the northern apex of the GTA's golden triangle. Newmarket is striving to maintain its small-town atmosphere combined with big-city amenities, and to provide quality employment within its boundaries so it doesn't become one of Toronto's dormitories.

The town is the administrative centre of the Regional Municipality of York with its spectacular, sprawling headquarters designed by architect

Douglas Cardinal. The old York County Hospital has morphed into the growing campus of the Southlake Regional Health Centre, one of the province's foremost treatment centres. York Regional Police headquarters are also located in Newmarket, and the town's east-side industrial parks have rapidly filled with new plants.

Old Main Street and its nineteenth-century brick buildings, which survived the great fire 1871, remain the nucleus of a downtown heritage district with Fairy Lake as its jewel. Surrounded by a sprawling park and connected to a trail system that runs along the river from the north boundary of the town on Green Lane to the south boundary at St. John's Sideroad, this historic centre is the focus of many recreational, cultural, and arts activities. Local businesses provide restaurants and patio dining, live theatre includes a Shakespeare Festival, and the seasonal farmers' market continues to be a draw.

Outside this heritage core, Newmarket boasts more than seventy parks and natural trails. Close to the eastern boundary is the Magna Centre, a recreation complex with an Olympic-size and three NHL-size arenas, an eighty-foot indoor pool, a seventy-foot learning pool, and other facilities such as a gymnasium, restaurants, and a pro shop. An older facility, the Twinney Centre, with two arenas and a pool, is located west of Yonge Street.

Our Quaker settler forefathers might be surprised at what their little milling centre has become, but the entrepreneurs who quickly joined them on the frontier would approve, for the Newmarket of today is a busy commercial town with a keen appreciation of its past and the heritage that has brought it thus far.

# Sources and Notes

Newmarket's history stretches back to the earliest days of settlement in this province. Timothy Rogers laid claims to the first of the forty Yonge Street farms in 1800, and his settlers began clearing the land and building a mill on the Holland River the following spring. Other settlers were quick to follow and soon a community known as Beman's Corners sprang up. Over its first two hundred years the community, which gradually came to be called New Market after the War of 1812, participated in many of the colourful events that went into the making of this province. The fur trade was Newmarket's earliest source of commerce, rebellion flared in 1837, the first railway in the colony came through in 1852, a streetcar line from Toronto, and an unfinished canal to Lake Simcoe are part of the story, as are various wars and depressions.

When I first began searching out tales of these events in the 1970s for stories in *The Era,* where I was the editor, it was pretty hard going. No one in Newmarket seemed to know or care about this colourful past. The public library had almost no books on local history, there was no historical society, archives, museum, microfilm copies, or Heritage Newmarket. But there was *The Era,* continuously published since 1853 and with one of the best preserved runs of newspapers in any Ontario archives. My lucky break was that all the originals in bound volumes from the 1890s to the present lived on racks at the back of the old newspaper plant. Many a

Sunday afternoon was spent on those dusty volumes, searching out what newspapermen call the "human interest stories."

Over the years, as new sources of information came to hand, I updated these files. I am particularly grateful to the late Ned Roe, grandson of the indomitable fur trader William Roe, for his interest, his many conversations, and his occasional glass of good whisky. Another invaluable source of information were the articles written by Erastus Jackson, first publisher of the *Era* and a man with a keen sense of history. After he retired from his busy life as editor and publisher in 1883, he set about interviewing survivors of those early days and published their recollections. Ethel Trewhella's manuscript, *History of the Town of Newmarket*, printed in unedited form after her death in the 1950s and now long out of print, is a great source of stories and leads for more information. Although it has not been available for more than fifty years, many Newmarket homes treasure copies of her work.

## Part I: The Earliest Days

IN SOME WAYS stories about the first years of settlement are the hardest to come by, and it's necessary to rely on the old standard sources, in particular *Étienne Brûlé: Immortal Scoundrel*, by J. Herbert Cranston. Francis Parkman's monumental history (*Pioneers of France in the New World*, Volumes I & II, George N. Morang & Company Ltd., 1899) of the French in North America, a full set that I was fortunate to inherit from my grandfather, is another such resource. The journal of Timothy Rogers, *The Best Man for Settling a New Country: The Journal of Timothy Rogers, 1790–1810*, published in Toronto by the Canadian Friends Historical Association in 2000, provides a firsthand account of the earliest times of "Our First Settlement" and "Grinding the First Bushel," and the Millard family history, the Srigley history (both sets of family papers are in Newmarket Public Library), the Cawthra papers in Archives Ontario (AO), and the Bogart history contained in the Old Boys Reunion 1939 booklet (*Newmarket Old Boys' Reunion Souvenir Booklet*, 1939) were also very helpful for this period.

Information on the "Trading Tree" came from late Ned Roe, who in the 1960s and 1970s was retired and living in Newmarket. The *Atlas of York County 1878*, and the *Holland River Conservation Report*, History Section, also have a considerable amount of information.

To these sources can be added the Ethel Trewhella manuscript (*History of the Town of Newmarket*, printed in 1957 by the town's centennial committee), *The Quakers in Canada: A History* by Arthur G. Dorland (The Ryerson Press, Toronto, 1968), and Henry Scaddings's *Toronto of Old* (Willing & Williamson, Toronto, 1878) for information on Andrew Borland, William Roe, and the Rogers family. The British Army's "24th Regiment of Foot" is extensively documented on the internet (*www.britishempire.co.uk/forces/armyunits/britishinfantry.htm*), and additional information is found in the Simcoe Papers (AO). The story of "The Sword" used to lead the artillery party onto the Plains of Abraham came, of course, from Ned Roe, and he showed me the sword. Following Ned's death, the sword went to a relative living in Ottawa.

## Notes

1. J.H. Cranston, *Étienne Brûlé: Immortal Scoundrel* (Toronto: The Ryerson Press, 1949), 30.
2. James Mason, "Brûlé, Étienne, *www.thecanadianencyclopedia.com*.
3. Christopher Robinson came from a fairly impecunious branch of the wealthy and prominent Robinson family of Virginia. He had run away from William and Mary College to join the Loyalist forces during the American Revolution and became an officer in the Queen's Rangers, commanded by John Graves Simcoe during the American Revolution. As a United Empire Loyalist he settled in New Brunswick but had a difficult time supporting his family there. When Simcoe became lieutenant governor of Upper Canada, Robinson heeded the call to serve in the administration of his former commander and moved to Upper Canada.
4. Mary Robinson (1787–1863) married Stephen Heward; Sarah Robinson (1789–1863) married D'Arcy Boulton. Both Heward and Boulton were Family Compact stalwarts and lived in Toronto. Esther Robinson (1795–1811) died at an early age.
5. As reported in Ethel Trewhella, *History of the Town of Newmarket* (Newmarket, ON: printer nk, 1957), 89.

6. Audrey Saunders Miller, ed., *The Journals of Mary O'Brien, 1828–1838* (Toronto: MacMillan Company of Canada, 1968), 43.

7. Andrew Borland built a post at the Narrows between Lakes Simcoe and Couchiching and traded furs from as far north as the French River. He became fluent in Native languages and was a major figure in the area north of Orillia.

8. The Rouge River Trail connected the mouth of that river on Lake Ontario to Lake Simcoe, the Don River Trail followed that river from Lake Ontario. The trails met at the ford on the Holland River where Hill built his dam, and Newmarket's Main Street followed the route of the trail going north towards Holland Landing and Lake Simcoe.

9. Colonel Richard G. England, of the 24th Regiment of Foot, had been sent to Canada in 1783. After three years at Montreal and Quebec, the regiment was ordered to garrison Fort Detroit and the western posts. Colonel England became commandant of Detroit in 1792. When Detroit was finally handed over to the Americans in July 1796, he moved across the river and the post he built there became Amherstburg, Upper Canada. The information attributed to Colonel England is quoted in F.R. Berchem, *The Yonge Street Story, 1793–1860* (Toronto: Natural Heritage Books, 1996), 62.

10. Supplies coming up Yonge Street, then but a muddy trail, were stored at this depot until they could be shipped up Lake Simcoe and over the next portage to Lake Huron. By using this route the British supplied their posts on the Upper Lakes without having to send ships past Detroit.

11. From *www.britishempire.co.uk*.

## ৩৶ Chapter 2: The Real Pioneers ৩৶

ETHEL TREWHELLA PROVIDES a good deal of information on "Beman the Hustler," and the material is backed up by the *Upper Holland Conservation Report* (Ontario Department of Planning and Development, 1953) and *Three Centuries of Robinsons*, a fine family history by Julia Jarvis (published by the author in 1967). How the "Teenager," William Roe, saved the colony's treasury is another Ned Roe story (the article published in the

*Era* in January 1973) telling the story of his grandfather and the gold in the War of 1812, but it is also in *Toronto of Old* by Henry Scadding (Willing & Williamson of Toronto, 1878), and the story of the Srigley's ,"Some Sigleys," comes from the Srigley journal written by family historian Alvin Mylo Srigley (a typewritten copy is available at Newmarket Public Library, local history section). The Beswick ("First Doctor") mystery is found in the Bogart history in the *Newmarket Old Boys' Reunion Souvenir Booklet* (1939), available from Newmarket Historical Society Archives. Eli Gorham's tale is recorded many places, but the best is the "Bogart Journal" also found in *Newmarket Old Boys' Reunion Souvenir Booklet*. It may, in fact, be based on Gorham's own, now lost journal. The background for the "First Settler's House" comes from my earlier pictorial book, *Newmarket: The Heart of York Region* (Dundurn Press, 1994). Peter Robinson's adventures in the War of 1812 war are part of his biography in the *Dictionary of Canadian Biography* (DCB).

## Notes

1.  Robert Saunders, "Elisha Beman," Dictionary of Canadian Biography online, Vol. VI, *www.biographia.ca*.
2.  *Ibid.*
3   Trewhella, *History of the Town of Newmarket*, 369.
4.  Walter Roe, father of William, arrived in Detroit in 1789 while it was still under British control and built a thriving law practice there. He was the acting head of the British administration in Detroit at the handover of the fort to the United States. It was he who turned over the keys to the American officers. He then crossed the river to Amherstburg and continued with his law practice.
5.  Trewhella, *History of the Town of Newmarket*, 46, and also told to the author by Edward "Ned" Roe, grandson of William Roe.
6.  The story of the legend can be found in the Srigley family history manuscript, housed in the Newmarket Public Library.
7.  Julia Jarvis, *Three Centuries of Robinsons* (Toronto: self published, 1967), 165.
8.  Wendy Cameron, "Peter Robinson," Dictionary of Canadian Biography online, Vol. II, *www.biographie.ca*.

9. From a conversation with Marjorie Richardson of Whitchurch (now deceased), circa 1979.
10. Wendy Cameron, "Peter Robinson," Dictionary of Canadian Biography online.

## ❧ Chapter 3: Landmarks and Other Artifacts ❧

BACKGROUND INFORMATION ON ponds and kettle lakes comes from the *Upper Holland Conservation Report*, (Ontario Department of Planning and Development, 1953) and *A Legend Lives: The Story of Lake St. George* by John Kileeg and published by the Metro Toronto and Region Conservation Authority in 1989). Any good map of mid-nineteenth-century York County shows the locations of villages that are no more. *The Illustrated Historical Atlas of York County 1878* (Miles & Co., Toronto) is one good source. Digging out information about these now lost villages is a little trickier, but most areas now have local histories. Ethel Trewhella's book helped here in Newmarket's case. "The Road to Uxbridge" started out as local legend, but accounts in the *Upper Holland Conservation Report, 1953* (Holland Valley Conservation Authority), *The Life & Times of Joseph Gould* by W.H. Higgins (Fitzhenry & Whiteside, Toronto, 1972), and the *York County Atlas 1878,* helped to turn fiction into fact. Trewhella, the *Era* files, and the Alexander Muir Public School history (a paper by Linda E. Ross, entitled "The School and the Man" and printed in 1976 to mark the closing of the school), provided information on Newmarket's first schools.

Much about the pioneer cemetery is personal recollection, but the information on fur trader John MacDonald is to be found in *Documents Relating to the North West Company* by W. Stewart Wallace (published by The Champlain Society in 1934), and *The History of Simcoe County* by Andrew F. Hunter (published by the Historical Committee of Simcoe County in Barrie, 1948). The Carthews have an article in *DCB*, and *Lions in the Way* by Anne Wilkinson, a history of the Osler family (published by The Macmillan Company of Canada Limited, Toronto, 1956) provided more useful information for the story "Early Pioneers Buried in Eagle Street Cemetery."

**Notes**

1. Trewhella, *History of the Town of Newmarket*, 121–26. A quote from the now lost journal of Eli Gorham.
2. George Luesby, "Fairy Lake" Newmarket Historical Society Paper, Vol. 1, No. 4 (1986), 1.
3. Trewhella, *History of the Town of Newmarket*, 122.
4. *Ibid.*, 70.
5. A reform movement dedicated to bringing about responsible government grew up in Lower Canada in parallel with a similar movement in Upper Canada. Louis-Joseph Papineau was the leader in Lower Canada of the Patriots and rebellion was the result. In Upper Canada, William Lyon Mackenzie was the leader of the portion of the Reform movement that resorted to rebellion.
6. *Colonial Advocate*, August 1837.

## ❧ Chapter 4: Who Were These People? ❧

THE DEBATE OVER the first white child born in York County was found in the *Era* columns, with more information the *History of the Children of Peace* by Emily McArthur (published by York Pioneer & Historical Society in Toronto in 1898 and reprinted 1967). The Cawthras are still a well-known family in the Toronto area, and John Cawthra's account of the War of 1812 is in Henry Cawthra, *Notes from Past and Present*, published by James and Williams of Toronto in 1924. The account of the fire is taken from the unpublished manuscript, "Reminiscences of Former Days," by Clayton Webb, circa 1850, (a typewritten copy is in the author's collection) and "Recollections" by Rachel Webb Haight dated 1928, the unpublished manuscript is also in the author's collection.

The man known as Lord North in early Newmarket, North Richardson, told his friends his father had eliminated him from any possibility of title when he decided to settle in Upper Canada, according to page 13 of the *Newmarket Centennial Book*, published by the Town of Newmarket in 1957. He settled in Newmarket in 1805, and throughout his life held many positions such as court clerk and notary public, according to references in Ethel Trewhella's the *History of the Town of Newmarket*, pages 51, 91, 104, 222, 240. Richardson descendants still live in the area today.

The story of the veteran of Wellington's army who feasted on his enemies came from the *History of Simcoe County* by Andrew F. Hunter. Details of Richard Lippincott's troubles during the American Revolution are found in John Ross Robertson's *Landmarks of Toronto* (page 543), *The Man Who Dared Lightning* by Thomas Fleming (published by Morrow & Co. of New York in 1971, page 454), *The Yonge Street Story* by F.R. Berchem (Natural Heritage Books, 1977), and the *History of Toms River*, published by the Township of Toms River, New Jersey, in 1767, from the website, *www.tomsrivertownship.com.* The best source for Captain Joseph Hewitt and the North American Hotel is Erastus Jackson's interview with Eleanor Hewitt in the *Era* (November 5, 1897). Dr. John Dawson's arrival with all his family and goods comes from Trewhella's *History of the Town of Newmarket*, from conversations with Joyce Dawson Hughes, a descendant, and from Ernest Hemingway's October 1923 *Toronto Star* article.

## Notes

1.  Emily McArthur, *History of the Children of Peace* (Toronto: Baxter Publishing for the York Pioneer and Historical Society, 1967), 2.
2.  Benjamin Cody, letter to the editor of the *Era*, nd.
3.  *Ibid.*
4.  Arthur G. Dorland, *The Quakers in Canada* (Toronto: Ryerson Press, 1968), 104.
5.  James Keith Johnson, *Being Prominent: Regional Leaders in Upper Canada, 1791–1841* (Montreal: McGill-Queen's University Press, 1989), 181.
6.  Henry Cawthra, *Notes from Past and Present* (Toronto: James and Williams, 1924).
7.  *Ibid.*
8.  *Ibid.*
9.  *Ibid.*
10. Peter Whitely, *Lord North: The Prime Minister Who Lost America* (London, UK: Continuum International Publishing Group, 1996), 1.

11. An election open house meant voters could stay overnight at a local inn, and eat and drink at the candidates' expense. An individual was only expected to stay one night. Each candidate chose a tavern for their supporters.

12. The Holland Landing lift lock was one of three lift locks built on the Newmarket Canal between 1907 and 1911. The canal was to move barges from Lake Simcoe up to Newmarket and back down. None of the locks were completely built when the Conservative government of Robert Borden killed the project, but all remain as landmarks today.

13. Julia Jarvis, *Three Centuries of Robinsons*, 162.

14. The subdivision was built and sold. Success depends on which of the residents one talks to. They paid a premium for the homes, and many do not now feel it was worth it. Newer technology quickly outdated their "high-tech homes."

## Chapter 5: Things Happen

INFORMATION ON EVERYDAY life in the Yonge Street colony during the War of 1812 is scarce, but some good sources are Trewhella, *East Gwillimbury in the 19th Century* by Gladys Rolling (published by the Township of East Gwillimbury in 1967), the *Upper Holland Conservation Report 1953*, *History of Simcoe County*, *A Summary of the Historical Development of York Region*, (published by the Regional Municipality of York in 1974), and *The Quakers in Canada* by Arthur G. Dorland. An account of the shooting at Dye's Inn was in *At Home in Newmarket*, a 1980 publication of the Newmarket Historical Society written by Jan Choppin, an owner of the building at the time. The defeat of the Dye's Inn ghost was told to me by Agnes Pretty, the victor and at a later time an owner of the building.

The murder of poor Isaac James is found in *The Life and Times of Joseph Gould* by W.H. Higgins. The stories of the 1837 Rebellion have many sources including the Gould biography. *The Life and Times of the Patriots* by E.G. Guillet (University of Toronto Press, 1968), and *The Rebellion of 1837 in Upper Canada*, edited by Ronald Stagg and Colin Read (The Champlain Society, Ontario Series XII, 1985) are two of the best. The great nineteenth-century fire is well documented in the *Era* and by Trewhella in her *History of the Town of Newmarket*.

## Notes

1.  Letter from Thomas Selby to a brother living in New York, dated in May 1819, as recorded in Ethel Trewhella, *History of the Town of Newmarket*, 75.
2.  *Ibid.*
3.  Author conversations with Agnes Pretty during 1989.
4.  *Ibid.*
5.  Letter to *The Era*, specific date not known but likely in 1892.
6.  Andrew F. Hunter, *A History of Simcoe County*, Vol. II (Barrie, ON: Historical Committee of Simcoe County, 1948), 2.
7.  Henry Scadding, *Toronto of Old: Collections and Recollections* (Toronto: William and Williamson, 1878), 492.
8.  Captain Basil Hall, R.N., *Travels in North America in 1827–28* (Edinburgh: Cadell & Co., 1829), 36.
9.  Andrew F. Hunter, *A History of Simcoe County*, Vol. II, 15.
10. Albert Schrauwers, *The Children of Peace and the Village of Hope, 1812–1889* (Toronto: University of Toronto Press, 1993), 243.
11. "Recollections of Moses Hayter," Pioneer Papers, No. 1, Simcoe County Pioneer and Historical Society, Barrie, Ontario (1908), 14.
12. *Ibid.*
13. According to *The Rebellion of 1837 in Upper Canada*, edited by Colin Read and Ronald J. Stagg, the Champlain Society, Carleton Library Series, 1985. The number of petitioners was between 12,000 and 20,000.

## ❧ Chapter 6: In Victoria's Reign ❧

THE STORY OF Colonel William Beresford's mansion "Mud Brick Mansion Boasted Wine Cellar" is in *Whitchurch Township*, prepared by the Whitchurch History Book Committee, (Boston Mills Press, 1993). The accounts of the Butcher's Fair and the first industries on Fairy Lake are drawn from earlier issues of *The Newmarket Era*, circa 1885 and 1897.

Susan MacDonald of Hamilton, a descendant of the Mosiers, wrote an article for the Newmarket Historical Society newsletter (November1993) on the "Mansion House"; the manuscript is in my possession. Details of the buttered-bread incident in "Mansion House a Meeting Place for Rebels" are in Henry Cawthra's *Notes from Past and Present*. The story of how York County came to be the home of responsible government is taken from *The Union of the Canadas, 1841–57*, by J.M.S. Careless and published by McClelland & Stewart in 1967.

Many other stories in this section — the election of 1867, the search for buried gold, the North York County Fair, the May 24th celebrations in 1862, the Fenian scare, and the meeting opposed to Riel — all came from news stories in the back issues of *The Newmarket Era*.

## Notes

1. From a promotional brochure for a subdivision called "On Bogart Pond" built around the pond by the Rockport Group of Toronto in 1995.
2. *The Newmarket Era*, August 3, 1855, 3.
3. *The Newmarket Era*, May 31, 1871, 3.
4. Henry Cawthra, *Notes from the Past and Present*.
5. Robert Terence Carter, *Newmarket: The Heart of York Region* (Toronto: Dundurn Press, 1994), 32.
6. Letter from Susan MacDonald to the author, October 1993.
7. Captain John Mosier was a master mariner from Kingston who claimed he supported the government in a number of battles during the 1837 Rebellion. Among them was the attack on the steamer *Caroline* by a party led by Royal Navy Captain Andrew Drew. In a petition for compensation Mosier said that he had the charge of three brigades of boats, under the command of Captain Drew. In an 1842 petition to the Governor-General, Sir Charles Bagot, Captain Mosier claimed he suffered financial loss in his vocation as mariner because ports on the American side the St. Lawrence River and Lake Ontario were closed to him by American officials sympathetic to the rebels. He asked Bagot to sell him the government-owned Pigeon Island, a two-acre island in the St. Lawrence River about eighteen miles from

Kingston. However, he was opposed by Wolfe Island's fishermen, who said they had used Pigeon Island as a convenient base for the past thirty years. He didn't get the island. His petition can be found on *http://freepages.geneology.rootsweb.ancestry.com/~theislands*.

8. Source of quote currently not located.

9. See *www.sharontemple.ca/biographies/baldwin-lafontaine*.

10. Background and quotes from Newmarket Village Council Minutes, December 1866 and January 1867; *Newmarket Era*, December 28, 1866, and January 11, 1867; *Upper Canada Law Journal*, March 1867.

11. *Newmarket Era*, December 28, 1866, 2.

12. *Ibid.*

13. *The Newmarket Era*, January 11, 1867.

14. *Ibid.*

15. Percy J. Robinson, *Toronto Under the French Regime, 1615–1793* (Toronto: The Ryerson Press, 1933), 91.

16. Ethel Trewhella, *History of the Town of Newmarket*, 197.

17. Thomas Scott was an Upper Canadian whose 1870 execution by the firing squad sparked meetings of protest and concern over all of the Canadian provinces. He was from Ontario and was protesting against Louis Riel and the Provisional Government he established. The execution eventually led to the Wolseley Expedition being sent to quell the Red River Rebellion.

18. *The Newmarket Era*, April 22 and April 29, 1870.

19. *The Newmarket Era*, April 22, 1870.

## ⚜ Chapter 7: Fascinating Folk ⚜

THE BUFFALO BILL story was obtained from a member of the Cody family, Bob Cody, a lifelong resident of Newmarket except for his overseas service in the Second World War, circa 1983, and from an *Era* story on a Cody family reunion held in Newmarket, *The Newmarket Era*, July 27, 1939. Information for the lawyer Blackstone story came from a number of sources, including *East Gwillimbury in the 19th Century, History of Simcoe County*, and *Toronto of Old*. Samuel Holland's biography is contained in the *Dictionary of Canadian Biography*, and Fleetfoot Corbiére's story is in

*The Era* of July 23, 1942, and the *History of Simcoe County.* I learned about the Bishop's Throne from Ned Roe, and, in fact, he kept the chair in my home for safekeeping until the museum was founded in 1982. The account of Colonel Joseph Hill's life was supplied by a descendant, Mrs. A.M. Armstrong, in 1984, and more information came from *Lions in the Way*, the Osler family history.

Heroes of the plague came from Ethel Trewhella's work, and the story of Samuel Morse's telegraph demonstration is in a back issue of the *Era*, an interview with Eleanor Hewitt, November 5, 1897. A good biography on Morse is Carleton Mabee's, *The American Leonardo: The Life of Samuel F.B. Morse,* published by Alfred A. Knoff, 1943. The story of Reeve Gorham came from the *Era*, Gorham's obituary of July 1883. Mrs. Howard's donation of a church bell, which subsequently rang for the first time for her funeral, came from *The Old Boys Reunion Booklet.* For information on Benoni Irwin, the "Farmboy" artist, see David Dearinger, *Painting and Sculpture in the National Academy of Design, Washington, D.C.* (Manchester, VT: Hudson Hill Press LLC [Limited Liability Company], 2004). Other information on Irwin came from his obituary in the *Louisville Courier* (Kentucky), August 26, 1896, page 20; the Newmarket Historical Society Newsletter, March 1994; and the *New York Times*, October 1867.

## Notes

1.  *The Newmarket Era,* July 27, 1939
2.  F.J. Thorpe, "Holland Samuel Johannes," *Dictionary of Canadian Biography,* Vol. 5 (1801–1820), online edition *www.biographi.ca.*
3.  In 1832, a great cholera epidemic from Europe arrived in London in February of that year. See C.M. Godfrey, *The Cholera Epidemics of Upper Canada, 1832–1866* (Toronto: Seccombe House, 1968), 12, and Appendix A.
5.  Mary Bellis, "The History of Electric Telegraph and Telegraphy," *http://inventors.about.com.*
6.  Ethel Trewhella, *History of the Town of Newmarket*, 151.
7.  *Louisville Courier*, nd.

## ❦ Chapter 8: Growing into a Town ❦

NEWMARKET'S RECENT MILITARY history is well documented in books such as *The Queen's York Rangers: An Historic Regiment* by Stewart H. Bull (Boston Mills Press, 1984), and on the Rangers' own website *www.qyrang. ca*. I am also indebted to the late Major Knobby Sproule for his advice and the use of some of his library. G.S. Porter's assessment of Newmarket in 1852 was left to us by Erastus Jackson and was included in Jackson's January 1919 obituary in *The Newmarket Era*. The Irwin Report was also carried in *The Newmarket Era* and is in the town records of the day. The newspaper's own history I researched at Archives Ontario while editor of the paper and wrote a story for its 125th anniversary edition.

The three mayors from the Cane family are part of town records, and the story of the charcoal maker is put together from information in *The Newmarket Era* and *East Gwillimbury in the 19th Century*. Information on the Hisson family, the Tamars, and other families, the Quakers and the Underground Railroad is from Gladys M. Rolling, *East Gwillimbury In The Nineteenth Century* (Sharon, ON: self-published, 1967), and from the *Aurora Banner* of July 7, 1939. I learned about how to tend a charcoal mound from Eric Sloane's *America* (published by William Funk Inc. of New York in 1956, pages 339–41). Ned Roe told me about the founding of the Citizen's Band, and Major Philip Boylen gave me the actual petition, which is now in the Newmarket Historical Society Archives. The history of the Stickwood bricks came from the late Frances Stickwood Walker of Newmarket, the last family member to live on the eighty-eight-acre Stickwood farm on Mulock Drive, now the Stickwood-Walker Park. Stories of the strange societies came from files of the *Newmarket Era* and *The Era* and personal recollections.

## Notes

1. G.S. Porter started *The New Era* but he only lasted a year, complaining that not enough people in the town could read to make the newspaper and printing business viable. In the spring of 1853 he sold to Erastus Jackson and a partner, and left for Australia. The partner soon left too,

and, in 1861, Jackson changed the name from *The New Era* to *The Newmarket Era*.

2.  Milling stones for grinding grain came in pairs or runs as they were known. Four run would be eight stones.

3.  "Report of Census Commissioner," by E.P.Irwin, 1861, in the municipal records.

4.  *The Newmarket Era*, March 12, 1915.

5.  *The Newmarket Era*, October 11, 1879.

6.  For more information on the Hisson family, see Linda Brown-Kubish, *The Queen's Bush Settlement: Black Pioneers 1839–1865* (Toronto: Natural Heritage Books, 2004), 184–85. Included is a photograph of Edward John Hisson and his home in Glen Allen, Peel Township, Wellington County.

7.  The petition was mounted in a two-sided maple frame by Major Philip Boylen of Etobicoke before he donated it to the Newmarket Historical Society Archives in 1974. The petition remains in the archives.

8.  The name Kanata Festival was chosen by the organizers for the 1980 celebration of the centennial of Newmarket's incorporation as a town, held June 6–10, 1980. *Kanata* is an aboriginal word meaning "village." The organization's members then dubbed themselves Kanataites. Although the organization has disappeared, the town continues to apply "Kanata" as a name for a municipally-sponsored July 1 weekend festival.

9.  *The Newmarket Era*, July 5, 1867.

## ❧ Chapter 9: More Life In the Nineteenth Century ❧

THE STORIES OF the artesian well going wild, the oldest companies in town, the regatta, the missing Baptist Church clock, the merchant who was found murdered, the three town halls, the Boer War celebration that ended with a bang, and how Minnie murdered Susie, all came from files of the *Era*. The history of the Ontario, Simcoe & Huron Railway and its successors is detailed in *The Railways of Canada 1871* by J.M. and E.D.W. Trout, published by the Monetary Times of Toronto in 1871. Recollections of Glenville are from the *Early Settlement of King Township* by published by Elizabeth Gillham of King City in 1975.

## Notes

1. Ethel Trewhella, *History of the Town of Newmarket*, 98.
2. *The Newmarket Era*, February 26, 1890.
3. Robert Simpson arrived in Newmarket in 1856 at age twenty-two to work in his cousin's general store, D. Sutherland & Sons. In 1858, when Sutherland sold the business to William McMaster, Simpson went into business with a partner, William Trent. The partnership split after four years and Simpson took Moses Bogart as a partner. In 1870 their store burned down. Simpson quickly rebuilt across the road and reopened as the Robert Simpson Co. In June 1871 he closed the Newmarket store and moved the company to Queen Street in Toronto.
4. The Constitutional Act of 1791 set aside one-seventh of all Crown lands in Upper Canada for the support of the Protestant clergy. What remained of these lands in 1854 was secularized and the revenues transferred to government, including local governments.
5. *Newmarket Era*, May 19, 1882.
6. *Ibid.*, August 26, 1896.
7. *Ibid.*
8. *Ibid.*

## ❧ Chapter 10: New Century ❧

THE RADIAL RAILWAY has often been written about, but among the best sources are *Riding the Rails*, by Robert M. Stamp (Boston Mills Press, 1991), and the *Upper Canada Railway Society Newsletter 1973*, now part of the author's library. The society is now defunct. The *Newmarket Era* followed the move of area families to the west closely and sometimes printed settlers' letters home. A biography of Sir William Mulock is on Library and Archives Canada website, *www.collectionscanada.gc.ca*. The abandoned Newmarket Canal is well-documented in *A Work Unfinished* by James T. Angus (Severn Publications, 2000) and in George Luesby's Newmarket Historical Society Occasional Paper, "The Newmarket Canal" (1989), available through the Newmarket Historical Society, 134 Main Street South, Newmarket, Ontario, L3Y 3Y7.

"The First Santa Claus Parade," the search for gas and oil beneath Newmarket, and the first subdivision, all came from *The Newmarket Era* files. "Steam whistles sounded daily" drew heavily on an article by Elman Campbell in his *Some Early Memories of Newmarket* (Newmarket Historical Society, 1990), and information for the First Hospital came from a number of sources including *York County Hospital: A Story of Faith and Courage* by Dr. Crawford Rose (published by York County Hospital, now Southlake Regional Health Centre, in 1972), the hospital's website (*www.southlakeregional.org*), and *The Newmarket Era* files.

## Notes

1. *The Newmarket Era*, July 13, 1883.
2. *Ibid.*, May 18, 1883.
3. William Mulock's widowed mother, Mary, moved to Pearson Street in Newmarket, when William was four, to be close to her parents; John Cawthra was her father. William attended the Newmarket Grammar School, graduated from University of Toronto in 1863 and articled with Alfred Boultbee's law office in Newmarket before being called to the bar in 1867. In 1882, he entered federal politics, winning election in the York North riding, centred on Newmarket, which he held until 1905. He was knighted in 1902. He maintained a large summer residence and two-hundred-acre estate on the outskirts of Newmarket. The remnants of the estate remain in family hands. A major thoroughfare, Mulock Drive and a secondary school have been named for Sir William.
4. See *www.thesantaclausparade.com*.
5. *The Newmarket Era*, December 28, 1883.
6. *Ibid.*
7. "The Salvation Army Newmarket Corps (1883–1983) Centennial Souvenir Program," 13.
8. *The Newmarket Era*, January 4, 1884.
9. *Ibid.*, February 1, 1884.
10. *Ibid.*, May 9, 1884.
11. *Ibid.*, June 13, 1884.
12. *Ibid.*

13. *Ibid.*
14. *Ibid.*, August 22, 1884.
15. Ethel Trewhella, *History of the Town of Newmarket*, 153–54.
16. *Ibid.*
17. *Ibid.*
18. *Ibid.*, 154.

## ✤ Chapter 11: War and Depression ✤

THE STORY OF Newmarket's battalion, the 127th, and the one about Newmarket's First World War dead comes from *The Queen's York Rangers,* the *Newmarket Old Boys Reunion* booklet, and from the Newmarket Historical Society Occasional Paper *Newmarket's War Dead in World War One* by Robert Terence Carter (2008), available from the Newmarket Historical Society. MacGregor Dawson's biography *William Lyon Mackenzie King* (University of Toronto Press, 1958), details King's obsession with this riding, and more information came from election coverage in *The Newmarket Era.*

The Redmen's 1933 national title story is also from *The Newmarket Era.* The recollections of the 1940s and the army camp are mostly the author's, and "The Fifth Column Scare Triggered Wartime Paranoia" is taken from *The Newmarket Era,* with additional background from *The Beaver,* January 1994. The story of Bill Pipher, our first war casualty, came from an *Era* report and from personal recollections.

### Notes

1.  J.C. Boylen, *Newmarket Old Boys' Reunion Souvenir Booklet,* 1939, 32.
2.  Stewart H. Bull, *The Queen's York Rangers: An Historic Regiment* (Erin, ON: Boston Mills Press, 1984), 167.
3.  The 20th was fighting at Mons, Belgium, when the war ended on November 11, 1918. Following a week's rest, the battalion started on the long march into Germany on November 18. It reached the Rhine border early in December. For three months the men were billeted in a small town near Bonn, then returned to England where the battalion

took part in a great victory parade in London. From there the 20th left for home, arriving by rail on May 24, 1919, at the CPR Station on Yonge Street below St. Clair Avenue in Toronto. The 20th Battalion made a last route march down Yonge Street and along Bloor to Varsity Stadium for the final dispersal and welcome by families.

4. From a letter quoted in *The Newmarket Era*, June 3, 1917, in an article on Alexander Brodie's death from a shoulder wound.
5. *The Newmarket Era*, June 13, 1917.
6. *Express-Herald* (Newmarket), November 23, 1917.
7. McGregor Dawson, *William Lyon Mackenzie King: A Political Biography* (Toronto: University of Toronto Press, 1958), 269.
8. *Ibid.*, 289.
9. *The Newmarket Era*, October 30, 1925.
10. From *The Newmarket Centennial, 1857–1957*, published by the Newmarket Centennial Committee in 1957, page 71.
11. *Ibid.*
12. *Ibid.*
13. Larry Hannant, "Fifth Column Crisis," *The Beaver* (December 1993–January 1944), 24–28.

## 🌱 Chapter 12: Later in the Century 🌱

THE CREST THEATRE, founded and run by a wealthy Newmarket family, spurred a renaissance in Toronto's live theatre community. Conversations with Donald Davis, and many with Ruby Haskett, the *Era's* dedicated theatre expert for many years, came in handy here. And of course, "Tall Tales of Past Pranks" were personal recollections of the author and his friends. *Goodbye Sousa* was made by Tony Ianuzielo, one of the author's oldest friends, and that was why, after the premiere, the party was held at my place. Information on Fred Hagen came from Ontario College of Art staff lists, from post office publicity on him in 1986 the year the stamps he designed were issued, and from personal conversation.

The "Marsh Moonshiners" were almost folk heroes in this area during the "dry" days. The *Era* covered their trials and some information came from conversations with Arleigh Armstrong, the father of a boyhood friend, and with Holland Landing residents. The "Race to Build A Mall" was covered by the author as a reporter.

## Notes

1. From interview with Donald Davis as published in the *Town Crier* (Toronto), circa 1988.
2. *Ibid.*
3. *Ibid.*
4. *The Newmarket Era*, December 8, 1938.
5. *Ibid.*
6. *Ibid.*
7. Story told to author, circa 1947.
8. Personal recollection of the author.
9. Undated letter to author from Mrs. Elmer (Alma) Starr, circa 1975.
10. Interview with Alma Starr, during 1978.

# Selected Bibliography

Angus, James T. *A Work Unfinished*. Orillia, ON: Severn Publications, 2000.

Berchem, F.R. *The Yonge Street Story, 1793-1860*. Toronto: Natural Heritage Books, 1996.

Boylen, J.C. "The 127th Battalion." In *Newmarket Old Boys' Reunion Souvenir Booklet*. Newmarket, ON: Express-Herald, 1939.

Bull, Stewart H. *The Queen's York Rangers: An Historic Regiment*. Erin: Boston Mills Press, 1984.

Campbell, Elman. *Some Early Memories of Newmarket*. Newmarket, ON: Newmarket Historical Society, 1990.

Careless, J.M.S. *The Union of the Canadas, 1841–57*. Toronto: McClelland & Stewart, 1967.

Carter, Robert Terence. *Newmarket: The Heart of York Region*. Toronto: Dundurn Press, 1994.

Cawthra, Henry. *Notes from the Past and Present*. Toronto: James and Williams, 1924.

Choppin, Jan. *At Home in Newmarket*. Newmarket, ON: Newmarket Historical Society, 1980.

Cranston, J.H. *Étienne Brûlé: Immortal Scoundrel*. Toronto: The Ryerson Press: 1949.

Dawson, MacGregor. *William Lyon Mackenzie King: A Political Biography*. Toronto: University of Toronto, 1958.

Dearinger, Davis. *Painting and Sculpture in the National Academy of Design, Washington, D.C.* Manchester, VT: Hudson Hill Press LLC, 2004.

Densmore, Christopher, and Albert Schrauwers. *The Best Man for Settling a New Country: The Journal of Timothy Rogers, 1790–1810.* Toronto: Canadian Friends Historical Society, 2000.

Dorland, Arthur G. *The Quakers in Canada: A History.* Toronto: The Ryerson Press, 1968.

Fleming, Thomas. *The Man Who Dared Lightening.* New York: Morrow & Co., 1971.

Gillham, Elizabeth. *Early Settlement of King Township.* King City, ON: self-published, 1975.

Godfrey, C.M. *The Cholera Epidemic of Upper Canada, 1832–1866.* Toronto: Seccombe House, 1968.

Guillet, E.G. *The Life and Times of the Patriots.* Toronto: University of Toronto Press, 1968.

Hall, Captain Basil R.N. *Travels in North America in 1827–28.* Edinburgh: Cadell & Co., 1829.

Higgins, W.H. *The Life & Times of Joseph Gould.* Toronto: Fitzhenry & Whiteside, 1972.

Hunter, Andrew F. *The History of Simcoe County.* Barrie, ON: The Historical Committee of Simcoe County, 1948.

*The Illustrated Historical Atlas of York County, 1878.* Toronto: Miles & Co., 1878.

Jarvis, Julia. *Three Centuries of Robinsons.* Toronto: self-published, 1967.

Johnson, James Keith. *Being Prominent: Regional Leaders in Upper Canada, 1791–1841.* Montreal: McGill-Queen's University Press, 1989.

Mabee, Carleton. *The American Leonardo: The Life of Samuel F.B. Morse.* New York: Alfred A. Knoff, 1943.

McArthur, Emily. *History of the Children of Peace.* Toronto: York Pioneer & Historical Society, 1898. Reprinted 1967.

Miller, Audrey Saunders. *The Journals of Mary O'Brien, 1828–1838.* Toronto: Macmillan Company of Canada, 1968.

*The Newmarket Centennial Book.* Newmarket, ON: Town of Newmarket, 1957.

Robertson, John Ross. *Landmarks of Toronto,* Volumes 1–6. Toronto: *Toronto Evening Telegram,* 1894–1914.

Robinson, Percy J. *Toronto Under the French Regime, 1615–1793*. Toronto: The Ryerson Press, 1933.

Rollings, Gladys. *East Gwillimbury in the 19th Century*. East Gwillimbury, ON: Township of East Gwillimbury, 1967.

Rose, Dr. Crawford. *York County Hospital: A Story of Faith and Courage*. Newmarket, ON: York County Hospital, 1972.

Scadding, Henry. *Toronto of Old: Collections and Recollections*. Toronto: Willing & Williamson, 1878.

Schrauwers, Albert. *The Children of Peace and the Village of Hope, 1812–1889*. Toronto: University of Toronto Press, 1993.

Stagg, Ronald and Colin Read, eds. *The Rebellion of 1837*. Toronto: The Champlain Society, 1985.

Stamp, Robert M. *Riding the Rails*. Erin: Boston Mills Press, 1991.

Trewhella, Ethel. *History of the Town of Newmarket*. Newmarket, ON: Newmarket Centennial Committee, 1957.

Trout, J.M. and E.D.W. *The Railways of Canada 1871*. Toronto: The Monetary Times, 1871.

Wallace, W. Stewart. *Documents Relating to the North West Company*. Toronto: The Champlain Society, 1934.

Wilkinson, Anne. *Lions in the Way*. Macmillan Company of Canada, 1956.

Whitchurch History Book Committee. *Whitchurch Township*. Erin: Boston Mills, 1993.

Whitely, Peter. *Lord North: The Prime Minister Who Lost America*. London, U.K.: Continuum International Publishing Group, 1996.

# INDEX

Agincourt, Ontario, 116
Albert Edward, Prince of Wales, 159
Alexander Muir Public School
    (Newmarket), 36, 55, 143, 222,
    231, 248
Algonquin First Nation, 20
Allan, Lieutenant-Colonel J.A.W.,
    141, 241
Allan, James, 175
Allegheny Mountains, Pennsylvania, 84
Allen family, 57
Allen, Mrs. Mary, 124
Allied Occupation Force, 214
Allward, Walter, 184
American Army, 35
American Civil War, 71, 119, 123, 153
American Regiment(s), army, troops,
    66, 76
American Revolution (*see also* War
    of Independence), 28, 29, 42, 43,
    70, 142
Anchor Park (Holland Landing), 78
Andastes First Nation, 20
Anderson, Sergeant Anthony, 136
Anderson, Police Chief P.J., 185

Angus, James T., 198, 258
Ansnorveldt (Holland Marsh), 219
Antrim County, Ireland, 149
Armentières, Battle of, 214
Armitage, Amos, 50
Armitage, community of, 50, 188, 195
Armstrong, Mrs. A.A., 255
Armstrong, Arleigh, 237, 261
Armstrong, John, 216
Arnott, __, 46
Arthur, Lieutenant Governor Sir
    George, 91, 92
Arthur Township (Wellington
    County), 227
Ashworth, John, 102
Asiatic cholera, 132
Aurora, Ontario, 51, 52, 62, 96, 120,
    123, 141, 151, 155, 160, 165, 168,
    176, 182, 189, 191, 195, 196, 201,
    207, 203, 217, 256
Aurora Agricultural Society, 114
*Aurora Banner*, 147, 148, 166
Aurora Fair and Horse Show, 114
Aurora Rifle Company, 140
Aurora Sideroad, 53–54

Aylesworth, Allen B., 198
Aylesworth's Ditch, 198

Bache, Mr. __, 46
Battalions, Militia, Rangers,
    Regiments
    1st American Regiment (Simcoe's
        Queen's Rangers), 142
    25th Armoured Regiment
        (Queen's York Rangers), 141
    2nd Battalion, Canadian Railway
        Troops, 211, 212
    4th Battalion of the First
        Division, Canadian
        Expeditionary Force, 214
    12th Battalion, York Volunteers
        (York Rangers), 120, 122,
        140, 141, 158, 214, 182, 214
    20th Battalion (York Rangers),
        141, 214, 260, 261
    49th Battalion, Alberta Regiment,
        214
    127th Battalion (York Rangers),
        141, 211, 212, 214, 260
    220th Battalion (York Rangers),
        141
    4th Brigade Division for North-
        West duty (Wolseley
        Expedition), 122
    3rd Regiment, York Militia, 64, 212
    24th Regiment of Foot, British
        Army, 28–30, 245–46
    69th Regiment of Foot, British
        Army, 131
    1st York Militia, 43
    Associated Loyalists, 71
    Glengarry Regiment, 71–72
    Her Majesty's 64th Regiment, 58
    New Jersey Militia, 71
    Peel Militia, 214
    Queen's Rangers (Loyalist
        battalion), 140, 142
    Queen's York Rangers, 141, 142

Roger's Rangers, 141
Royal American Regiment, 125
Royal Regiment of Canada, 184
Scarborough Rifle Company, 14
Simcoe Foresters, 141
Upper Canada Militia, 71
York Militia, 43, 64, 140, 141,
    212, 214
Back, Captain George, 40
Baird, Alexander, 218
Baldwin, Robert, 44, 106–08, 137, 172
Ballantrae, Ontario, 53
Baltimore, Maryland, 134, 138, 36
Barrie, Ontario, 92, 130, 131, 145,
    164, 208, 248
Bastedo, J.B., 228
Bathurst District, Upper Canada, 43
Baxter, Major James, 148
Beck, Sir Adam, 190
Bedford, New York (now Brooklyn),
    97
Belfry, Joseph, 175
Bell, Alexander Graham, 167
Bell Ewart (steamboat port), 164
Bell Telephone Company, 168, 169
Beman
    Eli, 34
    Squire Elisha, 22–24, 27, 28,
        31–34, 40–42, 54, 57, 69, 77,
        79, 86
    Esther (Sayre) Robinson (Mrs.
        Elisha), 34, 57, 69
    Joel, 34
Beman's Corners (Newmarket), 22,
    31, 243, 246
Bentley, Dr. Thomas, 193
Bentley, John, 112
Beresford, Colonel W.H., 98, 99, 252
Beswick, Dr. Christopher, 24, 37, 38,
    57, 58, 247
Binns, G.M., 148
Birthplace of Responsible
    Government, 106, 108

Black Creek Pioneer Village
(Toronto), 189
Black Rock, New York, 120
Blackhall, Private Herbert, 213
Blackstone
Henry William, 124, 254
Henry William Jr., 124
Sir William, 124
Blackstone family, 57
Blizzard, Thomas, 192, 193, 182
Boer War, 29, 141, 257
Bogart
E.A., 97
Constable Joe, 174
John Sr., 92, 96
John Jr., 97
Mary (see also Mary Smith [Mrs.
R.H. Smith]), 175
Moses, 176, 177, 258
Bogart family history, 244
Bogart Creek, 33, 143, 160
Bogart Pond, 96
Bogarttown, community of, 50, 92,
96–98, 174, 203, 227, 238
Bonaparte, Napoleon, 68
Bond Head, Ontario, 58, 194, 195
Bond Lake, 49, 189, 191, 198
Booth, William, 49
Borden, Prime Minister Sir Robert,
198
Borland, Andrew, 23–26, 34, 35, 77,
86, 245, 246
Borland & Roe (merchant partners),
24, 43, 131
Borthwick, Reverend Hugh, 56
Bosworth, William L., 176
Botsford, John, 166
Botsford, Mary Anne (see Mary Anne
Simpson)
Boultbee, Alfred, 108–12, 148, 149,
194, 259
Boultbee family, 57
Bowden, W.A., 190

Bowman, J.W., 149
Boyd, Mayor Dr. S.J., 225
Boylen, Major J.C., 211
Boylen, Major Philip, 256, 257
Bradford, Ontario, 131, 160, 165, 194,
202, 208, 218–19
Brammar, Joseph, 89, 90
Brammar, Ellen (Lundy), 89
Brantford, Ontario, 167
Brantford Gas and Oil Syndicate, 205
Briggs, Robert, 193
British Army, military garrisons, 24,
28, 30, 37, 64, 71, 77, 98, 103,
114, 130, 131, 214, 245
British-Canadian Band, 191
British Empire, 117, 151, 195
Brock, Major-General Sir Isaac, 43,
64–66, 71, 140, 212
Brock, Private Sherman, 213
Brodie
Private Alexander, 214, 215, 261
George, 214
Robert, 102
Brodie family, 57
Brown, George, 146
Brown, William, 175
Brown Bess (musket), 29
Brûlé, Etienne, 16, 19–21
Brunton, Lieutenant Reginald
Ruston, 213
Brunton, T.H., 75
Bucks County, Pennsylvania, 22, 36, 84
Buffalo, New York, 90
Bull, Major Stewart, 212
Burkett, Wright, 132–33
Burnham, E.W., 149
Butcher's Fair, 99–101, 181

Cain, Herb, 221
Caldwell, James B., 61, 89, 95, 133, 134
Caldwell, Sarah Jane, 133
Caldwell Chair Factory, 94
Cambridge Leaseholds Limited, 240

Cambridgeshire, England, 160
Campbell, Dr. __, 186
Campbell, E.G., 122
Campbell, Elman, 206, 259
Campbell, John (Earl of Loudoun), 126
Canada Temperance Act (1878), 238
Canadian Family Sewing Machine
    Company (Newmarket), 143
Canadian National Railway (CNR),
    157, 165
Canadian Navy, 225
Canadian Northern Railway, 190
Canadian Pacific Railway (CPR), 189
Canadian Press Association, 146
Canadian Society of Graphic Art, 234
Canadian Society of Painter-Etchers
    and Engravers, 234
Canadian Territorial Defence, 141
Canadian Tire, 75
Cane
    Henry Stiles, 150
    W.H.S. "Howard," 150, 183, 187
    William, 149–54, 181
Cane family, 149, 256
Cane Woodworking Company (later
    Dixon Pencil Company) (see also
    William Cane & Sons Ltd.), 115,
    144, 153, 199, 207
Cape Breton Island, 126
Cardinal, Douglas, 242
Carrying Place Trail, 21, 113
Carthew, Colonel Arthur, 57–58
Cassidy's Flowers (Newmarket), 94
Cataraqui (Kingston), 127
Cathers, C.A. "Tiny," 148
Cawthra
    Henry, 104, 105, 249
    John Joseph, 23, 64–67, 69, 70,
        80, 155, 172
    Mary (see Mary Mulock)
    William "Will," 105, 172
Cawthra family, 77, 86, 104, 194, 244,
    249

Cawthra House, 33
Cawthra's Mills, 67
Cedar Point (Newmarket), 47
Central Hotel (Glenville) 173
Central Hotel (Newmarket), 93
Champlain, Samuel de, 19, 20
Chapman, John, 193
Chappell, Sterling, 92
Charcoal maker, 153–54
Charleston, South Carolina, 135
Charlottetown, Prince Edward Island,
    126
Chicago, Illinois, 109, 111, 165, 178
Children of Peace (Sharon), 62, 90, 107
China Hall (Newmarket), 176–77
Chouaguen (Oswego, New York), 113
Christian Baptist Church, 157, 159,
    170, 171
Christian Church (now Christian
    Baptist Church), 25, 157, 159
Christian Society (Newmarket), 137
Christie, Michael, 82–84
Clarke, Colonel F.F., 211–12
Clarke, W.A., 102
Clarke Township, Upper Canada, 105
Clergy Reserve, 89, 180
Clergy Reserve Fund, 180
Cleveland, Ohio, 123
Clinton, Sir Henry, 71
Cobourg, Upper Canada, 146
Cochrane, Frank, 198
Cody
    Benjamin, 62, 63, 123
    Mrs. Benjamin, 238
    Bob, 254
    Isaac, 123
    Joseph, 62, 123
    Philip, 123
    William "Buffalo Bill" Frederick,
        123–24
Cody Family Association, 124
Colborne, Lieutenant Governor Sir
    John, 43, 44, 58

Collingwood, Ontario, 142, 164, 165, 231

Collins, Dodger, 221

Community Malls Inc. (Toronto), 240

Confederation, 121, 278

Connaught Gardens (Newmarket), 208, 209

Connecticut, 24, 38, 71, 137, 139

Cook, Francis, 229

Cook, Captain James, 126

Cook, LAC Ross, 229

Cook's Bay, Lake Simcoe, 157

Coombs, Major Albert, 202

Corbiére, Carlos (Charles Kirby), 131

Corbiére, Eli "Fleetfoot," 130, 131, 254

Cork, Ireland, 43, 48

Cornwall, Upper Canada, 23

Corporate Properties Limited (Newmarket), 240

Couchiching, Lake, 20, 32, 35, 103, 218, 246

Council of Quebec, 126

Cox Report, 205

Cranston, J. Herbert, 21, 244

Crest Theatre, The (Toronto), 230, 231, 261

Crew, William Babcock, 136

Crickmore, Evelyn (Hawes), 148

Culloden, Battle of, 37

Cumberland, Frederick, 166

Cummings, David, 79

Currie, Mathew, 23

Curry, Hannah (Kinsey), 132–33

D. Sutherland & Sons, 177, 258

Dales
    Beatrice, 209
    Joe, 209
    Dr. Lowell, 209–10

Davis
    Andy, 221
    Barbara Chilcott, 230–31
    Donald, 230–31
    E.J., 231
    Murray, 230–31

Davis family, 231

Davis Leather Company, 231

Davison, R.J., 175

Davisville Brickyard, 160

Dawson, Squire Dr. John, 57, 74, 75, 250

Dawson, Joyce (*see* Joyce Hughes)

Dawson, MacGregor, 216, 260

Dawson Manor (Newmarket), 73–75

Day, Professor William, 218–19

de Havilland Aircraft, 224

Denne, William, 208

Depression years, 148, 190, 209, 218, 219, 224

Detroit, Michigan (Fort Detroit), 22, 28, 29, 57, 65, 67, 77, 140, 246, 247

Detroit River, 65, 127

Dieterlie, Mr. __, 93

Dixon Pencil Company, 144, 206, 222, 223

Doan
    Abraham, 84
    Ebenezer, 84
    Elizabeth (Mrs. E.), 84
    Elizabeth (Reid) (Mrs. A.), 85
    G.R., 193
    George M., 192, 193
    Jesse, 192, 193
    John, 193

Dolan, George, 155

Dominion Junior Hockey Championship, 221

Doran, Silver, 221

Dorland, Arthur G., 64, 245, 251

Douville, Captain Alexandre, 114

Druery, James, 193

Druery, Thomas, 193

Drummond Island, 77

Dufferin, Governor General Lord, 137, 157, 158, 170

Duffin's Creek (Pickering Township), 52, 53

Duke and Duchess of York (later George V and Queen Mary), 159

Duncombe, Dr. Charles, 136

Dunlop, Captain Robert, 213

Dunn, John Henry, 44

Durham, Region of, 52

Dutchman's Bay, 46

Dye, Daniel, 24, 79

Dye, Michael, 24, 79

Dye's Inn (Newmarket), 24, 79–81, 251

Dymond, A.H., 112

Eagle Street Pioneer Burying Ground, 57–59, 132, 157, 248

East Gwillimbury, Township of (York County), 62, 63, 78, 83, 149, 151–54, 237, 251

East India Company, 36

Eaton, Timothy, 198

Ecobichon, Rodney "Rod," 167

Edmundson
Charles, 113
Charlie, 113
William, 113

Eldridge, Sergeant William G., 213, 215

Elgin, Lord, 108

Elton, Luther, 89

Elvidge, Corporal William, 213

Empy, Michael P., 173, 174, 176

England, Colonel Richard G., 28, 29

Era, The, 14, 15, 72, 111, 122, 144

Era Banner, The, 148–49

Erie, Fort, 120

Erie, Lake, 77

Evans, Arthur, 227

Express-Herald, 149, 216

Fairgrounds Park (formerly Newmarket Fairgrounds), 115, 116, 146

Fairy Lake (see also The Pond), 25, 33, 41, 45, 47, 48, 118, 133, 143, 161, 163, 169, 183, 222, 242, 252

Fairy Lake Gardens, 46

Falconbridge, Chief Justice William G., 186

Family Compact, 22, 23, 27, 34, 40–42, 64, 69, 74, 90, 166, 245

Fenians, 119–20

Festubert, Battle of, 214

Fifth Column, 226–28

First Nations people, traders, 19, 42, 45, 53, 74, 75, 77, 85–87, 113, 114, 236

First World War, 29, 141, 184, 209, 211, 216, 218, 223, 227, 228, 233, 260

Fleury, Lieutenant W.J., 141

Forder, Ran, 221

Forhan, Mayor Bob, 240

Forsythe, Mrs. Nellie, 180

Forsythe House (Newmarket), 100, 110, 180

Fort Alexander, 60

Fort Detroit (see Detroit)

Fort Erie, 120

Fort Frederick (Saint John, New Brunswick), 126

Fort Niagara, 114, 131

Fort Michilimackinac, 43, 64, 77

Foster, Morrice, 175

Foster, Tom, 236–37

Fourth Riding of York, 106, 107, 137, 172

Fox, __, 46

Fox, George H., 148

Franklin, Benjamin, 71

Franklin, Lady Jane, 57, 59, 61

Franklin, Sir John, 40, 57, 59, 61

Franklin, William, 71

Freddy Thompson's City Service (Newmarket), 223

French gold, 113–14

French Huguenots, 124
French River, 26, 246

Gain, Thomas, 155
Gamble, Nathaniel, 50
Gananoque, Upper Canada, 32
Garbutt Hill, community of, 51, 17
Gardners Foundry (Newmarket), 115
Gaudaur
  Francis, 103
  Jake Sr., 103
  CFL Commissioner Jake Jr., 103
Geer & Byers (Newmarket), 223
George, King V, 159
George, King VI, 159
Georgetown, Ontario, 190
Georgian Bay, 19, 32, 64, 196
Gibraltar Point (Toronto), 67
Gill, Jacob, 23
Gill family, 57
Gillham, Elizabeth, 172, 257
Givenchy, Battle of, 214
Gladman, H.M. "Herb," 228
Glengarry County, 66, 71
Glenville, village of (Cawthra Mills),
  51, 67, 172, 257
Glenville Distillery, 172
Glenville Methodist Church, 173
Glenville Pond, 232
Glenville school, 173
Glenville Temperance Hall, 173
*Goodbye Sousa*, 234, 261
Gorham, Eli, 24, 38, 39, 114, 135, 136,
  247, 249
Gorham, Nelson, 39, 121, 135, 136,
  205, 255
Gorham family, 39, 113, 136
Gorham Woollen Mills, 38, 39, 113,
  143, 167, 204
Graham
  Adam, 62
  Peter, 62
  Colonel William, 62

Grand Trunk Railway (GTR), 165,
  192, 196, 207, 209
Great Fire of 1862, 93, 94
Great Fire of 1871, 242
Great potato famine (Ireland), 132
Green Bay, Michigan, 165
Greensides, Rebecca, 186
Guelph, Ontario, 146, 153, 190, 218
Guinness Book of Records, 37

Hackett, George, 155
Hagen, Sir Frederick "Fred," 234–35,
  261
Hagen, Isabelle (Heald), 234
Haines, Walsley, 184
Haines family, 184
Haldimand, Frederick, 126, 127
Hall, Captain Basil, 86
Hall, Maurice "Mo," 224
Hamilton family, 57
Hancock, Bill, 221
Harrison, James, 155
Hartry, Fred, 46
Hartry's tannery, 46–47
Harvey, J.F., 149
Hastings County, Upper Canada, 106,
  108
Hawkes, Arthur, 148
Hawkstone, Upper Canada, 58
Hawley, Elijah, 24
Hawley, W., 23
Hayter, Moses, 91, 92, 252
Head, Lieutenant Governor Sir
  Francis Bond, 58, 89, 91, 104, 105
Heald, Isabelle (*see* Isabelle Hagen)
Hearst, William Randolph, 30
Hebb, Andrew, 148–49
Helmer, W.H., 184
Hemingway, Ernest, 73, 250
Henderson, E.R., 144, 145, 167
Henderson's Grocery, 94
Hewitt, Eleanor (McNulty), 104, 250,
  255

Hewitt, Captain Joseph, 71–73, 104, 105, 250
Hill, Edwin, 193
Hill, Joseph, 21, 22, 24–28, 32, 33, 38, 40, 41, 45–47, 101, 131–33, 246
Hill, Captain Joseph, 255
Hillsdale Dairy (Newmarket), 224
Hisson
    Edward John, 153, 257
    Henry, 151, 153–55, 256, 257
    Israel, 153
    Samuel, 153
    Sarah Jane (Mrs. H.), 151, 153
Historic Naval and Military Establishment (Penetang), 29
Hogg's Hollow (Toronto), 89, 190
Holland, Major Samuel Johannes, 125–27, 254
Holland Landing, Ontario, 23, 25–30, 32, 34, 40, 42, 64, 69, 72, 73, 76–78, 85–87, 91, 103, 113, 124, 125, 130–32, 173, 193, 196, 236, 237, 246, 251, 262
Holland Landing Depot, 78
Holland Marsh, 125, 218, 219, 236
Holland Marsh Drainage Commission, 218
Holland River, 19–21, 24, 31, 32, 34, 36, 45, 46, 48, 51, 73, 76, 77, 85, 113, 125, 132, 196, 218, 237, 246
Holland Trail, 19
Hollingshead, George, 236–37
Home District, Upper Canada, 32
Home District Court of Requests, 42
Hook and Ladder Company (Newmarket), 94, 117
Hoover, Private Levi, 214
Howard, Amelia (Wakefield), 137, 255
Howard, Brook, 137
Howard family, 27
Huddy, Captain Joshua, 71
Hudson's Bay Company, 57, 59, 60, 120, 178, 240

Huggins, Frank, 221
Hughes, C.M., 174
Hughes, George, 148
Hughes, John, 155
Hughes, Joyce (Dawson), 75, 250
Hughes, Colonel Sam, 214
Hull, General William, 65, 66
Humber River, 21, 28, 113
Humber Trail (Carrying Place Trail), 113
Hunter, Dr. James, 108–12, 117, 148
Huron, Lake, 28, 29, 64, 77, 64, 191, 246
Huron First Nation, 19–21
Hutchcroft, William, 155
Hutt, Dr. Walter G., 209

Ianuzielo, Tony, 234, 261
Illumination Ceremony (Sharon Temple), 107
Independent Order of the Daughters of the Empire (IODE), 212
Indian and Northern Affairs Canada, 88
Inland Publishing Company, 148, 167
Inverness, Scotland, 177–78
Iroquet, Huron Chief, 20
Iroquois First Nation, 20
Irwin
    Adelaide "Adela" Vellejo (Curtis), 138
    Benoni, 137–39, 255
    Charles, 138
    Constance, 138
    Daniel, 137
    Edith, 138–39
    Edwin P., 110, 138, 142–44, 257
    Jared, 138
    Lizzie B. (Bunner), 138
    Lydia (Kennedy), 138

Jackson, Erasmus, 15, 111, 122, 144–46, 148, 149, 167, 174, 244, 250, 256, 257

Jackson, Lyman G., 68
James, __, Mrs. E., 82, 83
James, Ezekiel, 82
James, Isaac, 82, 251
Jarvis, Aemilius, 114
Jarvis, Julia, 40–42, 246
*J.C. Morrison* (steamer), 165
Johnson, Sir William, 114
Johnson's Landing, community of, 69
Jones-Poirier Publishing Company, 149
Jonquière, Marquis de la, 113

Kanataites, 161, 257
Kansas, 123
Keffer's service station (Newmarket),
    223
Kelly, Pep, 221
Kempenfeldt Bay (Lake Simcoe), 60,
    76
Kent, Duke of, 67
Kettleby, Ontario, 173
King George Hotel (Newmarket),
    180, 187, 188
King George Public School, 222
King Infantry Company, 140
King Street Gaol, 90
King Street Market, 90
King Township, (York County), 20,
    21, 50, 63, 113, 136, 172
King, William Lyon Mackenzie, 182,
    195, 215–18, 225, 260
Kingston, Ontario, 34, 108, 127, 132,
    253
Kingston Penitentiary, 89
Kingston Road, 189
Kinsey, Hannah (*see* Hannah Curry)
Kinsey, James, 21, 22, 27
Kirby, Charles (*see* Carlos Corbiére)
Kirstine, John, 169
Kitely, Henry, 193
Kitely, Marshall, 193
Kodak plant (Mount Dennis), 212

LaFontaine, Sir Louis-Hippolyte,
    106–08, 136, 172
Lake St. George, 49, 248
Lake Wilcox (Lake Willcocks), 48–49
Landing, Lower or Steamboat, 69,
    76–78, 85–86
Landing, Upper or Canoe, 69, 77, 78,
    85–86
Lapointe, Justice Minister Ernest, 227
Laughton, Ann (*see also* Ann Roe),
    30, 57
Laughton, Lieutenant John, 30
Laughton, William, 23
Laurier, Sir Wilfrid, 182, 183, 195,
    215–17
Lawrence (or Laurence), Morris, 22, 28
League of Patriotic Action (Toronto),
    228
Lee bakery, 94
Lee the shoemaker, 94
Legislative Assembly of Upper
    Canada, 67, 90
Lennox, Colonel Herb, 217–18
Liberty Hall (Newmarket), 89
Lippincott, Esther (Borden), 71
Lippincott, Captain Richard, 70, 71
Lloyd, David, 168–69
Lloyd, Lieutenant-Colonel Thomas
    H., 141, 182, 184
Lloyd, William, 172
Lloydtown, Ontario, 198
Lloydtown Rifle Company, 140
Lorne, Marquis of (Governor
    General), 159
Lount
    Gabriel, 37
    George, 69, 122
    Samuel, 90–92, 113, 138, 140
    Mrs. Samuel, 91–92
Luesby, George, 13, 48, 249, 258
Lundy, C.F., 193
Lundy, Ellen (*see* Ellen Brammar)
Lundy, Isaac, 83

Lundy, Reeve Fred, 225
Lundy, Robert, 193
Lundy's Lane, Battle of, 71

Macdonald, Sir John A., 120
MacDonald, John, 248
MacDonald, Susan, 104, 105, 253
Macdonell, Colonel John, 23
Machell's Corners (Aurora), 165
Mackenzie, Sir William, 189–90
Mackenzie, William Lyon, 39, 58, 72–74, 88, 89, 103, 107, 113, 131, 135, 136, 138, 140, 216–17, 249
Mackie, William, 192
Mackie, William Jr., 193
MacLean, Lieutenant Archibald, 67
Madison, President James, 66
Manitoulin Island, 87
Manitoulin Island Treaty (1868), 87
Mann, Normie, 221
Mansion House (Newmarket), 103, 105, 253
Market Square (Newmarket), 100, 101, 178, 180, 181, 188, 223
Markham Plank Road, 53
Markland, George Herchimer, 44
Marsden flour mill (Newmarket), 46
Marshall, Aubrey "Aub," 221
Marshall, James, 176
Massey Hall (Toronto), 199
Mathews, Norman, 225
Matthews, Peter, 90–92
McArthur, Emily, 62, 245
McArthur, Red, 221
McCabe, Bob, 221
McDonald
    Catherine, 60
    John, 57–61
    Marie (Poitras), 59–61
McDonell, Colonel John, 66–67
McDougall, Honourable William, 146
McFarland, R., 193
McKay, J.D., 149

McKay, John, 23
McMaster, William, 102
McMaster, William Jr., 102, 180, 258
McMaster & Sutherland (general store), 102
McMillan, Dan, 184
McNulty, John J., 105
McNulty, Nancy Ann (see Nancy Ann Mosier)
Mechanics' Hall (Newmarket), 109, 110, 112, 118, 121, 146, 201
Merrickville, Upper Canada, 146
Métis, 121
Metroland Publishing Company, 148, 167
Metropolitan Street Railway Company, 189, 191
Meyer, John, 148
Michigan, Lake, 77, 165
Michigan, 66, 92
Millard
    B.H., 175
    John, 185
    Joseph, 94, 95, 16
    Mordecai, 24
    Timothy, 22, 24, 72
Millard Block, 102
Millard family, 24, 214, 244
Mitchell, Sergeant Douglas Gordon, 213
Mitchell, Captain Tom, 200–02
Molyneaux, Larry, 221
Monmouth County, New Jersey, 71
Montagnais First Nation, 19–20
Montcalm, Marquis de, 30
Montgomery's Tavern (Toronto), 89, 90, 103, 105, 113, 131, 136, 138, 140
Montreal Telegraph Company (Newmarket), 167
Moore, Robert, 55–56
Moore, Robert, 89–90
Morrison, Bert, 228

Morrison, Dr. John, 205
*Mornimg* (steamer), 165
Morse Code, 135
Morse, Samuel, 73, 133–35, 255
Mosier
    Jack, 104
    Captain John, 105, 253
    Nancy Ann (McNulty), 104–05
    Thomas, 104–05
Mosier family, 104, 253
Mosley's (John) general store, 176
Mount Albert, Ontario, 50, 201, 203
Mount Dennis, community, 212
Muir, Alexander, 55, 56, 61, 137, 143,
    158, 204
Muir, Captain J. Murray, 211
Mulock
    Marion (*see* Marion Boultbee)
    Mary (Cawthra) (Mrs. T.H.), 138,
        194, 259
    Dr. Thomas H, 194
    Colonel W.P., 14
    Sir William, 50, 109, 138, 149,
        182, 193–96, 198, 258
    William Thomas, 193, 194, 259
Mulock family, 50, 193
Murray, W.S., 169
Musselman's Lake, 52, 53, 198

National Film Board (NFB), 233–34
Natural gas (Newmarket), 203–06
Navy Island (Niagara River), 136
Nesbitt's service station, 223
Netherlands Emigration Foundation,
    219
*New Era, The*, 148, 166
New Brunswick, 42, 71, 126, 245
New Hampshire, 126
New Jersey, 71, 126
New Jersey Loyalist, 70
New Jersey Militia, 71
New York City, 30, 75, 126, 127, 133,
    135, 138

New York State, 126
Newcastle District, Upper Canada, 43
Newmarket
    Incorporation as village in 1857,
        93, 109, 161, 165, 257
    Incorporation as town in 1880,
        149, 150, 165, 257
    Arthur Street, 226
    Bathurst Street, 73
    Bayview Avenue, 56, 70, 222
    Botsford Street, 72, 89, 94,
        100–02, 104, 133, 134, 158,
        160, 166, 169, 175, 181, 188,
        203, 216, 223, 224, 233
    Boulton Street (now D'Arcy
        Street), 132
    Charles Street, 145, 148
    Church Street, 30, 41, 88, 129,
        184, 223, 233
    D'Arcy Street, 55, 129, 132, 184
    Davis Drive, 21, 51, 143, 153,
        158, 173, 196, 197, 208, 209,
        222, 240, 241
    Dufferin Street, 52
    Eagle Street, 22–24, 34, 38, 40,
        41, 45, 79–81 101, 117, 188,
        223
    Fred Hagen Crescent, 235
    Gamble Road (now Mulock
        Drive), 50
    Gorham Street, 24, 28, 33, 38, 39,
        51, 114, 136, 143, 204
    Grammar School Lane (now
        Millard Avenue), 180, 181
    Green Lane, 84, 198, 242
    Huron Street (now Davis Drive),
        51, 143, 158, 196, 207, 222
    Leslie Street, 50, 92, 97, 152, 160,
        203, 240
    Lorne Avenue, 174–75
    Lot Street (now Millard Avenue),
        72, 143, 201
    Lowell Street, 226

Main Street, 15, 22, 24, 26, 38, 41, 51, 55, 57, 64, 67, 72, 92–95, 99–103, 113, 116–18, 127, 128, 133–35, 137, 144–46, 148, 156–61, 163, 166–68, 170, 171, 173–78, 180, 181, 184, 188, 203, 206, 209, 210, 222–24, 228, 234, 238, 242, 246

Millard Avenue, 56, 72, 121, 143, 159, 169, 175, 180, 194, 201, 203, 223

Mulock Drive, 50, 52, 56, 70, 92, 97, 98, 188, 195, 203, 208, 256, 259

Muriel Street, 226

Parkside Drive, 232

Pearson Street, 56, 168, 194, 259

Pleasantview Street, 209

Prospect Street, 36, 39, 51, 54–56, 68, 97, 117, 143, 163, 169, 208, 209, 223

Queen Street (formerly Mill Street), 145, 166, 188, 189, 203, 208, 223

Raglan Street, 56, 188

Srigley Street, 35, 160, 208, 209, 226

Superior Street, 143

Timothy Street, 22, 24, 26, 36, 143, 54, 55, 89, 90, 95, 109, 111, 112, 115, 117, 119, 143, 170, 174, 176–78, 180, 203, 206, 208, 223, 228

Victoria Street, 176

Water Street, 27, 46, 69, 81, 93, 101–03 117, 128, 132, 157, 170, 180, 184, 207, 223

Wellington Street, 151, 152, 203

William Roe Boulevard, 37

William Street, 188

Woodbine Avenue, 52, 98, 151–52

Yonge Street, 21, 24, 28, 31, 32, 36–38, 42, 48–52, 62–64, 72–78, 82–85, 91, 103, 123, 140, 188, 191, 193, 195, 240–43, 246, 252

Newmarket Agricultural Society, 110

Newmarket Canal, 15, 216, 251, 258

Newmarket Canoe Club and Camel Corps, 161

Newmarket Cemetery, 102, 186

Newmarket Citizens Band, 47, 155–57, 234

Newmarket Civic Guard, 228

Newmarket Corps (Salvation Army), 199–203

*Newmarket Courier*, 148

Newmarket Development Company, 205

*Newmarket Era, The*, 62, 68, 84, 92, 111, 119, 146, 148, 149, 158, 161, 166, 182, 191, 201–04, 217, 219, 220, 236, 243, 252–54, 256–60

*Newmarket Era & Express, The*, 149, 227

*Newmarket Express & Advertiser*, 149

Newmarket Fairgrounds (*see also* Fairgrounds Park), 146

Newmarket Grammar School, 56, 194, 259

Newmarket High School, 56, 228, 234

Newmarket Historical Society, 48, 206, 216, 251, 253, 259, 260

Newmarket Historical Society Archives, 247, 246, 257

Newmarket Hydro, 45, 80

Newmarket Infantry Company, 140

Newmarket Mechanics' Institute, 146

*Newmarket News*, 149

*Newmarket Post*, 149

Newmarket Public Library, 13, 14, 244, 247

Newmarket Redmen, 219–22

Newmarket Regatta, 169–70

Newmarket Veterans Association, 227

North American Hotel (Newmarket), 58, 72, 73, 94, 104, 133, 174
North Fair Palace (Newmarket), 115
North West Company, 29, 43, 57, 59, 60
North York Agricultural Society, 146
North York federal riding, 112, 195, 196, 215–18
*North York Intelligencer & Advertiser*, 149
*North York Reformer*, 148–49
*North York Sentinel*, 148
North, Lord Frederick, 2nd Earl of Guilford, 68
Northern Railway Company of Canada, 165
Northridge Community Church of the Salvation Army, 203
North-West Rebellion, 122, 141
Novelty Company, The (Newmarket), 102

O'Brien, Mrs. Mary, 24
Oak Ridges, 37, 49, 63, 76, 113
Oak Ridges Moraine, 191
Odd Fellows' Hall (Newmarket), 72
Office Specialty Manufacturing Company Limited, 47, 115, 119, 144, 150, 206, 223
Ogilvie, Mac, 221
Ojibwa First Nation, 33, 74, 75
Old Town Hall (Newmarket), 101, 160, 178–82, 188, 216
Onondaga, town of, 20
Ontario, Lake, 20, 28, 34, 52, 53, 63, 77, 83, 113, 127, 135, 191, 246, 253
Ontario Agricultural College, 218
Ontario Hydro, 190
Ontario Science Centre, 80
Ontario, Simcoe & Huron Railway, 102, 142, 164, 257
Orillia, Ontario, 87, 130, 131, 165, 246
Osler, Canon Featherstone, 58
Oswego, New York, 113

Paddytown, community of, 51
Parachute Joe, 231–33
Parry, Jimmy, 221
Partridge, George, 186
Patstone, Reverend Arthur, 128–29
Pearson
    Ann, 63
    Benjamin, 63, 148
    J.J. (justice of peace), 186
    Mary, 63
    Susannah (Mrs. B.), 63
Peel, County of, 123, 166
Penetanguishene, Ontario, 29, 30, 60, 64, 76–78, 86, 87, 103, 130, 131, 176
Pennsylvania, 20–22, 24, 28, 36, 37, 84, 92, 126, 172, 205
Penrose, Fred, 228
Petchville, community of, 51
Peterborough, Ontario, 23, 43
Peters, Bob, 221
Peterson, Howard, 221
Phantazmagloria Society, 161–62
Pheasant Run Golf Club, 153
Phelps' Tavern, 69
Phoenix Mill (Newmarket), 39
Pickering College (Newmarket), 138, 150, 157, 205, 234–35
Pickering Township (Durham Region), 52
Pine Orchard, community of, 52
Pine Orchard Road, 52–53
Pipher
    Sergeant-Pilot Bill, 228, 229, 260
    Earl, 228
    James, 180
    Lelia, 228
Plains of Abraham, 30, 35
Playter
    Dr.__, 148
    Glenn, 167
    Jackie, 167
    W.W., 169

Wesley, 167
Wray, 167
Pleasantville, community of, 52
Pleasantville House, 99
Poitras, Marie (*see* Marie McDonald)
Porter, George S., 142, 144, 145, 167, 256
Pottageville, community of, 173
Present Island, 87
Preston, Gar, 221
Pretty, Agnes, 80–81
Prince Charles Public School, 36, 160, 226
Prince of Wales (1860), 159, 162
Pringle, Ellis, 221
Provost, Edward, 151, 153

Quaker(s) (Society of Friends), 27, 36, 37, 40, 50, 64, 123, 151, 152, 237, 256
Quaker Hill subdivision (Newmarket), 240
Quaker Meeting House (Armitage), 50, 123
Quaker settlers, settlement, 21, 27, 28, 31, 52, 63, 77, 82–84, 90, 91, 123, 133, 144, 242
Queensville, Ontario, 50, 105, 149, 152, 164, 192, 193

Rachar, C.C., 227
Railway Hotel (Newmarket), 115
Ramsay, Canon S.P., 121–22
Raper, Frederick, 155
Rebellion of 1837, 23, 39, 72, 73, 75, 88–91, 103, 104, 105, 113, 121, 136, 140, 176, 243, 249, 250, 251, 253
Red Cross, 212
Red Mill (Holland Landing), 42
Regional Municipality of York, 164, 241
Regional Shopping Centres Limited, 240

Reid, Elizabeth (*see* Elizabeth Doan)
Reid, William, 83
Rest, Robert, 155
Richardson
    H., 175
    Marjorie, 42, 248
    North, 23, 67, 68, 249
    William Edwin, 68
    Major William North, 68
Richardson family, 24, 57, 250
Richardson Park, 222
Richmond Hill, Ontario, 48, 70, 71, 136, 182, 187, 189, 190
Ridout, Surveyor General Thomas, 34
Riel, Louis, 120–22
Roadhouse
    John, 166
    Samuel, 166
    William, 193
Roadhouse & Rose Funeral Service, 145, 166, 167, 221
Roadhouse Furniture, 115
Robert Simpson Co., The, 176, 178
Robertson, John Ross, 124, 250
Robinette, R.C., 198
Robinson
    Christopher, 22, 31, 42, 245
    Emma (Walker) (Mrs. J.B.), 43
    Esther, 23, 245
    Esther (Sayer) (*see* Esther Beman)
    Frederick, 42
    Isabella, 42
    John Beverley, 22, 23, 28, 34, 42–44, 166
    Mary, 23, 245
    Peter, 22–24, 24, 32, 33, 42, 43, 61, 77, 86, 195, 247
    Sarah, 23, 245
    William Benjamin, 22, 23, 40, 42, 68, 69, 86
Roe
    Albert E., 155, 175
    Ann (Laughton), 57

Edward "Ned," 14, 15, 30, 127–29, 244–47, 255–56
Frederick "Fred," 155, 157
Walter (father of William), 35, 247
Walter (son of William), 155, 157
William, 22–26, 30, 34, 35, 55, 68, 77, 86, 106–08, 127, 128, 137, 155, 172, 181, 244
Roe family, 127–29,157
Rogers
    Augustus, 63
    Elmsley, 63
    Enoch, 75
    Isaac, 63
    Lydia (Mrs. Rufus), 63
    Olive (Mrs. Isaac), 63
    Rufus, 63
    Sarah, 63
    Sarah (Mrs. Timothy), 63
    Timothy, 21, 27, 50, 52, 123, 132, 243–44
Rogers family, 24, 245
Roger's Rangers, 141
Rogers, Robert, 142
Rolph, Dr. John, 44
Ronto Developments, 70
Rose, Donald, 167
Rose, Lyman, 167, 221
Ross, Private Irvine Dudley, 213
Rouge Trail, 113–14
Rowen, Peter, 89
Roxy Theatre (Newmarket), 234
Royal Canadian British Bank (Newmarket), 65
Royal Canadian Legion, Branch 426, 226
Royal Hotel (Newmarket), 159
Royal Navy, 64, 77, 78, 86, 253
Royal Navy storage depot, 29, 64, 78
Royal Regiment of Canada, 184
Royal Regiment of Wales, 29
Royal Rink (Newmarket), 119
Rupert's Land, 120

Russel, R., 23
Russell, Douglas & Longford (Mills), 39
Russell, Honourable Peter, 32, 48

Salvation Army, Newmarket Corps, 199–203
Sand Bank Hotel (Glenville), 173
Sandfield-Dorion administration, 146
Santa Claus Parade, 198–99
Savage, Constable John, 174, 186
Saxton, Frederick, 155
Saxton, Minnie, 184–86
Saxton, Susan "Susie," 184–86
Saxton's Jewellery, 94, 95
Schickedanz Developments Limited, 240
Schomberg, Ontario, 102, 189, 190, 196
Schomberg Agricultural Fair, 114
Schreyer, Governor General Edward, 157, 159
Scott, Dr. Stuart, 174
Scott, Thomas, 121, 185, 186, 254
Second World War, 29, 47, 116, 141, 208, 222, 224, 228, 232, 254
Selby, Receiver-General Prideaux, 35
Selby, Robert, 79
Selby, Thomas, 79
Seven Years War (1756–62), 37
Sharon, Ontario, 50, 79, 83–85, 89, 90, 107, 115, 131, 141, 153, 155, 193
Sharon Brass Band, 119
Sharon Colony, 192–93
Sharon Temple, 62, 84, 85, 90, 107
Shell service station, 223
Shrigley, Enoch, 26
Shrigley, Mary, 36
Shrigley family, 36
Simcoe, County of, 23, 60, 70, 113, 125
Simcoe electoral district, 43, 67, 69
Simcoe Foresters (see Battalions)
Simcoe, Lake, 13, 20, 23, 25, 26, 43, 46, 76, 85–87, 92, 157, 164, 165, 187, 195, 196, 218, 243, 248, 251

Simcoe, Lieutenant Governor John
Graves, 22, 28, 31, 32, 34, 35, 42,
49, 58, 60, 68, 71, 97, 142, 245
Simcoe's Queen's Rangers, 71, 142
Simpson, Mary Anne (Botsford), 178
Simpson, Robert, 155, 174, 176–78,
258
Simpson & Bogart (general store), 176
Simpson & Trent Groceries, Boots,
Shoes and Dry Goods, 177
Simpson family, 57
Simpson's Department Store, 155, 178
Simpson-Sears Limited, 178, 240
Slavery Abolition Act (1834), 151
Sloane, W., 23
Smith
Ida (Mrs. R.A.), 174, 176
John Marshall, 174, 176
Mary (Bogart) (Mrs. R.H.),
174–75
Robert Arthur "R.A.," 174, 175
Robert Hall "R.H.," 112, 173–76
Smith family, 174
Smith, Reverend A.A., 122
Smith, A.P., 193
Smith, Alf, 27
Smith, Felicia, 174
Smith, G.P. Jr., 193
Smith, Captain L.L.F., 141
Smith R.A., 176
Smith, Stan, 221
Smith, W.H., 52
Smith & Empy, 174, 176
Smith Bros., Newmarket, Ont., 151
Snor, John J., 219
Snowball, community of, 173
Souch, J.E., 175
Soules, John, 193
Soules, Silas C., 193
Southlake Regional Health Centre
(Newmarket), 209, 210, 242, 259
Srigley
Alvin Mylo, 247

Christopher Beswick, 36
Elisha Beman, 36
Jane (Heacock), 36
Richard, 36
Robert, 22, 36
Wellington, 36
Srigley family, 35, 36, 55, 244, 247
St. Andrew's College, 62, 123
St. Andrew's Presbyterian Church, 27,
33, 41, 101, 180
St. George, Laurent Quetton, 49
St. John's Sideroad, 242
St. Paul's Anglican Church, 99, 121,
127–29
St. Paul's Anglican Church (Old),
128–29, 157
Stallard, J., 175
Starr, Alma, 237, 239, 262
Starr, Elmer, 237, 239
Starr, Francis, 237
Starr, Reverend J.H., 203
Stauffer's Mills, 53
Steam whistles, 206–08
Stephens, Miss __, 36
Stephens, Shadrick, 70
Stephens brothers, 36
Steven Court (Newmarket), 148
Stickwood
__ (Mrs. Charles), 161
Charles, 160
Isaac, 160
William, 160
Stickwood Brickyard, 160, 208
Stickwood family, 160
Stickwood-Walker Park, 256
Strachan, Bishop John, 23, 127–29
Strogdale, S., 23
Stuart Scott Public School
(Newmarket), 222
Sullivan, Robert Baldwin, 44
Superior, Lake, 77, 103
Sutherland
Donald, 102, 109, 112

James, 175
Mrs. James, 177
Sutherlands Pond, 169
Sutton, Ontario, 141
Sutton Agricultural Society, 114
Sutton Fair & Horse Show, 114
Sydenham, Lieutenant Governor
    (Charles Poulett Thomson), 106

T. Eaton Company, 198, 199
Tamar, Taylor, 151, 153
Taylor, James, 193
Tecumseth, 66
Terry, Mort, 193
*The Beaver*, 226
The *Caroline* incident, 105
The Cedars (Newmarket), 174–76
"The Maple Leaf Forever," 55, 137,
    158, 204
The Pond (*see also* Fairy Lake), 25,
    45–48, 101, 118, 119, 170
Thoms, Bill, 221
Thorold, Camp, 120
Toronto and York Radial Railway,
    187, 189
Toronto Suburban Street Railway, 190
Toronto Transit Commission (TTC),
    190
Toronto, Sarnia & Lake Huron
    Railway Company, 164
Trading Tree, 24–26
Traviss
    Charles, 192, 193
    Stephen, 193
    Thomas, 193
Trent, William, 177, 258
Trent-Severn Waterway, 195
Trewhella, Ethel, 22, 114, 244, 246
Trinity United Church (Newmarket),
    160
Twinney Centre (Newmarket), 242
Typhus, 61, 132–33

Underground Railroad, 151
Union Army, 119, 123
United Empire Loyalist (UEL), 22, 41,
    42, 70, 127
Upper Canada Law Society, 124
Upper Canada Mall, 240–41
Upper Canada Militia, 71–72, 82
Uxbridge, Ontario, 37, 52–54

Vail, Sparkie, 221
Valcartier, Quebec, 214
Vale, Deputy Reeve Joe, 225
Vermont, State of, 21, 27, 89, 126
Victoria, Queen, 67, 96, 117, 118,
    135, 161
Vimy Ridge, 184
Virginia, State of, 22, 31, 42

Wakefield, Brook, 137
Wakefield, Amelia (*see* Amelia
    Howard)
Walker, Emma (*see* Emma Robinson)
Walker, Frances (Stickwood), 256
Wallis, William, 94, 95, 133
Wallis' Saddlery and Harness, 94
War of 1812, 21, 23, 25, 33, 35, 54,
    63–67, 71, 76–78, 92, 119, 140,
    223, 243, 247, 249, 251
War of Independence, 142, 153, 245,
    250
Warren, Mrs. Stephen, 163
Warren, Stephen, 163
Washington, General George, 70, 71
Watson, N. David, 218
Watson and Hall Funeral Home, 166
Watt, Constable Ron, 236–37
Wayling, Major J., 141
Webb, Thomas, 79
Webster, Fred, 172
Wellington, Duke of, 68, 69, 70, 90,
    91, 250
Wells, Joseph, 44
Wells, Richard, 201

Wesley, Dr. J.E., 209
Wesley Brooks Conservation Area
    (Newmarket), 45
Wesleyan Methodist Church
    (Newmarket), 122
Wesley Street, 209
West, Angus, 149
West family, 57
*West Sutton Herald*, 149
Whitchurch Township, 32, 42, 49,
    52–54, 62, 63, 83, 89, 98, 214
White Rose, community of, 51
White, John, 23
White, Philip, 71
Widdifield, W.C., 185
Wiley, W.E., 149
Willcocks, William, 48–49
William Cane & Sons Ltd., 153,
    206–207
Willson, David, 62, 107
Williams farm, 205
Williams, Constable Vern, 236–37
Willson, Hugh D. 62–63
Wilson, Don, 220–21
Windsor, Lance Sergeant Clifford
    Dare, 213
Wolfe, General James, 30, 35
Wolseley Expedition, 122
Women's Christian Temperance
    Union (WCTU) (Newmarket),
    237–38
Wood
    Benjamin, 63
    Mary (Mrs. Robert), 63
    Robert, 63

Yonge Street Monthly Meeting, 64
York, County of, 36, 50, 52, 61, 70,
    73–75, 98, 106, 108, 114–16, 136,
    142, 146, 149, 150, 153, 164, 191,
    192, 211, 212, 215, 248, 249, 253
York County Hospital, 209, 242
York County Police Force, 236

York Manor Home for the Aged
    (Newmarket), 239
York Mills, 199
York Rangers (*see* 12th Battalion)
York Regional Police, 242
York Volunteers, 120